W9-BVQ-532

Learning to Be Old

Gender, Culture, and Aging

Margaret Cruikshank

ROWMAN & LITTLEFIELD PUBLISHERS, INC.
Lanham • Boulder • New York • Oxford

ROWMAN & LITTLEFIELD PUBLISHERS, INC.

Published in the United States of America
by Rowman & Littlefield Publishers, Inc.
An Imprint of the Rowman & Littlefield Publishing Group
4720 Boston Way, Lanham, Maryland 20706
www.rowmanlittlefield.com

12 Hid's Copse Road, Cumnor Hill, Oxford OX2 9JJ, England

Copyright © 2003 by Margaret Cruikshank

All rights reserved. No part of this publication may be reproduced, stored in a retrieval
system, or transmitted in any form or by any means, electronic, mechanical,
photocopying, recording, or otherwise, without the prior permission of the publisher.

British Library Cataloguing in Publication Information Available

Library of Congress Cataloging-in-Publication Data

Cruikshank, Margaret.
    Learning to be old : gender, culture, and aging / Margaret Cruikshank.
        p.   cm.
    Includes bibliographical references and index.
    ISBN 0-8476-9848-3 (cloth : alk. paper) — ISBN 0-8476-9849-1 (pbk. :
alk. paper)
    1. Aging—Psychological aspects.   2. Aged—United States.   I. Title.
    BF724.55.A35 C78   2002
    305.26—dc21   2002005352

Printed in the United States of America

♾ ™ The paper used in this publication meets the minimum requirements of American
National Standard for Information Sciences—Permanence of Paper for Printed Library
Materials, ANSI/NISO Z39.48-1992.

for Donna

Contents

Preface		ix
Acknowledgments		xi
Introduction		1
1	Cultural Myths and Aging	9
2	The Fear of an Aging Population	25
3	Sickness and Other Social Roles of the Old	35
4	Overmedicating Old Americans	51
5	Healthy Physical Aging	69
6	The Politics of Healthy Aging	93
7	Gender, Class, and Ethnicity	115
8	Ageism	135
9	Prescribed Busyness and Spirituality	159
10	Gerastology: A Feminist's View of Gerontology and Women's Aging	173
Conclusion: The Paradoxes of Aging		203
References		207
Index		233
About the Author		245

Preface

"Perhaps, with full-life spans the norm, people may need to learn how to be aged as they once had to learn to be adult."

—Ronald Blythe, *The View in Winter*

Two ideas run through this book. The first is that aging in America is shaped more by culture than by biology, more by beliefs, customs, and traditions than by bodily changes. In other words, it is socially constructed. The second is that awareness of social constructions and resistance to them is crucial for women's comfortable aging.

Nonetheless, our aging bodies matter greatly. No matter how clearly we understand the complex and interconnecting forces of social aging, we age in our individual bodies.

Sometimes chronological age holds great significance and sometimes it does not. Accepting this fact is an important part of learning to be old. Equally important is a willingness to imagine what aging would be like if we could free ourselves, even partially, from negative beliefs about it and if social, political, and economic policy favored healthy aging.

My title has two meanings. The first is that aging in contemporary America is so complex and multidimensional that studying it is worthwhile, even necessary, for those who wish to do it consciously and without fear. Secondly, "learning to be old" means unlearning much of what we think is true. The misconceptions about aging will have less power to limit our experience if we can examine them carefully. Entering the third (or fourth) stage of life with no preparation or forethought would perhaps not be dangerous in a society organized for the well-being of its oldest members. In our market economy, however, mindless aging leaves us vulnerable to many forms of exploitation. This is especially true for women.

Learning to Be Old falls somewhere in the large space between practical guides to aging and theoretical work. I have attempted to bring together matters usually treated separately: health, politics, the humanities, feminist gerontology, and cultural analysis. At the same time, I have not taken up except in passing some topics important to women's aging such as housing, transportation, Medicare, and nursing homes.

At sixty-two, I do not presume to write "we" and "us" when referring to "the old," but the emotionally-distancing pronouns "they" and "them" have not felt quite right, either. My motivation for writing this book is the belief that neither gerontology nor women's studies has really come to grips with the fact that most of the old are women. *Learning to Be Old* is but one of many possible responses to the remarkable and unremarkable longevity of women.

Women's aging is like the Chinese ideogram that means both danger and opportunity.

Acknowledgments

I first learned about aging from my professors in the graduate gerontology program of San Francisco State University and from members of Montefiore Senior Center in San Francisco. I gratefully acknowledge the many gerontologists cited in the following pages, especially Martha Holstein and Sally Gadow, whose work I particularly admire. I thank colleagues who commented on early drafts of chapters: Sharon Blake, Tara Healy, Lisa Johns, Diana Long, Nancy Manahan, Donna Murphy, Matile Rothschild, and Mary Tyrrell. Many conversations about aging with Lisa over the past several years have broadened my perspective. I thank both the Bain Center at the University of California, Berkeley, for the opportunity to be an affiliate scholar there and the Resource Center on Aging at UCB for access to its materials. The University of Maine Fogler library staff, especially Libby Norton in interlibrary loan, reference librarian Nancy Lewis, and Bonnie Garceau and Ethel Leclair in circulation, were most helpful.

Students in my Women and Aging classes at the University of Maine and at the University of Southern Maine stimulated my thinking. I thank my women's studies colleagues, especially Ann Schonberger and Mazie Hough of the University of Maine, for their support. I am indebted to my editor at Rowman & Littlefield, Jennifer Knerr, for her valuable contribution to the book and guidance, and to her assistants, Renee Legatt and Brigitte Scott. I thank Jill Rothenberg for believing in this book when it was only an idea.

My greatest debt by far is to Donna Murphy, who was with me every step of the way.

Margaret Cruikshank
Corea, Maine

Introduction

In this book I propose alternatives to the ways aging is usually understood in popular culture and mainstream gerontology. Although my chief concern is women's aging, I try to place it in a broad context by considering issues that may also affect men. Because of age denial, it is hard to see how common beliefs limit our perceptions of the aging process. Customarily we think of aging as something that happens to our individual bodies, slowly, imperceptibly, inevitably. Learning to be old means fully experiencing the physical, bodily changes that accompany aging while at the same time recognizing that those changes occur in a particular social setting, influenced by our ethnicity, class, and gender, and by the political and economic climate. It is also shaped by developments such as the burgeoning population of elders. Our condition in old age is largely determined by forces over which we have no control, although it is also partly determined by heredity and by our earlier life choices and habits.

I believe that the survival of large numbers of old women is desirable. It may help to balance the bland and homogenizing tendencies of globalization, for example. Instead of fearing that a tidal wave of elders will engulf our society, I note that declining fertility makes population aging possible. Usually this decline is associated with improvements in women's lives and is therefore deemed beneficial. From a woman's perspective, aging may have unforeseen dimensions. But the potential created by longevity will not be realized until conventional views of aging are set aside.

The vigor with which feminists have challenged notions of biological determinism leaves us in an awkward position with aging, because this process happens in and to our bodies. The spin of social construction offers nondeterministic ways to view aging, but for nearly everyone, aging means some

1

bodily decline. For many of our mothers and grandmothers, a common interpretation was, "We fall apart and there's nothing to be done about it." For many today this attitude still holds true. An alternative is to say, yes, some loss is likely but what else defines my aging? *Learning to Be Old* attempts to answer this question.

In the following chapters, several examples illustrate the ways aging is socially constructed. It is 1) medicalized; 2) stereotyped; 3) regarded as frightening both for individuals and for society; 4) genderless; and 5) stripped of class and ethnicity.

To the extent that we are conditioned to view aging through these paradigms, we must learn to be old. It is not just a natural process like breathing but requires initiation, and we learn to be old partly in response to the ways we are treated. The other meaning of learning to be old is discovering that aging is a creation of this time and place, more cultural than biological, determined by social institutions, or, more optimistically, a set of life experiences we can consciously shape once we see how others are attempting to shape them for us. Thus learning to be old requires that we both observe how aging is socially constructed and find ways to resist being molded to its dictates.

A popular idea, "successful aging," is now circulating in the media and among gerontologists, for example in *Successful Aging,* the report of a ten-year aging study by the MacArthur Foundation, edited by John W. Rowe and Robert L. Kahn. The authors challenge the disease model of aging and offer many insights into late-life potential. When success is proposed as an aging model, however, a competitive or business standard measures a complex human process and a white, male, middle-class professional outlook is taken for granted. While business success can be gauged by profits and athletes succeed by winning competitions, aging well has no such definitive marker. Successful aging overlooks the very important role class plays in determining not only how healthy we are in old age, but even whether we get to be old. The phrase is prescriptive. Our physical health may be rated good or bad, but it is intertwined with our psychological health and depends on factors that may be elusive, changing, or knowable only by intuition. Research in a positivist spirit will not grasp them. A poor and sick old woman ages unsuccessfully by material yardsticks, but suppose she raises two grandchildren and helps out a neighbor who is older and sicker than she is. Does this constitute "success"?

Another problem with successful aging and its counterpart, "productive aging," is its implication that aging depends mostly on our own efforts. Throughout their book, for example, Rowe and Kahn state that we are responsible for our aging. Even for affluent and powerful men, this is manifestly untrue. This belief about aging is a cultural artifact, a small stone bearing the inscription "rugged individualism." The success model overlooks the elements of luck and mystery in aging.

Although personal responsibility undeniably plays some role, being white and middle-class are powerful predictors of the late-life health and well-being of Americans. No amount of individual effort or sturdy self-reliance can gain for working-class people or people of color the advantages enjoyed by the white middle class, and especially by men. Working-class people and people of color can obviously make healthy choices that narrow somewhat the gap between themselves and the more favored old. But the often substantial differences in aging created by ethnicity, class, and gender are covered up by the falsely universalizing phrase "successful aging."

When it means such things as creative adaptation to loss of function or to the death of a spouse, successful aging is clearly desirable, but this model misses much of the context in which we age. It cannot tell us if the aging lobby in Washington is strong or weak or if supermarket food is laced with sugar and salt. It cannot tell us the prevalence of elder abuse or weigh the impact of media stereotypes, and it cannot guarantee that when journalists write about proposals to "privatize" Social Security, the probable harmful effects on women and people of color will be carefully considered. Perhaps the concept of successful aging is popular with gerontologists because of its positive connotations, but it is simplistic and its promise of mastery is false.

"Comfortable aging" is preferable to successful aging because it emphasizes ease rather than external measurement, and because we can judge for ourselves whether or not we are aging comfortably. While successful aging implies that failure is possible, comfortable aging has a more neutral and nonjudgmental opposite. Comfortable aging also carries a faint hint of emancipatory hedonism, for which we have little time in youth and middle age and too little permission at any age. I would broaden the definition of "hedonism" to include the pleasures of breathing deeply and being still.

Another aging model uses an analogy: the old are like a colonized people. The term "ageism" denotes negative attitudes and unjust treatment but the dehumanization of older adults is more profound than ageism indicates. Seeing old women as a colonized people risks trivializing victims of colonial domination in other countries, for in important respects the analogy does not work. Forced labor, common to colonization, is not demanded of old women, nor are they deprived of political rights. They are not beaten or jailed for being old, although the dependent among them may suffer physical and psychological abuse. Old women share with colonized people the follow-ing characteristics, however: they are thought less intelligent than the domi-nant group. They are judged solely by appearance. They are encouraged to imitate the dominant group. They are figures of fun. They are scapegoated. They may internalize messages of their inferiority, and their movements may be controlled.

Because old women are seen as old bodies, physical appearance encom-passes their whole being. Just as dark-skinned people under colonization are viewed only as manifestations of color, the old are equated with declining bodies. In both cases, physical difference from the dominant group is the key to lesser status. By a process called "internal colonization," one group dominates another within the same country, causing a wide range of inequal-ities and dis-ease for the subordinate group.[1] The educational needs of the old are neglected, for example, most doctors have little preparation for treat-ing them competently, and psychoactive drugs are overprescribed for them (Green, 138). Furthermore, the colonized are manipulated by the colonizers who see them as incapable of managing themselves and in fact benefiting from being managed (139). Old women may respond to systematic devalua-tion by becoming docile or by taking on a "colonized personality" (Franz Fanon's phrase). The old may demonstrate their oppression, that is, by "obsessive self-concern, passivity, clowning, fear of aging, and failure to iden-tify themselves as old" (Green, 141). According to this interpretation, such traits, usually thought of as aspects of individual personality, reflect power-lessness. If friends and family of older adults understood internal coloniza-tion, they might have more patience with parents and grandparents who seem self-absorbed, docile, or afraid of aging. Instead of reacting with amuse-ment to elders' disavowal of the label "old," they would see why it appears so undesirable.

Old women are not confined to certain parts of the country or neighbor-hoods as South African blacks used to be. The most obvious way their move-ments are controlled is by confinement in nursing homes, where many are given an average of eight medications a day. This amounts to massive social control of the institutionalized old, under the guise of medical need. Less obvious physical control takes two forms: encouraging the old who are not institutionalized to see sickness as their natural condition and overmedicat-ing them. Whenever drug-induced slowing down or confusion are mistaken for normal aging or medication causes a fall that causes an injury, the drug industry's role in colonizing old women is apparent. Sometimes families dis-courage an elderly parent from continuing an activity, traveling, or initiating a sexual relationship when no danger is involved, a subtle form of physical and psychological control.

When an old woman becomes "the Other," fundamentally different from others, those in the dominant group create emotional distance from her by exaggerating difference and overlooking shared characteristics. An old woman is an alien creature, costly and crabby, and her life stage is seen as disconnected from youth and midlife rather than as an outgrowth of them. At seventy, Baba Copper wrote that she felt socially segregated, "as if I had a disease that might be catching" (80). A white person who "others" a black will not herself become black, but a thirty-year-old who "others" someone over seventy-five may well live to join the minority that now seems so distant. Conscious aging requires that we become aware of being seen as other by resisting impositions of difference.

The view that old women are a colonized people seems to account for more aspects of aging than are covered by successful aging or productive aging, but it tends to view them as a monolithic group, captured by biology as if they were specimens in amber. When the old are defined by a total category, a false homogeneity is imposed on them (Hazan, 81). Decline is their characteristic mark. They are the group gerontologists and social workers want to help. The category is meaningful to the extent that people who get Social Security and Medicare share something in common and face certain forms of prejudice and discrimination, but "old," in and of itself, is merely a site on the life span. If a person over seventy lived alone on an island, age would not be very relevant. No social cues would evoke it. Just as the concept of race is deeply entwined with ideas of racial superiority, the term "old" carries connotations of dependency and non-productivity. It tells who is less powerful, compared to others, and less respected.

If "old" is a fluid and changing identity, one that comes from outside of us rather than from within, then arranging people by years accumulated seems highly arbitrary, especially given the great diversity among people over sixty-five. It is not the changes in our bodies that define old; it is the meanings given to those changes. If our culture interprets these changes as shameful decrepitude, we can resist being pinned down by the category "old" by naming them challenges instead. When "old" seems to be a woman's whole identity, however, her ability to act on her own behalf and to resist ageist stereotypes is lost sight of.

The inexactitude of "the old" is revealed when another life stage is used for comparison. Childhood is only eighteen years but it has distinct periods of infant, toddler, school child, preadolescent, and adolescent. Someone in her early sixties may not wish to be grouped with everyone from sixty to one hundred. "Young old," the designation gerontologists use, is a foolish oxymoron but at least it acknowledges differences between seventy and ninety.

Some have suggested seeing aging as part of the life course rather than as a unique time. This emphasis has the advantage of finding roots of old-age problems or conditions in earlier decades, for example, the problem of low-paying jobs leading to inadequate Social Security later on, and it stresses the continuities of aging. But a life course interpretation may de-emphasize the role prejudice plays in aging in our society. Just as some whites like to say that skin color doesn't matter and blacks reply that whites have the privilege of not seeing what difference it makes, saying "old" is a stage in human development obscures the fact that youth is favored, while age is not.

The challenge, then, is to see the politics of aging and personal/individual aging simultaneously. From this perspective, the injustice of late-life poverty is exposed but the subjective experience of poverty is acknowledged to vary. The poverty of a group comprised equally of old black women and white women, for example, was found to be "a mold both strong and loose" (Black and Rubinstein, 20). Social inequality characterizes American aging but the emotional and spiritual growth possible in late life deserves equal attention.

In an autobiographical and anecdotal book on aging, Paul Tournier tells of a Swiss doctor assigned to several old and severely ill patients in a psychiatric hospital who used exercise, games, group therapy, and the telling of life stories to bring about "unexpected revival of the personality" (38). These same four activities would be extremely beneficial for elders outside of institutions, too. Why group therapy (admittedly a middle-class activity)? The speed, fragmentation, and noise of American life take a toll on minds and bodies; thus old women and men might benefit from sessions in which recovery is a theme. Perhaps an important purpose of late life is to recover from the harried pace of earlier times. A person who tries to make healthy choices about diet, exercise, medication, relationships, and activities cannot very easily tune out the materialism of our society, its addictive cravings for bigger and more. To be old and psychologically healthy in a society marked by destructive impulses requires great equilibrium and balance. In supportive groups, older women could perhaps come to regard moving slowly not as humiliation but as a chance to tap into the life force that is unnaturally suppressed by speed and fragmentation. As for life stories, elders who take time to reflect on their own stories and share them with others participate in an ancient ritual of most other cultures across time.

Aging is a process socially constructed as a problem. Public discussion of aging in America is narrowly focused on politics and economics, while a wide range of other relevant topics is ignored. Old women and men are seen in a utilitarian light of cost rather than potential. Who can they become is an unasked question. Can they be socially useful in ways that do not exploit them? In designating 1999 the International Year of Older Persons, Kofi Annan said that "a society for all ages is one that does not caricature older persons as patients and pensioners. Instead it seeks a balance between supporting dependency and investing in lifelong development" (P5). Learning to be old may be the last emotional and spiritual challenge we can agree to take on. While aging is shrouded in denial or shame, it will be seen simply as defeat. For many Americans, inability to think about being old, to plan for late life psychologically and not just financially, or to look squarely at its many complexities precludes conscious aging. Stoic resignation or despair may be their only reaction to bodily decline. The promise of other ways to age is exhilarating, though, if we can imagine late life as the time when we are most fully ourselves, a time to strengthen our survivor fiber. Women, especially, may flourish in old age if we can "break out of the confines of youthful adaptations" (LaBouvie-Vief, 163–164). In the following chapters, I suggest some ways of accomplishing this transformation.

Note

1. Brent Green, "Internal Colonialism vs. the Elderly," *Berkeley Journal of Sociology* (1979): 129–149. Green adopts a concept first applied to black Americans by Robert Blauner.

CHAPTER ONE

∾

Cultural Myths and Aging

Learning to be old means knowing that the way you age depends on where you live. In the mountains of Peru, you may be expected to do hard physical labor in your eighties. In Japan, your children may house you from a sense of filial duty but wish you could live alone. As an elderly woman in the Chagga tribe of Mt. Kilimanjaro, you have the right to pick a grandchild to live with you and help with daily chores, a custom practiced by some Navajo in the Southwest. In many societies, your tasks of child care and food preparation fully integrate you into your group. Infirmity may lower your status, for "nowhere is decrepitude valued" (Nydegger, 76), but if you live in Vatican City and wear a red hat, your power will draw attention away from your infirmities.

The commonplace that the old are devalued here in America and venerated in other societies is oversimplified. In nonindustrial societies, treatment of the old depends on wealth, gender, political role, and religious function (Foner, 390–395). Professed attitudes of regard for the old do not necessarily reflect actual treatment, and respect for a few powerful old people can be mistaken for respect for the old in general (Nydegger, 74–75). Nevertheless, high status for some of the old in some cultures, past and present, sharply contrasts with the relatively low status of the old in the U.S. today.[1]

A key to conscious aging is the ability to think critically about the culturally determined place one is assigned, so that discriminatory attitudes and questionable assumptions can be challenged, quietly within ourselves if not in words. When we receive a chirpy letter from AARP at fifty or later when a Medicare card arrives, no insert tells us that long-held cultural myths strongly influence the ways Americans age.

9

Self-Reliance

One of the most obvious and pervasive American myths is self-reliance, expressed by the phrase "rugged individualism." Is this myth useful for old age, or should it be discarded or at least reconsidered? The people best able to embody the extreme individualism of American culture are the young and strong. The middle-aged can do fairly well, but the old are bound to fail if this is a measure for judging them. To be sure, some old women and men have the physical and psychological energy to be as self-reliant and autonomous as anyone else. More often, to be old, at least to be over eighty, means needing some help; it means acknowledging that total independence is no longer possible. In America, this recognition often brings anguish and humiliation. In other cultures, where interconnectedness is lifelong and often necessary for survival, old-age dependency is not so radically different from dependency during other life stages.

The cultural myth of self-reliance suggests pushing against barriers and obstacles, dogged perseverance, and left-brain logic. It connotes competition, action, and freedom in separation. Self-reliance appears to be a male model, for women are often depicted as being in relation to others, whether by choice or conventional expectation. Women, like the poor, disabled people, or members of minority groups, may also lack the control over their life circumstances that is often a precondition for self-reliance, a value better suited to Anglo America than to the culturally diverse population reflected in the 2000 census. Despite these inherent limitations, self-reliance is commonly urged upon the old as if they were a monolithic group.

Emerson's essay "Self Reliance" (1841) is a classic text on this American virtue, but for Emerson the phrase does not suggest the ability to take care of oneself without depending on others. The focus of the essay is independent thinking. Emerson expresses the Transcendentalists' faith in the individual's inner light. He praises nonconformity.

Those over sixty-five who scorn senior centers, saying that they do not want to be around "all those old people," may unconsciously be avoiding the unpleasant truth that some people cannot *be* totally autonomous as they age. Elders who stay away from senior centers avoid seeing signs of dependence in age: canes, wheelchairs, walkers. Self-imposed isolation from others who are old allows one to preserve the fiction that one will never lose autonomy and thereby join a devalued group. The fact that people at senior centers have banded together for a common purpose, however, suggests the limits of late-life individualism.

A curious pattern in gerontological research is that when questioned about their health in relation to their age, subjects tend to express a gloomy view of the health of the old in general, but consider themselves lucky exceptions to the decline they think characteristic of their life stage. This pattern clearly illustrates the cultural emphasis on individualism. Caught in its grip, many of the old are unable to imagine large numbers of their peers as favored as they are. By viewing themselves as *not like* all of the others, the healthy old stress separation from their group. Distancing strategies, a form of denial, may also be a reasonable response to ageism, a way of resisting oppressive expectations of sickness or decrepitude. Such attitudes work against group solidarity among old women and men. Seeing oneself as an exception, a queen bee of aging, limits awareness of the large social and cultural factors that shape the category "old."

If I emphasize that I differ from the "typical" old who are deteriorating, I try to dodge the scorn often heaped on them. Unlike the dependent old, whom I perceive as weak, I stand as a strong individual. And the more I claim difference, the better I feel about myself. Like light-skinned blacks who pass for white and thus escape the stigma borne by the dark-skinned, the old who deny they are like the other old try to be taken for someone they are not. They assume that dependency and self-reliance are complete opposites.

Many old women and men cling fiercely to their right to drive because they well know that anyone too old to drive is indisputably old. Loss of the ability to drive is an informal rite of passage to the next life stage, in which autonomy, self-reliance, and freedom from interference are all threatened. What does this important transition mean for the psychological well-being and social life of the old? Is it more traumatic for men than for women? A driver controls her own schedule and her movements. When she stops driving and must then ask others for rides, she is in a subordinate position, created not by her age itself but also by culture.

Fifty-four percent of our communities have no publicly-funded senior transportation and the rest have limited systems (Freund). The lack of good public transportation in most places, especially rural America, helps to keep an elderly person at home. The belief that she shouldn't ask others for help becomes another reason to stay there (Nelson, 89). "Surviving without driving" is such a challenge, in fact, that a transportation expert has recommended a national education campaign to persuade elders that if they stop driving, they are still worthy persons (Freund), a proposal that vividly illustrates the power of the self-reliance myth to lower self-esteem among those who can no longer follow its dictates.

The primacy of the automobile is understood to be a threat to the environment, but it is also a factor in colonizing elders who no longer drive, a group that is predominantly female. When lack of transportation leads to loss of mobility and that in turn leads to physical decline, the problem is rooted in social status. If old citizens really had the political clout politicians and the media like to attribute to them, every community in America would have appropriate transportation for them and the system would be seen not as a special favor to an interest group but as a necessity like paved streets. The obstacles to such a system are not only cost but the myth of self-reliance. It casts normal physical change as a stigmatizing deficit.

The ultimate failure, according to self-reliance, is confinement in a nursing home. "I'd rather die than go there" is a commonly heard statement from people who have passed seventy-five. Their understandable fear comes not only from threatened self-reliance, of course, but from oppressive conditions in some nursing homes. Moving into a nursing home looms as a hateful eventuality partly because of our cultural myth of individualism. Conditioned to link old age with dependency and dependency with nursing homes, we prefer not to think about aging. Psychologist Ellen Langer has shown how the dependency nursing homes foster can be reversed when residents make many ordinary daily-life choices. Mindfulness exercises and activities that encourage independence can reverse memory loss and actually lengthen lives (81–89). The Eden Alternative nursing home model was developed by William Thomas to decrease the boredom and loneliness of life there. Among its strategies are care-giving teams who share in decision-making, visits by pets and children, and an emphasis on freedom of movement (Deaton et al., 196).

The bad image of nursing homes results from widespread abuses and unnecessary regimentation, but irrational fear of them impedes creative thought about their possibilities. Major problems of nursing homes are low pay and extremely high worker turnover, as much as 100 percent a year in some homes. Many aides are recent immigrants. A sensible nursing home plan would be to offer English as a Second Language classes to workers, who would be encouraged to practice their skills by talking to residents and writing down some of their stories. Workers would then have an incentive to pay attention to the individuality of residents and to keep their jobs at least until completing their classes.

Shame, depression, or a sense of unworthiness may result from trying to conform to a cultural ideal of individualism. Each loss of function is humiliating. For many old women and men, having to ask for help is regarded as a weakness. "I don't want to be a burden to anyone," one of the most frequently heard statements from the old, has a hidden subtext: "I will cling to my independence as long and as fiercely as I can, and you can count on me not to ask for help until I absolutely need it." This attitude is expected of the old; someone who said she looked forward to being helped would lose face. "The claim 'I can do it myself' reverberates throughout the lifecycle, perhaps becoming a dominant note in individualist competitive cultures." (Ruddick, 59). Rural old women especially value self reliance; their "world-views strongly condition the extent to which they accept nontraditional sources of assistance" (Kivett, 361). Naming needs discloses that the flame of self-reliance is sputtering. Another possibility is that a woman may fend off efforts to place her in a nursing home by saying she wants to live "independently," even though she may be both "heavily dependent on and heavily discounting her daughter's financial and emotional support" (Nelson, 87). In such a case, it is hard to disentangle strong social pressure to be self-reliant from the expression of an individual's wishes.

In the introduction to his cultural history of American aging, *The Journey of Life,* Thomas R. Cole recalls that his grandmothers felt ashamed of their old bodies, feelings that reflect "our culture's intractable hostility to physical decline and mental decay, imposed with particular vengeance on older women. Their shame and revulsion also reflects the scientific management of aging—which encouraged them to think of growing old not as part of the human condition but as a solvable problem" (xxiv). People are known through their bodies, and therefore, as Sally Gadow says, "repudiation of the body as a failed object, or worse, as an enemy, jeopardizes that connection of persons and their world" (Gadow, 1983, 45). A massive shift in consciousness would have to occur before old American women who are frail could love their bodies or women not yet frail could see old bodies in decline as simply old and not ugly. Jacqueline Hayden's life-size nude photographs of old women and men are startling because they disrupt our culturally sanctioned notions of beauty. Whose body merits representation?[2]

An individual's desire to be self-reliant when increasingly frail becomes especially poignant when early signs of dementia appear. "Early" is imprecise and easily contested, as I discovered when the niece of a woman I had befriended wanted to move her to the Jewish Home for the Aged in San Francisco. My friend, Frieda Walter, clearly suffered from mild dementia, but she was able to walk by herself everyday to the neighborhood senior center. She told me that when she couldn't remember what day it was, she called the child care center next door. To me these were signs that she could still look after herself. When the niece took Frieda to the Home and asked her to fill out an application, she refused. The niece interpreted this as a sign of dementia; to me it seemed the rational choice of someone not ready to surrender her freedom. Frieda's social worker was appalled that she had not seen a doctor in four years, even though she was eighty-six. But her disengagement from medicalized aging could also be seen as a calculation that she had more to lose than to gain by seeing a doctor. The social worker assumed Frieda was incapable of choosing wisely. At the Home, Frieda was immediately put on drugs. Soon her ankles were badly swollen and she broke her wrist in a fall. Placement in the dementia ward ensured her rapid mental deterioration. Drugged dependency was forced upon her. Population aging, especially, the coming large increase in the number of women over eighty-five, insures that some version of Frieda's story will be repeated often.[3]

Although people of any age are vulnerable to disease, disability, loss of friends, and lack of respect based on some arbitrary characteristic, the old are especially vulnerable to these and other conditions. Holding up self-reliance as a cross-generational ideal is singularly inappropriate. Too great an emphasis on self-reliance "reinforces the norm of living in single family units, the belief that the old should look after themselves, and the belief that their problems are their own and of no concern to the rest of us" (Tronto, 273). Such attitudes of course may characterize white middle-class life far more accurately than for example the lives of American Indians, many of whom are accustomed to interdependence and reciprocity throughout their lives, in contrast to whites; consequently, among them, "dependency and need in old age are judged less harshly" (John, Blanchard, and Hennessy, 309). The same may be true of Latinos accustomed to letting adult children take over responsibility for them. The notion of individual autonomy familiar in white, middle-class life is also out of place among Chinese Americans in the case of hospitals' policy of informed consent because families are expected to make decisions for their elders, sometimes deciding not to tell a parent that she is terminally ill (Yeo, 77). Similarly, among Korean Americans, conveying a fatal diagnosis seems disrespectful.

A deeper understanding of late-life frailty and dependence would not seriously challenge a mainstream cultural value as deeply entrenched as self-reliance, but it might take away some of the shame now associated with the end of complete autonomy. Dependency comes in many forms, some of which do not entail powerlessness, and dependency must be distinguished from incompetence (Baltes, 11), an insight that mitigates age shame. Frailty, after all, is only one dimension of a person, is not the same as withering away, and is a more or less apt description depending on circumstances. Most important, frailty can coexist with strengths. Someone who walks with great difficulty may have a strong voice, a strong will, or strong self-esteem. The intertwining of frailty and strength was brought home to me in a dramatic way several years ago when I heard Sir Georg Solti conduct the San Francisco Symphony during one of his last U.S. appearances. The stage door opened and out walked a very old frail man who moved slowly and stiffly. I watched nervously, wondering if he would make it to the podium. As soon as he raised his baton, though, he became a powerful figure. The orchestra played beyond its usual capacity. At the end of the concert as the musicians clapped loudly for Solti, the audience shared in the intensity of the moment. Then the conductor left the podium, once more a frail old man, walking with very small steps. The musicians and the audience intuitively knew that frailty made mastery more triumphant.

"Frailty is dialectical," writes Sally Gadow, "containing within itself its apparent opposite, new life and strength." She cites Florida Scott-Maxwell's description of "fierce energy" possible through frailty, when the life force appears in full strength as it cannot at times of "busy engagement with the world" (Gadow, 1983, 146). The idea that the life force does not depend on physical energy is arresting. It implies that frailty is relative and contingent rather than a fixed quality. Moreover, in Gadow's view, frailty is "essential to the making of a self" (146), a viewpoint better suited to late life than successful aging or productive aging.

Images of the old that romanticize individualism appear to counter ageist stereotypes in that they depict the old as able and honorable. But such images perpetuate the myth of self-reliance as preeminently worthy. This is true, I think, of "Alice Bell," a powerful story at the end of Pat Barker's Union Street. The eccentric old woman in the story is heroically self-reliant, fights off attempts to subdue her into dependency, starves herself to pay for her funeral, and finally kills herself. Her suicide is portrayed as a noble expression of her idiosyncratic self. Similarly, in May Sarton's novel As We Are Now, the suicide of Caro Spencer that also kills others in her nursing home represents a triumph of individualism over an oppressive, dehumanizing environment. Self reliance is portrayed as a transcendent virtue even in a violent and murderous form.

Another example: a severe ice storm in Maine early in January 1998 caused many people to be evacuated to shelters. For several days, homes had no power. Conditions were so dangerous that an elderly couple in Hancock County froze to death on the way to their mailbox. After the storm subsided, newspapers were filled with stories of neighbor helping neighbor, but special praise was reserved for the old who refused to leave their homes. No one mentioned the possibility that stubbornness might have shaded into foolhardiness. Naturally, the bravery of people for whom uprooting would have been a hardship evokes satisfaction in their triumph over adversity. In this case, however, the story of the unflappable old Mainers who said no to help illustrates the extremely high value placed on self-reliance, even when its exercise might be life threatening.

Learning to be old is hard when it means being able to accept dependency with grace. For women especially, whose struggle to become whole human beings often requires a great degree of self-sufficiency, at least in white, middle-class life, letting go of triumphant individualism must be painful and shaming. But the willingness to ask for help and the acknowledgement that one is not wholly self-sufficient are signs of emancipation from socially-constructed aging. Autonomy is incompatible with many of the facts of old age, and held up as an ideal, leads inevitably to disappointment (Moody, Age, 1993, 418).

In their study Life Beyond 85 Years: The Aura of Survivorship, Colleen Johnson and Barbara Barer found that their subjects reconstituted themselves as they increasingly needed help from others and that their adaptations were highly individualized (192). Even when their disabilities increased, they maintained their equilibrium (219). Compared to a group of 70–84 year olds, the people over eighty-five accepted dependency more easily and gave up control over some aspects of their lives, changes that usually did not undermine their sense of well-being (224). Perhaps these findings show that the people in the study outgrew the cultural norm of self-reliance. Were they exceptional? Is it futile to expect individualism to lose its central place in our system of values even when we are no longer able to exemplify it?

The need to be self-reliant may not press as heavily on women as on men because women are expected to relate to others and see to their needs. On the other hand, since most men who reach old age have a spouse to help them and most women do not, women have more opportunity to display self-reliance. Traditional female socialization might be advantageous in old age if it prepares women to accept dependence. In practice, it seems not to work this way. The cultural exhortation to stand on one's own two feet is stronger than the social message that caring for others and being cared for are equally admirable. At the same time, a male-identified woman whose life has been shaped by her autonomy may have a harder time in late life than a woman who has lived out a subordinate role.

Social historian Stephanie Coontz points out that the pioneer families who settled the West saw themselves as self-reliant but in fact were subsidized by the federal government, for example by military campaigns that took land from Indians and appropriated half of Mexico. She believes that "depending on support beyond the family has been the rule rather than the exception in American history" (214). And as feminist theorist Josephine Donovan notes, the "vision of the independent, autonomous individual (male) ignores the network of supporting persons (usually female) who enable his autonomy" by food, clothes, shelter, and nurture (15). Seen from these perspectives, the old who can no longer be self-reliant are like other Americans, in need of a web of support. Without a framework of interconnectedness and a critique of rugged individualism, however, old women and men are more likely to see themselves as failures when their self-reliance slips away. Old-age policies that assume that independence is necessary ignore or devalue women's life-long connections with others (Rodeheaver, 745).

At the same time that self-reliance is overvalued as an ideal for the old to embody, many suffer from learned helplessness. "Older people often end up in a Catch-22, caught between a social ethic of independence on the one hand, and a service ethic which constructs them as dependent on the other" (Robertson, 82). They or their families think they should give up an activity or avoid trying something new because of their age. "Mindsets about old age confirm a sense of incompetence" (Langer, 1989, 87). When a doctor questioned a middle-aged nurse about her mother, she replied tartly, "Why don't you ask *her*; she's right here." Several experiences of this kind condition an old woman to be silent. In other situations, "well-meant protectiveness gradually undermines any autonomy" in the old, especially among those who are institutionalized. Tying them in their wheelchairs for long periods amounts to "coercive interference" (87).

Self-Reinvention

An American cultural myth that fits the aging process better than self-reliance is the belief that we can reinvent ourselves. Originally subjects of a king, white Americans remade themselves into rebels. When life in the East became too confining, some went West. And when they arrived, nobody cared about the status, occupation, or wealth of their families. We mobile Americans know instinctively that if things don't work out where we are, we can go elsewhere, if we can afford to. Hard times decrease mobility but can also drive people out of their places. "Americans have always had second acts. They have been immigrants beginning anew. They have left behind families and scrawled 'Gone to Texas' on the walls of their houses. Second and third marriages are routine. And even in the most conventional lives, retirees leave familiar worlds behind for the Florida sun" (Applebome, 1). Cutting loose has always been the prerogative of the young, but today millions of Americans over sixty-five are settling in towns and regions far from where they raised families. And a surprising number are going home again after having tried Florida, Arizona, and California.

Since Gold Rush days and especially since the end of the Second World War, California has been the quintessential American place for reinventing the self. Judy Garland left Grand Rapids for Hollywood. Young people who worked as waiters and clerks in the Midwest kept similar jobs after moving to California but called themselves writers and artists. Women and men who led closeted lives in other places came to California for the freedom to be openly gay. Particularly since the 1960s, California has been the place to go after divorce, although the end of free community college tuition in the early 1980s made it less attractive for divorced mothers of college-aged children. The high cost of living in California has dissuaded some retirees from moving there, but the climate remains a draw for others.

Today the myth of reinventing the self plays out in the immigrant communities. Parents of community college students from China, Vietnam, and the Philippines, for example, typically work long hours in low-paying jobs, but the older brothers and sisters of these students often work in professions. Political upheavals in Central America in the 1980s resulted in the displacement of many Latino families, newcomers to California whose members include aged parents. Also in the 1980s, many Russian Jews relocated to San Francisco. Some elders who settled in suburbia are moving back to the city, a trend that may revitalize some American cities.

The more interesting aspect of reinventing the self is not the geographical move but the interior one. When the old come to a new place, they may choose to develop facets of themselves that found no expression earlier. New activities, new friends, and a new community all contribute to a sense of possibility. This is more true of course of the white middle class than of those who "age in place" because they have no other choice. People who have endured years of uncongenial work may take renewed pleasure in life. Some people stop going to church or find religion for the first time. Although colleges and universities have not been welcoming places for older students, many have found taking college classes the occasion for reinventing selves. Simply discovering that they have the ability to do college work can be exhilarating. Some of the ablest reentry students are working-class women for whom higher education was unattainable at eighteen.

The American myth of reinventing the self has traditionally been a male myth, one sometimes involving deception or a criminal past.[4] In Willa Cather's story "Paul's Case," the reinvention myth is beautifully rendered. Paul escapes a smothering bourgeois family, crass teachers, and a dull job for the aesthetic pleasures of New York. Although reinvention ends tragically in this instance, it is portrayed in such psychologically satisfying and enlarging terms that its possibility seems not completely denied by Paul's death.[5]

The prospect of reinventing the self in old age has special relevance for women, who may not have been able earlier to express their full individuality. Family responsibilities, work pressures, constraints imposed by sexism, and the expectation that they will juggle many things at once without complaint all hamper women's self-development. For healthy women, life after seventy may present unanticipated opportunities. Sometimes they are more willing to risk social disapproval for their choices. For those conditioned to meet all demands made of them, the simple act of saying "no" is freeing. The death of a husband may be the occasion for unexpected change. Redefinition of self is almost inevitable for married heterosexual women because many are widows by age sixty-five. More black women than white are widowed by then. Perhaps an older woman reinvents herself when she marries a man younger than herself, a good strategy for preserving companionship in late life, but not yet a common one.[6] "Some of us who are old," writes Carolyn Heilbrun, "suspect that a transformation of the self may require an abandonment of all that our consumer society identifies as woman's nature" (4). Deference, compliance, and attentiveness to men are examples.

A woman who has never expressed anger may find late in life that she has much to be angry about. Families have trouble dealing with this shift in a parent's or grandparent's behavior. Too often, an old woman's anger, particularly if it is uncharacteristic, signals to her family that she should be given drugs to calm down. Another way to view the unexpected anger is as a sign of growth or newly discovered power. If old women don't stifle anger, they appear intractable. In a story by Mary Wilkins Freeman, "The Village Singer" (1891), Candace Whitcomb is dismissed from her position of honor, lead soprano in the church choir, because she is old and her voice is fading. She erupts with anger and plots revenge. As she argues forcefully with her minister, the only way he can cope with her is to order her to pray with him. She refuses, defying his authority to silence her. For a woman of her time and place, that was an act of extreme rebellion. Even when the anger of the old seems justified by losses and humiliations, those around them may resist letting the anger play out.

At seventy-nine, Jeannette Picard was told she was too old to become one of the first women ordained as Episcopal priests. She and her sister priests dramatically reinvented themselves from laywomen to authority figures. Imogene Cunningham conceived of her late-life development as "a process of constant refocusing of the self" (Mitchell, 17). A Minneapolis woman, Nina Draxten, cast off the role of retired professor when she was eighty to become an actor, first in commercials and later in the movie *Far North*. Jon Hendricks tells of a concert clarinetist who turned his instrument into a lamp when he retired, explaining that he wanted new challenges (Creativity, 1991, 105).

Sometimes adaptations are as meaningful as reinventions. DeBeauvoir describes Renoir in his sixties, unable to hold a paintbrush in his paralyzed hand, continuing to paint until he was seventy-eight by having a brush taped to his wrist (313). People over eighty-five in the study cited earlier were found to "reinvent a self-concept that [takes] their survivorship into account" (Johnson and Barer, 163). Accepting help is not traumatic for them, for example. Some who had been very engaged socially now "cherish peaceful solitude" and do not feel lonely (156).

Lately gerontologists have suggested that "self" is really "selves" that require social interaction to call them forth (Hendricks, Practical, 1999, 200; Ray, 2001, 22). Despite all the changes we undergo, nevertheless, "something called 'I' always tells the stories about my many successive, lost, and parallel identities" (Gullette, 1999, 229). Baba Copper describes her aging as a "familiar process to which I bring an ever-expanding self," (91), suggesting that the self in "reinvention of the self" evolves. The conflict old women may experience between their inner selves and who they appear to be may ease if they value their aging faces and their aging selves (Meyers, 32), a difficult feat, perhaps, for younger women to imagine. Seen from these perspectives, reinvention is more a process than an event, interpersonal as well as intrapersonal. In contrast to some of its past guises, in late life the reinvention myth is anti-heroic and rooted in the ordinary. "Grandma Climbs Mountain" may be a less compelling story than "Helen Wong Says No to her Neighbors for the First Time."

Social class, a source for many of assumptions about the world, exerts a powerful influence on self-concept. "Far from being simply a mosaic of occupational, educational, and financial resources, social class wields considerable sway over all aspects" of our lives, including what we perceive as meaningful and how we age (Hendricks, Practical, 1999, 203–204). Moreover, the great variation observed among old women and men, usually assumed to reflect individual personalities, may be explained by "a lifetime's experience of social class" (207). Class privilege facilitates creative late-life reinventions but these take place in people of all classes. Consider for example the poor women of Argentina whose sons and husbands disappeared. Unable to protest in the usual ways, they gathered in small groups in their communities to make *arpilleras*, small drawings or weavings that told what happened and commemorated their family members. Through their ingenuity, they were not silenced.

Creativity

It would be worthwhile to study the late-life creativity not of artists such as Käthe Kollowitz, Louise Nevelson, and Georgia O'Keeffe, revealing as their stories are, but of women whose creativity could not flourish until they were in their seventies or eighties. It may take a lifetime for conventionally socialized women to throw off self doubt and focus intently on whatever engages them. The ninety-year-old narrator of Doris Grumbach's powerful novel *Chamber Music* embodies the unexpected, emotionally deepening changes that may accompany old age. Creating in some form is a way past despair, bodily decline, or the absence of friends who have died. Drawing and painting, singing, gardening, playing, laughing, breathing deeply, and being surprised all hold promise for our still developing selves.

Old women's lives may be seen as improvisations, an insight of Mary Catherine Bateson, who notes that women have always lived "discontinuous and contingent lives" (quoted in Friedan, 246). This is probably more true of heterosexual mothers than of lesbians who have no children, but many lesbians experience the major discontinuity of closeted lives followed later by more open lives. How do life improvisations for women in their nineties differ from those of women in their seventies? A good example of improvisation in a working-class setting is Mary Wilkins Freeman's story "A Mistaken Charity" (1887), in which sisters run away from an old-age home to which they have been sent. Middle-class norms of propriety, dress, and unfamiliar food displease them.

Notions of creativity are rooted in a particular time and place, although playfulness is probably a cross-cultural sign of creativity. In small-scale societies, the old may be expected to pass on what is known without any embellishment reflecting their individuality, as individuality is understood in large technological societies. However we conceive of it, creativity is an important aspect of late life, and pondering its manifestations may be a way of correcting the cultural myth of aging as inevitable decline.[7] Making new connections with one's past illustrates creativity. In a National Public Radio interview, for example, Lisa Simeoni asked Alfred Brendel why he recorded works he had already recorded years ago (April 28, 2000). Going back to a Mozart sonata after a long time, he explained, can "start a new chain of experiences." Creativity may also be sparked by participation in a stimulating activity. For many years, Elizabeth Wenzel has led literary discussion groups in senior centers and retirement homes in the Philadelphia area. Favorite works include *The Best of Simple* by Langston Hughes and stories with aging themes from writers such as Paley, Mansfield, Chekhov, O'Connor, and Brecht.

Creativity is usually regarded as an individual attribute, but it depends on opportunities for expression and on a receptive audience (Hendricks, Creativity, 1999, 96). In interviews, Alice Walker has said in response to questions about her early artistic leanings that she thought of becoming a musician but there was no money for a piano and then she thought of becoming an artist but there was no money for paints. Writing was within her means. In the landmark essay "In Search of Our Mothers' Gardens," Walker pays tribute to the old black women artists whose quilting and gardening nurtured their creative talent.

Reinventing the self may also be thought of as a strategy for maintaining self-respect. Usually I will be respected if seen as exerting power or influence on others or as controlling my own life. If I can drive, climb stairs, use a computer, carry bags of groceries, handle tools, arrange for services I need, and refuse whatever does not suit me, I exercise mastery over my environment without having to think about it. Others tacitly acknowledge my competence by not interfering. What happens when I can no longer drive, manage stairs, etc? My self-respect must rest on some other set of competencies. How can I feel worthy without the independence that previously marked my life? Will I respect myself when I hear "poor thing" in the voices of those who speak to me? How can I feel able when my sphere of movement shrinks? Perhaps if I know others like me, who have a sense of irony and a healthy self-regard, I can more easily base my self-worth on some inner qualities and thus avoid the shame that seems to accompany waning physical capacity. If I am no longer one who lives completely independently, who exerts her will in hundreds of small ways, can I become a woman who accepts this change with detachment? Will I have a context for understanding it that leaves me dignity? Can I simultaneously admit that I miss my former activities and see them as not so important now? If I project a sense of power when I can no longer move about freely, will others treat me as competent? If they see me only as diminished, can I parallel that partial truth with other truths about myself?

It is easy to admire the eighty-year-old woman who jogs or the eighty-year-old man who plays tennis. Our admiration reflects dominant cultural values. The ultimate countercultural stance is forcefully to declare one's worthiness in the face of irreversible physical decline. To do so requires setting aside the belief that aging is a falling from grace.[8] Avoiding the numbing effect of age denial and challenging cultural values can sharpen my awareness of aging's relativity. Others may see me as a pitiable wreck, but I know that in another society I would have meaningful tasks to undertake, my opinion would be sought, and no one would be embarrassed by my appearance.

Conclusion

It may be that those best suited to sustaining self-esteem are old women and men characterized by the same sturdy individualism that earlier in the chapter was judged a poor value to carry into old age. Perhaps instead of outgrowing this value, we need only transmute it. When we are too slow for competition, too buffeted by life to look down on others as weak or inept, and too appreciative of our friends' regard to overvalue material possessions, our individualism can soften. We can then see exaggerated forms of it as thwarting our development. If needing much help from others does not fill us with shame, we may readily accept Emerson's view of self-reliance as freeing our minds of common opinions, especially when these common opinions devalue ourselves.

Trying to live up to the contemporary American myth of self-reliance, on the other hand, may undermine our psychological health in late life. Seeing its limits and resisting it may free us from shame when we are no longer totally self sufficient, when the value of interdependence comes into sharper focus. No greater challenge faces women growing old in America than the preservation of self-worth in a culture of extreme individualism.

Notes

1. For overviews of anthropological work, see "An Anthropological Perspective on Aging," the introduction to Pamela T. Amoss and Steven Harrell, eds., *Other Ways of Growing Old* (Stanford: Stanford University Press, 1981); and Christine L. Fry, "Anthro-

pological Theories of Age and Aging," in *Handbook of Theories of Aging*, ed. Vern L. Bengtson and K. Warner Schaie (New York: Springer, 1999). See also Barbara Myerhoff, "Rites and Signs of Ripening: The Intertwining of Ritual, Time, and Growing Older," in *Age and Anthropological Theory*, ed. David Kertzer and Jennie Keith (Ithaca: Cornell, 1984); and Sharon Kaufman, "Narrative, Death, and the Uses of Anthropology," in *Handbook of the Humanities and Aging*, 2nd ed., ed. Thomas R. Cole, Robert Kastenbaum and Ruth Ray (New York: Springer, 1999).

2. Jacqueline Hayden's work was featured in Zoe Ingalls, "In the Unrelenting Eye of the Camera, Images of Our Own Mortality," *Chronicle of Higher Education* (January 7, 2000): B2. Illustrating the article is a striking nude photo of a woman crouching that evokes power and intensity rather than mortality.

3. I tell Frieda Walter's story in more detail in "Old in Spirit," in *Fierce with Reality: An Anthology of Literature about Aging*, ed. Margaret Cruikshank (St. Cloud, Minn.: North Star Press, 1995).

4. For a good discussion of the American myth of reinventing the self, see Frank Rich's essay "American Pseudo," on the Anthony Minghella film *The Talented Mr. Ripley*, *New York Times Sunday Magazine* (December 12, 1999): 80.

5. "Paul's Case," in *The Troll Garden* (1905), has an intriguing homoerotic subtext.

6. This theme is comprehensively treated in Lois Banner, *In Full Flower: Aging Women, Power, and Sexuality, a History* (New York: Knopf, 1992).

7. For creativity and aging, see Robert Kastenbaum, "Creativity and the Arts," in *Handbook of the Humanities and Aging*, 2nd ed., ed. Thomas R. Cole, Robert Kastenbaum and Ruth Ray (New York: Springer, 1999); and Anne Wyatt-Brown, introduction to *Aging and Gender in Literature*, ed. Anne Wyatt-Brown and Janice Rossen (Charlottesville: University Press of Virginia, 1993). This collection includes Margaret Morganroth Gullette's excellent essay, "Creativity, Aging, Gender: A Study of their Intersections 1910–1935." See also "Creative Uncertainty," chapter 6 of Ellen Langer's *Mindfulness*, and *Creativity and Successful Aging: Theoretical and Empirical Approaches*, ed. Carolyn E. Adams-Price (New York: Springer, 1998).

8. Margaret Morganroth Gullette's book *Declining to Decline* (Charlottesville: University Press of Virginia, 1997) discusses aging as a fall from grace. For a perceptive commentary on the decline narrative, see Hilde Lindemann Nelson and James Lindemann Nelson, "Care at Home: Virtue in Multigenerational Households," *Generations* 22, no. 3 (1998).

CHAPTER TWO

⌒

The Fear of an Aging Population

Another cultural myth, of more recent origin than those described in the preceding chapter, is that an aging population threatens the non-old. In the U.S. and other industrialized nations, population aging is a major trend. Here the old make up nearly 13 percent of the population, while the figures for other countries are slightly higher: 15 percent in Germany, for example, and 16 percent in Japan. Improved longevity is the most obvious reason for the growing numbers of older people, but another important and often overlooked reason is the decline in the fertility rate. Worldwide, women today have only half as many children as they had in 1972 (Longman, 31). The *combination* of these two trends from opposite ends of the life course is needed to make the old as numerous as they now are in western nations. Increased longevity has been defined as a menace by conservative commentators. Using appeals to emotion rather than evidence, they have constructed population aging as a fearful development. A few gerontologists have challenged their assumptions and refuted their claims, but the mass media has unquestioningly accepted the equation of an aging population with danger to the common good.

People over eighty-five comprise the fastest growing group of Americans, now outnumbering teenagers. Fear of this change rests partly on the stereotype of the old as parasites expensive to maintain. In fact, the old contribute a great deal to their families and friends in goods and services and in nonmaterial terms. Their contributions are often invisible in economic calculations: taking care of a spouse, for example, helping a neighbor, teaching or guiding grandchildren, volunteering, or simply being available to talk. An old woman or man who is currently not able to give to others should be seen as someone who has contributed in the past.

The Language of Fear

Fear of an aging population is sometimes communicated in ways that suggest that the old are alien creatures who are not a part of our common life. A *Boston Globe* article began, "Just as societies gird for the greatest onslaught of people ever to cross the threshold of old age" (Knox, 40).[1] "Society" here is defined as the not old. The war metaphor is telling. Its effect is not to inform but to create fear. The implied "we," those facing the "greatest onslaught," have no connection to the Others, who are not just different from us but menacing. Words like "onslaught" were also used to attack immigration in the nineteenth and early twentieth centuries.

Other examples of language used to create fear of increasing longevity are instructive. The Hoover Institute at Stanford, for example, issued a report called "Facing the Age Wave" by David A. Wise (1997). A wave can't be controlled, keeps coming, and may be harmful. "Age wave" is a popular usage in the media. "Facing" goes with a problem or crisis. If the Hoover Institute report had been called "Preparing for Demographic Change," the emotion would have been stripped away. Another usage is "grey hordes" (Bytheway, 60) to suggest barbarian invaders climbing over city walls. Disaster metaphors are common, for example, the use of "flood" or "epidemic" of old age to describe the society that lies just ahead. Nations with aging populations face "mountains of debt. . . that could destabilize the world economy" (Longman, 34). Dire predictions such as these have been repeated uncritically until they sound familiar enough to be plausible. World economic health obviously depends on multiple factors, of which population aging is only one.

Statements suggesting that population shifts in and of themselves bring disaster imagine passive politicians and economists unable to plan or react. They assume that the economic dimension of aging supercedes all others. When writers like Daniel Callahan refer to "the baneful effects of longer lives" (189), their comments are taken as self-evident facts rather than as emotionally-laden value judgments.

Another word that deserves attention is "entitlement," which conveys an impression of "self-interested demands upon government and its taxpayers" (Ekert, 526). A more accurate term would be "deferred compensation" to acknowledge that people over sixty-five are both contributors to the system and its beneficiaries. And, if Social Security were seen correctly as an earned benefit, a way to preserve living standards, or a program that shields families over the life course (Quadagno, 1996, 398), attempts to reduce confidence in it would appear destructive.

A Sunday *New York Times* full-page ad for Peter G. Peterson's book *Gray Dawn: How the Coming Age Wave Will Transform America and the World* pictures a huge and ominous iceberg with many jagged edges (February 14, 1999, p. 19). The caption reads, "A Demographic Iceberg Threatens to Sink the Great Powers." Beneath the caption are alarmist quotes from conservative luminaries such as Peggy Noonan and Sam Nunn. Paul Volker, former chairman of the Federal Reserve Board, cautions that the aging of America is a "time bomb." The phrase "great powers" has a lovely Victorian ring to it, suggesting imperialist glories. Making a connection between an iceberg and a group of citizens requires a leap past logic into irrational fear. Countries with aging populations, we are told, will "stagger under their weight." The personification of a country uses emotion to convey a sense of intolerable burden. Despite its arctic setting, the ad displays a lush garden of metaphor.

Grim prophecies such as these have been described as "apocalyptic demography" and "alarmist demographic discourse."[2] They may also be termed "demographic demagoguery" because they attempt to stir up fear by inventing a social problem. Similarly, in the 1970s and 1980s, some conservatives imagined a homosexual takeover of America, a myth that has lost much of its potency except when the issue is marriage. If lesbians and gay men replaced Communists as the alien group most to be feared, perhaps the old are now replacing gay people, although since September 2001, no one has seemed more frightening than terrorists. The rhetorical intent implicit in the iceberg ad is to divide old from young by creating a huge disparity of interests, just as enemies of immigration in the late nineteenth and early twentieth century portrayed a great gulf between Anglo-Americans and immigrants. Demographic demagoguery is a weapon used against women, people of color, and workers (Estes, 2001). Beyond curbing old-age benefits, its real aim is "to challenge and undermine the legitimacy of all government social welfare provisions" (Olson, 1999, 14). That is why conservative rhetoric about population aging is so emotionally charged.

Aging Politics and Economics

Americans for Generational Equity, founded by former Republican U.S. Senator David Durenberger and others, rests on the assumption that the young and the old are mutually antagonistic.[3] A similar philosophy shapes the Concord Coalition, created by former Republican U.S. Senator Warren Rudman and others. The latter group took out a full-page ad in the *New York Times* to attack a proposal to use part of the budget surplus to strengthen Social

Security and Medicare and to add a prescription drug benefit to Medicare (August 15, 1999, p. 23). The bill for these federal programs is "exploding," according to the ad, and in forty years they will "swallow" nearly half of U.S. payrolls. In fact, future costs of these benefits could easily be met if corporations were taxed today at the same rate as they were taxed in the 1950s (Minkler, 1997, 10). Liberals, too, may have negative views of population aging or concerns about Social Security and Medicare funding, but they usually do not resort to the elder bashing practiced by Americans for Generational Equity and the Concord Coalition.

A flaw in the thinking of such groups is the assumption that the old live in complete isolation from others. In fact, most live in families, either in the same family unit or in contact with nearby or distant family members. That means, for example, that a cut in Social Security benefits might require an adult child to give money to an aged parent, a change that would clearly harm the economic interest of the younger person. Or, if a grandparent who parents because she has the time available goes back to a paid job to cover increasing health care costs, the child suffers. Benefits to the old do not come from the pockets of the young and middle-aged.

Furthermore, wealth is passed downward to the young as well as upward to the old. Without Medicare, parents of baby boomers would have spent much more of their savings on health care. The often-cited fact that programs for the old take up one-third of the federal budget is usually stripped of its context: without Social Security and Medicare, the old would be entirely dependent on savings or families, if they had either one. Thus payments to the old can be seen as payments the young and middle-aged need not make. Without these so-called entitlements, the old would have fewer assets to pass on to their children. Not much ability to think abstractly is required to understand that the old are a part of society, interconnected with others, not an invasive species like kudzu.

Words and phrases such as "epidemic," "onslaught," and "time bomb" scapegoat old women and men. Instead of being seen in multiple roles or as having diverse economic needs, they are caricatured as parasites, "living too long, consuming too many societal resources, and robbing the young," a perception that justifies cuts in their benefits (Estes, Critical, 1999, 29). According to Meredith Minkler, this viewpoint falsely assumes 1) that the old are a monolithic group and 2) that spending on the elderly directly harms young families and children. In fact, many of the old, especially women over eighty-five and single women of color, are poor. Nearly 20 percent of older Americans are poor or near poor, the highest rate for any group except children

(Minkler, 9). The claim that old-age benefits increase poverty among minority children is unsubstantiated. In fact, these benefits are especially important in minority communities because family units are interdependent (Wallace and Villa, 242).

False assumptions can influence large numbers of people, however, and the result of conservative arguments that the old threaten future generations is that we have lost the social contract of the Lyndon Johnson era, according to which the old should be cared for. They were often mistreated in the past, as Robert Butler's book *Why Survive: Being Old in America* (1975) makes abundantly clear, but most citizens believed in providing an adequate safety net for them. The social contract began unraveling in the late 1970s, according to former Labor Secretary Robert Reich, who argues that it defined our sense of fairness but was not based on redistribution of wealth (21). Humane values have been supplanted by a view of the old as an economic drain. Thus the 1997 budget was balanced only because of large cutbacks in Medicare, particularly in home health care. Many agencies went out of business in 1998 and 1999 because they could not provide care at the reimbursement level of 1994, the date arbitrarily chosen by Medicare.

The attack on entitlements used to evoke fear of an aging population seems ironic considering that the old are better off than their grandparents *because* of increased Social Security benefits and Medicare. "The aggregate well-being of today's aged is largely the result of a half century's governmental action on their behalf" (Hudson, 11). Conservatives have been attacking a success. The white middle class benefits more than the working class from deferred compensation, and if benefits are cut, the greatest suffering will occur among the working class and people of color. They are less likely to own property or to have pensions, two cushions that help protect the economic interests of white middle-class people over sixty-five. And their interests are usually not promoted by the American Association of Retired People (now known as AARP) unless they coincide with the interests of the middle class.

Conservative politicians' hostility to AARP extends far beyond partisanship. Exaggerating its influence is a favorite ploy to discredit it. On a CNN news interview in September 2000, former U.S. Senator Alan Simpson launched into a long tirade against AARP, finally calling it "evil." No politician demonizes other citizen interest groups such as NAACP in this way. Women and men over sixty-five are resented for having a voice, even as muted a voice as AARP.

The dangers to the economic health of older Americans posed by conservative attempts to "fix" Social Security have been thoroughly analyzed by others.[4] I simply note that these proposals would lack credibility if widespread fear of an aging population were not part of the popular mythology. The chief beneficiaries of privatizing Social Security would be banks, insurance companies, and brokerage houses, because they would have access to money that now goes to the government in payroll taxes. Zeal for privatizing Social Security has dissipated as a result of the September 11 attacks and the disappearance of the budget surplus, but its security remains somewhat threatened by fear of an age wave swamping younger taxpayers. The importance of keeping Social Security intact was reinforced by the Enron collapse that wiped out the 401k retirement plans of many of its employees.

Conservatives' success in frightening many citizens about population aging is illustrated by the results of the 1999 Retirement Confidence Survey: two-thirds of current workers are not confident that Social Security and Medicare will give them benefits equal to benefits received today.[5] Multiple sources feed into this fear. An important one must be workers' fear of their own aging. With that dread already implanted they are susceptible to more abstract fears. If someone told these workers that a projected huge increase in the number of teenagers threatened the country's economic future, they would probably not be very alarmed.[6]

The mass media have not communicated to citizens a far more plausible outcome than slashed benefits: with reforms and adjustments, both Social Security and Medicare can be maintained at their present levels. The second scenario lacks drama. No scary graphics can be brought out to illustrate it. The conservative scenario imagines us victims of numbers. In fact, a modest improvement in the health of old Americans would result in Medicare savings, and a modest shift towards health promotion for the old, in place of the current disease model, would bring these improvements. No utopian schemes are needed to assure the continued security of old-age benefits.

Health care costs will increase with population aging, but a major cause of escalating Medicare costs is fraud. A report by the General Accounting Office estimates that fraud costs Medicare $13 billion dollars a year, but the actual amount may be much higher.[7] Some doctors pad bills for treatment, and now widespread fraud results from the entry of organized crime into Medicare. The old did not cause the huge increases in health care costs in recent years. They did not create the Harry and Louise ads that insurance companies used to defeat the Clinton health care plan. They did not compel drug companies to test a thousand new drugs, to spend millions giving free samples to doctors, or to carpet bomb television with their commercials. The

U.S. spends more of its GNP on health care than Canada and gets less in return, an imbalance that the old did not create. Furthermore, the very old cost less to care for at the end of life than people in their sixties and seventies. The ten-year MacArthur Foundation study *Successful Aging* concluded, surprisingly, that once people reach sixty-five, their added years do not have a major impact on Medicare costs (Rowe and Kahn, 186). The reason is that people in their eighties are less likely than fifty-year-olds to have major surgery or dialysis. Requiring fewer resources, their care is less costly.

In fiscal year 1999, Medicare spending declined for the first time in its history. Although this may not happen again, the fact that it could happen even once tends to cast doubt on doomsday scenarios of right-wing analysts. A big question about the future is whether breakthroughs in genetic research and biotechnology will increase or decrease the cost of health care.

No one knows the future economic impact of population aging; the large number of variables makes predictions unreliable. While the percentage of the old is growing, their actual numbers may not increase substantially. In the coming decades, longevity may level off. According to one calculation, human life expectancy will not exceed eighty-five years. Even eliminating cancer, stroke, and diabetes would not boost the figure to ninety-five or 100 (Roush, 42). While it is true that the ratio of workers to retirees is shrinking, the trend in itself is not the menace that conservatives make it out to be. Even if the economy grows only 1.3–2.0 percent over the next thirty to sixty years, the U.S. can absorb the costs of population aging "without placing undue burden on future cohorts of workers" (Kingson and Quadagno, 356).

Even when economics is the only lens through which population aging is examined, the cost of the old should be calculated not only by Social Security and Medicare but also by less obvious factors. Women and men over sixty-five, for example, have a crime rate that is "remarkably low," according to Richard Posner (128). The car accident rate for male drivers over eighty-five is one-fourth the rate for teenaged males and one-half the rate for males aged 25–29 (125). Even though the old as a group have fewer accidents than younger people, their accident rate per mile driven is comparable. Posner strongly disagrees with other conservatives on the meaning of population aging. He believes that when both costs and benefits are calculated, there is "no solid basis for concluding that the aging of the population has been or in the foreseeable future will be a source of net diminution in the overall welfare of the American people" (363). No icebergs, tidal waves, epidemics, floods, onslaughts, gray hordes, or time bombs dramatize this assessment.[8]

Although misleading, conservatives' fear-inducing rhetoric deserves study because it frames the public discussion of aging policy issues that will affect every citizen. As a result, drastic proposals for change can look moderate, and the interests of women, minorities, and the poor can be ignored (Kingson and Quadagno, 346). An example is the option of raising the retirement age for Social Security to seventy, a change that would particularly harm low-income early retirees and unemployed older workers and would result in a 40 percent benefit reduction for workers who retire at sixty-two (351). In addition, people of color would be disproportionately harmed because of their lower life expectancy. If progressives led the discussion about reforming Social Security, allowing people of color to collect benefits a few years earlier than whites might be proposed. That would be unwieldy and unpopular with middle-class whites but such a proposal would call attention to the great disparity in U.S. life expectancies.[9] And any proposed changes in Medicare would take into account women's longer lives, higher incidence of chronic illness, greater risk of poverty, and greater need of long-term care insurance.

Conclusion

The issue of old-age benefits is not only economic and demographic but also moral (Vincent, 147). Generational equity assumes a narrow view of reciprocity: you get back what you have given. A broader view, one that acknowledges interconnectedness, is that benefits bestowed by the generation ahead of us will be returned to the generation following us (149). A related moral issue is the limits and dangers of the adversarial mindset implicit in visions of generational conflict, a white, middle-class, male, competitive, and Western mindset. The communal traditions of many blacks, Latino/as, Asian Americans, and American Indians and the value systems of many whites (especially white women) stress cooperation and harmony between generations rather than opposition and struggle. They are not the ones who formulate aging policy.

Because unfounded fears of population aging have spread widely, progressives must respond to demographic demagoguery when their energy would better be spent finding solutions that do not pit one group of citizens against another. The time bomb and the iceberg are, after all, large numbers of our mothers, and aunts, our neighbors, and co-workers, and ourselves. This is not a reason to ignore implications of increased longevity, but it is a reminder that numbers tell only part of the story and that other numbers give a different account. When the story is frightening, when metaphors carry the weight of argument, when the powerful feel victimized, it is time to turn on our flashlights in the dark room and find no rough beast lurking there after all.

Notes

1. The writer must have seen the popular new button available at senior centers, "We Will Bury You," available in German and Japanese as well as English.

2. Ann Robertson, "Beyond Apocalyptic Demography," in *Critical Gerontology: Perspectives from Political and Moral Economy*, eds. Meredith Minkler and Carroll L. Estes (Amityville, N.Y.: Baywood, 1999). Stephen Katz uses the phrase "alarmist demographic discourse" in *Disciplining Old Age: The Formation of Gerontological Knowledge* (Charlottesville, Va.: University Press of Virginia, 1996).

3. For a history of Americans for Generational Equity and a refutation of its claims, see Jill Quadagno, "Generational Equity and the Politics of the Welfare State," in *Aging for the Twenty-First Century*, eds. Jill Quadagno and Debra Street (New York: St. Martin's, 1996). Quadagno points out that benefits for the old do not cause child poverty and that Social Security is a "highly visible target for conservative attacks" because the U.S., unlike Europe, does not have a wide range of family support programs (413–14).

4. See, for example, "Social Security—It's a Women's Issue" by the National Council of Women's Organizations' Task Force on Women and Social Security (Washington, D.C.: National Council of Women's Organizations' Task Force on Women and Social Security, n.d.). See also Jill Quadagno, "Social Security and the Myth of the Entitlement 'Crisis,'" *Gerontologist* 36 (1996): 391–99.

5. Paul Yakoboski, *1999 Retirement Confidence Survey* (Washington, D.C.: Employee Benefit Research Institute, 1999). Worker confidence was slightly lower in 1994 and 1996 surveys conducted by Yakoboski.

6. For more on internalized ageism, see chapter 8.

7. *NRTA Bulletin* 40, no. 11 (December 1999): 2.

8. "Demographics is not Destiny," published by the National Academy on an Aging Society, also concludes that no crisis looms because many factors will determine the solvency of Medicare and Social Security. See Paul Kleyman, "Report Questions Basing Policy on Fear of Aging Demographics," *Aging Today* 20, no. 2 (March-April 1999): 4.

9. "Surprises in a Study of Life Expectancies," *New York Times* (December 4, 1997): A9. Male Indians in South Dakota live to fifty-six years; black men in Washington, D.C., to nearly fifty-eight; white women in central Minnesota to eighty-three; and white men in Utah to seventy-seven. For the population as a whole, the figures are seventy-nine years for women and seventy-two for men.

CHAPTER THREE

~

Sickness and Other Social Roles of the Old

Wherever meaningful social and religious roles exist for the old, physical health is only one dimension of aging. In a materialistic culture, on the other hand, having no designated role for elders, the state of the body is all-important. "Our society views aging through the prism of illness" (Hazan, 20). In other societies, the old may be peacemakers or mediators. They may be keepers of traditions or repositories of special knowledge. In some African tribes, old women have the power of naming the newborn. In Asian cultures, the time of gradual loss of physical strength is thought to be the time for deepening spiritual power. In North America, minority communities are generally the only ones in which any comparably high status for the old is found. Old Indian women assume roles such as wisdom keeper, leader, and artist, for example (John, Blanchard, and Hennessy, 305). They too name children (Long, 111). Everyone has a place in the talking circle of the Manitoba Cree, but it is the elder who begins the talk. Black women typically exert strong influence when they are old, often through their churches.

One mark of the social construction of aging is overemphasis on bodily decline. The meaning of old age then becomes physical loss. When the old are reduced to deteriorating bodies (which change in infinitely varied ways), they can easily be marginalized. No one regards childhood or adolescence solely as a physical condition. Seeing old age in this narrow way has many consequences, of which the most significant is the medicalization of aging.

The Sick Role

Thirty years ago, the distinguished anthropologist Margaret Clark pointed out that the old in the U.S. have only one important social function: getting sick. This viewpoint is even more persuasive today because of the increasingly large role that corporate health care plays in aging, both in shaping public policy and in limiting individual choice. In America, where usefulness is defined as productivity, many of the old do not appear to themselves or others as useful because their paid work role has ended. In a market economy, however, the old do produce something of great monetary value: illness. The business of the old is to be sick.

As the number of young people decreases and the number of those over sixty-five and especially over eighty-five rapidly increases, biomedicine depends more than ever on the old for its profits. American elders use a third of all prescription drugs. Decreased use would result in big losses for the drug industry. If most of the old could manage without drugs and hospitals, who would fill the beds? In addition, population aging creates potential expansion for businesses that provide illness-related products and services.

If the financial interests of big medicine, insurance companies, and the drug industry were served by healthy old people, the center of aging would be health promotion and not illness. But as Carroll Estes has written, the old in America are "instrumental in the development and expansion of a large and profitable medical-industrial complex." Under capitalism, the needs of the old are commodified ("Critical," 1999, 26). Therefore, the illnesses of the old have far more than biological meaning; they are not just individual occurrences. Looking at illness as *characteristic* of the old, especially old women, misses its social function. A resurgence of health among large numbers of them would slow down expansion of the medical-industrial complex. On the other hand, if this slowing down occurred, pension funds that invest in drug companies would be hurt, IRAs and CDs might decline in value, and other ripple effects might cause economic harm to the old.[1]

In industrial nations, the *healthy* old are expected "to behave psychologically and socially" like sick people of any age (Arluke and Peterson, 275). To fill their social function of illness, the old must be conditioned to believe that aging is a disease requiring heavy consumption of medical services. The drug ads that saturate television encourage this belief, especially since old women and men appear in few ads for the products healthy people use. Magazines geared to them advertise medicines and props for illness. Newspapers cover the disease aspects of aging as if the two were interchangeable. Families assume that an elderly parent needs more drugs than before simply because she is old, and this assumption is shared by nurses, doctors, and social workers. Medicare's emphasis on acute illness rather than health promotion is a major factor in conditioning the old to see sickness as their chief concern.

Instead of having federally funded recreation programs for the old, or a jobs program, we have Medicare. When aging is viewed as socially constructed, however, as something more than what happens to our bodies, the focus on illness seems skewed.

The accuracy of Clark's comment on the sickness function of the old can readily be tested by eavesdropping on conversations in a senior center or any-where people over sixty-five gather. It is soon apparent that illness serves as one of the main staples of conversation. More significantly, the old with seri-ous health problems gain status by having them. They quote their doctors at length, speculate about the progress of their disease, cite examples of others who have had it, and manage to stay in the spotlight by emphasizing their illness. Other facets of their lives recede in importance. Sometimes elders will try to outdo each other in boasting of the severity of their condition. A sentence that begins, "My doctor says . . ." is a status marker for an old woman or man. It links him or her to culturally valued workers and institu-tions. It announces participation in an important world.

Once during a healthy aging workshop I was conducting, a woman in her seventies said proudly and defiantly, "I live with pain." She offered no other information about herself. As I thought later about her words, I guessed that she was staking a claim to be taken seriously. Without her pain, how would she present herself? The woman's pain is a physical condition, but the mean-ing she gives it is culturally determined. In a society where sickness conferred no status she might experience pain, but its meaning would be slight com-pared to its very large meaning in modern America.

Those who come into contact with old women and men sometimes com-plain about their preoccupation with illness and disease. Perhaps they would have more compassion if they could see how the world of the old often excludes much of what used to make life meaningful and now focuses on illness. The old woman who constantly complains about her ailments expresses not only an individual personality but a cultural pattern. At the same time, she is breaking an unwritten rule that requires her to suffer silently. Reporting on one's physical condition is not the same as complain-ing, but old women often are not granted the psychic space to explore the differences between reporting and complaining.

The doctor may be the one person outside the family than an elderly woman regularly sees. Often those perceived as frail and dependent are not making new friends or discovering new interests. The importance of sickness may become magnified if isolation removes other sources of meaning and self-definition. The very old typically have little power or influence, and society has few expectations of them. Illness is absorbing, ever-changing, seldom dramatic but eventful. It fills up time. Illness may be the only process occurring in the life of an old person that others regard as meaningful. No wonder many of them emphasize it. It takes both an awareness that one can easily become enmeshed in the medical system and a strong ego consciously to avoid the sick role when old and ailing, or to resist exploiting sickness to gain attention.

The understanding that old-age illness is partly socially constructed does not deny widespread health problems among the old, blame them for being sick, or assume they are victims. Whether we age from wear and tear or because we are genetically programmed to age, the fact is that late life and sickness are more closely linked than youth or middle age and sickness. But this general truth is no reliable predictor that any given individual will get sick, nor does it mean that a disease or health problem in old age is incurable. People fall ill for complex and mysterious reasons. Even in the case of the chain smoker who gets emphysema or the heavy meat eater with heart disease, we cannot know the brain chemistry disorders that may have predisposed them to addictions. Although programmed to accept illness as natural to their life stage, many of the old navigate the health care system without becoming victims. For some, seeing a doctor is comforting and reassuring without entanglement in a sick role.

Furthermore, certain groups are sicker than others. Black women are more likely than white women to die of heart disease, stroke, and breast cancer and are less likely to get mammograms. Their rate of diabetes is 50 percent higher. High blood pressure is a problem for 19 percent of white women but 34 percent of black women (Flaherty, 3). American Indians have very high rates of diabetes. Poor whites as well as people of color are more likely to have been exposed to environmental toxins and less likely to have had their illnesses diagnosed and treated before they reach old age.

Today, Alzheimer's stands for aging in America. The great attention paid to the disease by the media reinforces the link between aging and sickness. The devastating impact of Alzheimer's on individuals and their families warrants concern, but media coverage has also contributed to an unreasonable fear of aging. John Bayly's memoir about caring for Iris Murdoch, in which the great novelist is described playing with Teletubbies, received far more press than any of her works. Fear of getting Alzheimer's is disproportionate to its incidence. Approximately one in ten older Americans suffers from the disease (some estimates say one in eight) but media emphasis creates the impression that it is far more prevalent. Students are surprised to learn that it is does not afflict most older people.

Loss of one's mental capacity is especially terrifying in societies like ours where rationality is so highly valued. Here Alzheimer's excludes one from the circle of life in ways not characteristic of other societies. A person with Alzheimer's becomes a manifestation of disorder rather than an individual who is ill. The ideology of Alzheimer's sharply contrasts normal aging with "total and remitting pathology; in so doing, it both denies the complex experience and the personhood of old persons it would represent and shifts attention away from the social origins of much of the weakness of old age" (Cohen, 1998, 303). Social origins include learned helplessness, expectations of decay and decline, the lack of health promotion programs for the old, media stereotypes, and inattention to the dangers of multiple prescription drug use.

Elizabeth Markson has observed that memory loss may be a way of coping for women whose roles have disappeared and consequently, what we term dementia may be a "social interaction and the appearance of more primitive, unsocialized, emotional or cognitive states" (1986, 268). A similar interpretation suggests that memory loss may be an attempt to return to the "safe haven of a past universe of meaning" (Hazan, 86). Nonetheless, Alzheimer's is a dreadful affliction, striking many people over eighty-five, the age group in which women outnumber men four to one.

An insidious aspect of the sick role is that it may actually create illness. A telling example of socially-constructed incapacity occurred when a group of English people in a long-term geriatric ward was moved into attractively decorated bungalows during renovation of their ward. As they began to exercise more and to perform household tasks, both their incontinence and their mental confusion declined, and they began to cast off their sick role (Townsend, 37). This dramatic change suggests that older people may perform sickness when their environment gives them the appropriate cues. If they assume their illnesses are natural concomitants of their age, they may feel fatalistic about their health. "Fatalism implicit in metaphors of deterioration, decline, and disease as aging" may prevent older adults from re-establishing their levels of physical, psychological, and social health (Davidson, 177). It may even prevent them from imagining recovery.

Learning to be old, then, means knowing that late-life illness has both cultural and biological origins. It means believing in one's capacity to recover completely from illness, accident, or disease in the face of skepticism or insensitivity from families and doctors. It means knowing that political and economic institutions are structured to offer some support for the sick old but very little for their health maintenance or improvement.

Aside from normalizing illness, the sick role of the old is damaging because it places them in a dependent, relatively powerless position. The old woman or man who frequents doctors' offices performs subordination. His or her infirmities receive far more attention than strengths and innate healing powers. Rarely will a doctor view an old patient as capable of returning to full vigor. Rarely does a patient have the opportunity to tell the whole story of her illness in a way that emphasizes not only its severity but also her coping strategies and her resilience. She may escape the most blatant forms of gender bias in her medical care, being diagnosed as demented if she expresses anger, for example, but gender may determine how seriously her symptoms are taken and whether or not a psychotropic (mood-altering) drug is prescribed.

To remain healthy in old age is to defy expectations. Good luck, class privilege, college education, and high status of one's former work help increase chances of health as do exercise, good habits, and access to well-trained alternative healers. A nonconforming spirit seems essential, too. What Rowe and Kahn call "usual aging" has not been the fate of the very healthy old. Since the robust among them tend not to appear on the radar screens of policymakers, their numbers are probably greater than anyone realizes. The ordinariness of late-life vigor goes unreported. This is a hunch based on letters I received from potential contributors to an aging anthology. The writers told me about their pursuits and their experience of aging. If they had ailments, they didn't mention them, even though most were well over eighty. A composer in his nineties expressed disappointment that he no longer got commissions. People assumed he had stopped working but he hadn't. The caregiver of an elderly woman, herself quite old, described her pleasure in gardening with the older woman. The helper let her do all she could before taking over a task so that the garden was a real collaboration. A retired professor who had come out in his sixties described the surprises and pleasures of his new life. An herbalist in Tennessee told of a local television program where she described the lore passed down to her from her mother. People such as these are invisible to most younger Americans. Thousands of their stories would give aging America a different face.

The conventional view inextricably linking disease with old age must give way to a newer idea that good health characterizes large numbers of the elderly. If very healthy people in their eighties and older could become known beyond their circle of family and friends, the assumption that being old is a medical condition could be challenged. Fear of an aging population rests on this belief. Fear of our own possible deterioration is surely intensified if the lives of the only old we know are circumscribed by illness.

Other Social Roles

Are there alternatives to the sick role for old women and men? Social gerontologists often call modern aging a "roleless role" because no special tasks, responsibilities, or leadership functions are expected of people resulting solely from old age. Recently it has seemed that the social role of the old is to extend mid life as long as possible so that neither they nor others will be discomfited by thoughts of what comes next. Those who favor rationing health care do not forthrightly say that the social role of the old is to hurry up and die, but they regard their prolonged living as a threat to the common good. The description "roleless role" better fits the white middle class than Indians, Asian Americans, Latinos, and blacks, whose communities often seem to have a variety of roles for elders. Gender bias lurks here, too, because very often a woman's caregiving role lasts for her whole life.

Service
What are the old supposed to do or be? A common view is that their role is to serve others. Since those who serve others are unquestionably useful, the service role has some appeal, but it masks doubt that the old are worthy in and of themselves. Designated server is a demeaning role for the old; it assumes they are a monolithic group, and locates their value in action, not in being. Designated server is especially unsuited to old women, many of whom have served others all too faithfully for decades. The service ideal reflects middle-class bias, in that it disregards the fact that poor and working class women and men have often been coerced into the service of others. In her "Open Letter to the Women's Movement," Barbara Macdonald tells younger feminists not to expect her to serve them simply because they are younger (73).

Tillie Olsen's novella *Tell Me a Riddle* describes a woman who fiercely rebels against the expectation that she tend to others' needs. She is tired. She would rather sit quietly absorbed in her own thoughts than humor a grandchild by telling riddles. Service to others is not the special province of the old. They may be good at it from practice, and they may have more leisure than others to be of use, but this worthy ideal for people of any age should not be assumed to fit them automatically. Justifying the existence of old women and men on the grounds that they serve others is narrowly utilitarian and devalues those too infirm to give assistance to others. What they can provide is opportunities for others to serve them.

In grandparenting, the service role takes a benign form, but it is not an experience universal to aging, and it is a more complicated role than before because of high divorce rates, blended families, and the mobility that allows working families to live far from grandparents and grandparents to retire far from their grandchildren. The role has also changed significantly now that many grandparents have assumed parenting responsibilities. The term *abuela*, or grandmother, conveys "a romanticized image of older Chicanas that only serves to disempower women within their families and among the community" (Facio, 348). The individuality of an elderly Chicana may disappear into *abuela*. David Steinberg, who writes a column called "Seniorities" for the *San Francisco Examiner,* reports that when he auditions for television commercials featuring grandfathers, he wears a cardigan sweater because that's what grandfathers are expected to wear. The narrowness of role expectations is mirrored in the narrowness of this dress code.

As the population ages and more people over sixty-five are available to volunteer, the idea that their role is to serve others conveniently justifies the use of volunteer labor to replace the many paid workers whose jobs were cut in the 1980s and 1990s. Volunteer labor, it is true, keeps many programs and agencies afloat, but it cannot compensate for what has been lost.

A psychiatrist and gerontologist whose writings have encouraged a humanistic view of aging, Robert Butler, sees the role question in this light: "Older persons should be custodians of the finest elements of civilization, and active guides, mentors, models, and critics. Old age should be a moral powerhouse. Otherwise, does humanity deserve its newly acquired longevity?" (1999). Commendable as this sounds at first hearing, it assumes that the presence of large numbers of the old requires justification. It doesn't. Butler's view expresses a need that the non-old may have for mentors, moral guides, and preservers of culture, but the existence of that need does not mean that the old should be the ones to meet it. Barbara Macdonald thinks that the culture bearer role objectifies old women, for example (75). The statement that "old age should be a moral powerhouse" in effect prescribes a role for women, because it is they who survive to be old. In fact, life knowledge probably equips many old women to advise well, but this role should be freely chosen, not imposed. Number of years accumulated does not predict moral development.

A related prescription is that the old should be protectors of the environment. Many retirees have become ecologically sophisticated advocates for environmental causes, using their leisure for the common good. Many marched with groups such as the Sierra Club at the demonstrations against the World Trade Organization in Seattle in December 1999. The Colorado group Great Old Broads for Wilderness calls attention to damage caused on public lands by off-road vehicles and publishes the newsletter *Broadsides*. Perhaps late life encourages an awareness of future generations, of legacy, or of the transitoriness of human existence. It's likely, too, that women and men who are now over seventy remember clean air and clean water. Although the notion of the old as guardians of the environment is appealing, it is a variation of the idea that they exist to serve others.

The service role might look different if the old were paid for their labor. Designed for low-income people over sixty-five, the Foster Grandparent Program, Senior Companions, and Senior Community Service involve only one quarter of one percent of the elder population. The first two pay a tax-exempt stipend of $2.45 an hour and Senior Community Service pays the minimum wage. Since the number of tasks is limited, delivering Meals on Wheels, for example, the programs do not make use of a wide range of skills that participants could offer. Program limitations suggest "a cultural ambivalence about older adults as serious and capable service-providers" (Freedman, 2000, 215). This situation is especially discouraging because public institutions need so much work. Some problems in our underfunded schools might be solved, for example, if paid workers from the ranks of older women and men were given meaningful work to do in schools, such as mentoring, testing, or tutoring. The boredom and loneliness of nursing home residents might be alleviated if paid workers their own age visited them frequently.

In late life, people will keep on doing what they have been doing, especially if they are healthy. Others will learn something new or discover talents and abilities unknown before. Some will take up a cause like literacy or community work such as hospice. Some will be the mainstays of their parishes, congregations, synagogues, or covens. For some the role of bereaved spouse will be defining. Caregiving will be the social role of an increasing number of middle-aged and old women.

Wisdom

Another common view is that the old hand down their wisdom to others. This notion fit societies in which the survival of the young directly depended on acquiring the knowledge possessed by tribal elders. Among Pacific coastal tribes, for example, the art of catching salmon was passed down to the young. An understanding of how to behave, how to handle disputes, how to choose a partner, whom to avoid, and how to interpret the natural world all depended on received wisdom. Where to find medicinal plants, how to make tools, or how to fashion baskets reflected accumulations of knowledge whose possession gave status to old members of the group. On the other hand, in a technological society, in which information becomes obsolete rapidly, the wisdom role of the old all but disappears. Today a grandparent may impart knowledge, but with the dispersion of families and the proliferation of information, few grandparents have knowledge that a young person absolutely needs to survive. The life experience acquired by some elderly women and men, valuable as it is, does not provide a widely-sanctioned guide role for them, partly because age segregation is common now and individualism highly valued. In addition, cultural diversity and the dissimilarity of our various American traditions preclude a common guide role for older Americans, but particular forms of it exist among groups such as Indians and newly-arrived immigrants.

The role of wise elder appears to require a scarcity of candidates for the honor. In colonial America, where few lived to be old, that attainment carried with it an aura of God's favor. Now, with millions surviving past seventy-five and eighty and growing numbers of centenarians, figuring out what is special about them is difficult.

The wise elder is a comforting notion in times of upheaval and rapid change. But the automatic linking of wisdom and age overlooks the fact that not all of the old are wise and that the characteristics of modern America are manifestly not conducive to developing wisdom at any age. Those who attribute wisdom to the old romanticize them. This link is popular with young and middle-aged feminists, who understandably wish to counter ageism, for example by referring to the "wisdom. . . emerging from a lifetime of experience" as if this were universal.[2] A better way to honor old women than by invoking positive stereotypes is to value individual temperament and creativity. In some, wisdom will be a striking feature, but only in some. Or it will characterize certain aspects of an old woman's life but not others. The wisdom borne of a deep understanding of one's life experience differs from the wisdom that transcends an individual story.

At the same time, the wise elder archetype deserves some place in the modern scheme of aging if only because of its powerful, ancient, and cross-cultural manifestations. Surely old women and men who are highly developed emotionally, intellectually, and spiritually are worthy of being named wise elders. Whether they would choose this designation is another question. Recognizing high attainment in an elder requires both a generosity of spirit and freedom from ageist stereotypes on the part of a younger person. American Buddhists honor old women teachers such as Pema Chodron, Ruth Dennison, and Roshi Jiyu Kennett, and others can readily identify wise elders such as Eleanor Roosevelt and Margaret Mead, but none of these remarkable women needed to be old in order to be wise.

Retirement

Some gerontologists believe retirement is merely a position, not a role involving special rights and duties or determining social relationships (Atchley, 251). Retirees identify themselves by their former work, especially when meeting someone for the first time, suggesting that the retirement role has limited meaning for them. Since work has more status than leisure, the retiree who names past work links herself to what is valued. Paradoxically, retirees may be engaged in the most complex, demanding, and absorbing work they have ever undertaken, but it will not be defined as work if it brings no wage. (Retirement is analyzed in chapter 7.)

Gender Shifts

An aspect of social role and aging is the process by which some heterosexual men take on traits and attitudes thought characteristic of women such as nurturing and women become more assertive. This late-life gender-bending may become more common as gender stereotypes lose some of their formative influence, if that is a result of more women entering professions and more men growing through fatherhood. The late work of Georgia O'Keeffe reveals an "adventurous, expansive, self-asserting," woman, according to David Gutmann. By contrast, older men increasingly stress "their self-control, their friendly adaptability, and even their passivity."[3] Does this observation best fit white middle-class people? O'Keeffe's late-life independence resulted in part from the good fortune of having a male partner who opened the doors of the New York art world to her.

I saw confirmation of Gutmann's point, however, at the Montefiore Senior Center in San Francisco, where I observed women in their eighties leading groups in which old men were rather quiet participants, even though some had retired from professions in which their dominance was assured, labor union president, for example. The men were outnumbered, but that alone should not have been responsible for their willingness to defer to women.

One man memorably did not illustrate this pattern of late-life androgyny. He stood up in a discussion group and yelled, "Where are the men?" I explained that women outlive men. "Why is that?" he roared, and answered his own question, "Because women don't take good care of their husbands!"

Structural Lag

The phrase "structural lag" refers to a mismatch or imbalance between growing numbers of the elderly and "role opportunities, or places in the social structure, that could foster and reward" people at all stages of their lives (Riley and Riley, 16). Age integration would alleviate some of the problems caused by structural lag (30). The challenge is to figure out ways to achieve an age-integrated society (Quadagno, 1999, 184–86). From the vantage point of their nineties, Matilda White Riley and John W. Riley envision a society in which retirement will be replaced by alternating periods of leisure, work, and education; education will truly be lifelong; paid work opportunities will be available to people of all ages; and old age will not be considered a burden (33).

Structural lag is illustrated by the preoccupation with illness as a marker of old age, the lack of federal programs that involve significant numbers of low-income elderly, and media focus on Social Security and Medicare as the only important aging issues. It is one of the unacknowledged gender issues embedded in aging. In his book *Prime Time*, Marc Freedman notes that Americans lack "a compelling vision for later life" and institutions to match capable elders with opportunities for meaningful activity (21).

Colleges and universities keep older adults on the fringes with weekend courses, "senior college," and noncredit work. A major barrier to achieving an age-integrated society, according to John W. Rowe and Robert L. Kahn, is the unwillingness of many colleges and universities to adjust schedules and requirements "to encourage intermittent or sustained course work by adults of all ages" (196). Encourage is the key word here. At present, students over fifty or sixty are merely tolerated. They may take continuing education courses, usually shorter than regular college courses, and sometimes their fees are waived if they are over sixty-five. But colleges are currently set up to serve 18–25 year olds. There is no biological reason for restricting education and work to youth and midlife, but the association of old age with decline seems to justify this custom. In the 1970s and 1980s, however, The University of the Third Age was developed in Britain and Australia to offer low-cost higher education to older people. No previous education is required, and professors and administrators donate their time.

What if old women and men have no particular social role simply by virtue of being their particular age? The great diversity of this population, its size, the increasing number of minority elders, the growing gap between rich and poor, and the fragmentation of society all support this view. Shaped by decades of influences and accidents of race, class, and gender, those who happen to be over sixty-five or seventy may find other aspects of their being more salient than their chronological age. If they have no social roles unique to their life stage, then their value cannot be grounded there in utility and service. The idea that old women and men have special roles is condescending. They have the same roles as others. They choose them based on individual temperament, energy level, family needs, beliefs, habits, locale, income, friendship, skills and time available rather than on age.

Stories, Reminiscence, and Life Review

Another possibility, however, is that a social role for the old might be found in storytelling, reminiscence, and life review. The meaning older people see in their lives is part of the larger system of social and cultural meaning (Black and Rubinstein, 3). Life review was recently described by Robert Butler as a process marked by the return of memories and past conflicts that can lead to "resolution, reconciliation, atonement, integration and serenity. It can occur spontaneously, or be structured" (2000, 9).[4] Barbara Myerhoff hyphenates "re-membering" to distinguish it from ordinary recollection. It is a process of "focused unification" in which the members are our past selves and the people important to our story. In re-membering, the creation of an aesthetic or moral framework for a story may be preferable to fullness of detail (1984, 320).

Life review usually cannot be done alone; a recipient is needed to make the narrative coherent (Myerhoff and Tufte, 252). When the listener is young, the shared stories create intergenerational continuity (255). Women and men who live to be old accumulate much material to draw from, and the stories they write down or tell others constitute a legacy. Kathleen Woodward describes reminiscence as less analytical than life review and likely to create an "atmosphere of a certain companionableness" (1997, 152). When reminiscence is the focus of writing groups, it becomes a "highly malleable process subject to others' influence," so that the story is not simply a record of an individual's thoughts and feelings but a "social product" (Ray, 1999–2000, 57).

In one life writing workshop, participants encouraged to focus on positive, optimistic narratives rejected the invitation to romanticize their lives and instead presented "multiple and conflicting representations of old age" (Ray, 1999, 179). The patronizing view of the old as dwelling too much on past events misses an important dimension of reminiscence: the past is not simply over but "continually lived out in new terms as its storytellers speak of life" (Gubrium and Holstein, 297). A vehicle for expressing this continuity is reminiscence theater, developed by groups such as Elders Share the Arts in Brooklyn.

Eagerness to tell one's story signals a desire to live (Bruner, 9). Elders recounting their stories seldom follow the actual sequence of life events, a choice that probably heightens interest for their hearers. When a life review is elicited by an interviewer, he or she must be aware that if another interviewer spoke with the elder, the result would be a different story (Black and Rubinstein, 7). Looking back over one's past may hold special significance for members of stigmatized groups, particularly if survival strategies are a theme. Reminiscence and life review are healthy antidotes to the sick role.[5] Given the tendencies to project wisdom onto the old and to ask them to serve others, however, the emphasis in storytelling and life review should be as much on the pleasure and satisfaction of the elder as on the enlightenment of her audience.

Conclusion

The rise of HMOs and the concomitant loss of patient-centered health care have been especially harmful to the old, whose chronic illnesses need closer attention and a wider range of treatments than mainstream, drug-oriented medicine can provide. Thus sickness consumes more of their time, money, and attention than it should, and other social roles diminish in importance. The very healthy old women and men for whom this is not true find their individual solutions to the roleless role of old age, but few structures support them. Our sense of late-life possibilities may change as healthier women and men, especially those who are middle-class, choose activities and roles never before thought compatible with "old." For many poor and working-class Americans and for people of color, greater longevity may mean longer periods of chronic illness. The future dominance of the sick role will depend not only on elders' level of health but also on cultural attitudes magnifying the importance of sickness in their lives. As the numbers of the old increase, pressures to expand the sick role for profit will intensify. Awareness of these pressures and resistance to them will mark those who have learned to be old.

Notes

1. I thank Tara Healy of the University of Southern Maine Social Work Department for pointing this out to me.

2. Linda Gannon, *Women and Aging: Beyond the Myths* (New York: Routledge, 1999), 46. This excellent work, cited in the Healthy Aging chapters, interprets a large body of research on older women's health.

3. David Gutmann, *Reclaimed Powers: Toward a New Psychology of Men and Women in Later Life* (New York: Basic Books, 1987), 152–53. The author adds that "where old men seek to control their spontaneous urges, older women appear to seek out opportunities for vigorous action and lively interpersonal encounters" (153). Chapters 3 and 4 of Gutmann's book consider late-life androgyny. The author cites numerous anthropological studies to support his claim that this role shift is cross-cultural.

4. In his original formulation of life review, Butler wrote that it may cause depression, not serenity, a caution overlooked in current discussions of the concept. "The Life Review: an Interpretation of Reminiscence in the Aged," *Psychiatry* 26 (1963): 65–76.

5. For life review and reminiscence, see Joanna Bornat, ed., *Reminiscence Reviewed* (Buckingham, U.K.: Open University Press, 1994); Harry J. Berman, *Interpreting the Aging Self: Personal Journals of Later Life* (New York: Springer, 1994); Ruth Ray, *Beyond Nostalgia* (Charlottesville, Va.: University Press of Virginia, 2000); Anne Wyatt-Brown, "The Future of Literary Gerontology," in *Handbook of Aging and the Humanities*, 2nd ed., ed. Thomas R. Cole, Robert Kastenbaum, and Ruth Ray (New York: Springer, 2000); Kathleen Woodward, "Reminiscence and the Life Review," in *What Does it Mean to Grow Old?*, ed. Thomas R. Cole and Sally Gadow (Durham, N.C.: Duke, 1986); Sharon Jacobson and Beth Kivel, "The Narratives of Old Lesbians: Maintaining the Integrity," *Outword: Newsletter of the Lesbian and Gay Aging Issues Network of the American Society on Aging* 4, no. 3 (1998): 3, 5; Paul Kleyman, "Life Stories: A 'NonTherapy' For Elders and Their Families," *Aging Today* (July/Aug. 2000): 9; and Ronald J. Manheimer, "Refashioning Later Life," *Gerontologist* 41, no. 2 (2001): 275–79.

CHAPTER FOUR

Overmedicating Old Americans

People over sixty-five make up 12.4 percent of the population according to the 2000 Census, but use 34 percent of the prescription drugs (some estimates say 45 percent). Since early 1999, their prescription drug consumption, a subject previously confined to gerontology journals and geriatric publications, has been front-page news across the country as the exorbitant cost of drugs finally caught the attention of editorial writers and politicians. Stories described busloads of elders going to Canada and Mexico to buy cheaper medications, choosing between food and medicine, or taking lower doses than prescribed. Some women reported that they could afford to fill their husbands' prescriptions but not their own. Drug costs have been rising 15–20 percent each year, totaling $131.9 billion in 2000 and prompting predictions that total American health care costs would double by 2010 (McQueen, A3). According to a Health and Human Services Department report, total national spending on prescription drugs doubled between 1995 and 2000 (nytimes.com, Jan. 7, 2002). Older Americans paid twice as much for out-of-pocket health care expenses in 1999 as they had paid in 1987 (Knight and Avorn, 111). Some face an annual drug bill of several thousand dollars and many find the situation intolerable.

Clinton proposed drug coverage through Medicare in State of the Union speeches in both 1999 and 2000, and the need for coverage became an issue in the 2000 presidential campaign. In his State of the Union address in January 2002, President Bush proposed Medicare prescription drug coverage for low-income elders. In June 2002, House Republicans passed a bill that would provide a drug benefit through Medicare by paying subsidies to insurance companies to create insurance covering drug costs, a plan challenged by

51

Democrats for providing too little coverage and not tackling the issue of soaring drug costs.

The attention paid to the high drug costs for the elderly, while necessary, narrows public discussion of this key issue. Drug management and compliance are topics gerontologists usually consider. The unasked larger question is more abstract: should the old be taking as many drugs as they now take? This chapter offers a context for discussing an issue that has many more dimensions than economic.

The focus here is not on drugs taken for short periods for specific acute illnesses but rather on long-term use, especially of multiple drugs for chronic conditions. Most health problems associated with aging are chronic, for example arthritis and high blood pressure.

A typical reaction to statistics showing extremely heavy drug use by people over sixty-five is that the old need more drugs *because* they are old. But someone who steps outside the circle of medicalized aging has to wonder whether this is really so, whether drugs on the scale they are now being used are benign, health-inducing agents or instruments of social control, whether profit is not a hidden but defining factor in high drug use. According to a 2001 assessment, many people over sixty take six to eight drugs a day, but proper management could cut the number in half (Anderson and Wahler, 3). It may be true that as a group elders need more medical care than others, but the equation of medical care with drugs is socially constructed. In this culture, accepting the inevitability of multiple drug use is an essential part of learning to be old.

Overmedicating the old results from three interlocking problems:

1. The multinational drug industry has the money and power to control markets and heavily influence the way Americans think about aging.
2. As medicine and gerontology have increasingly become advocates of prescription-drugged aging, they have exaggerated the benefits of drugs, downplayed their risks, and left unexamined the assumption that multiple drug use promotes healthy aging.
3. The opposing, countercultural view is not taken seriously by professionals or by the mainstream media.

Together these developments create a serious threat to the health of older Americans. Understanding why requires a brief examination of body changes with age, adverse drug reactions, the drug industry, doctor training, pharmacy practices, the F.D.A., cultural attitudes, and alternatives to the present system.

Changes with Age

Changes in height and weight as we age influence our reactions to drugs. Because the metabolism slows down and organs tend to function less efficiently, drugs can have a very powerful impact on aging bodies. Loss of lean body mass affects the way we retain and eliminate drugs. In women, the percentage of body fat goes up from about 36 percent to 48 percent and consequently, fat-soluble drugs like sedatives and anti-anxiety medications are more concentrated in fatty tissue (Drugs and Older Women, 5). Blood vessels stiffen and decreased blood flow impedes the circulation of drugs and nutrients. Cerebral blood flow decreases by 25 percent. With less water in our bodies, drugs are more concentrated than in younger bodies. The filtering function of kidneys does not work as well in the old, resulting in drug accumulation. Decreased liver function can affect the way some drugs are metabolized, leading to toxic levels (Cameron, 10). The brains of older people are more sensitive to drug side effects than younger brains (Lamy, 1988, 9).

Because the lining of our intestinal walls loses cells as we age, we cannot absorb what we take in as efficiently as before, and because our stomachs empty more slowly, drugs remain in them longer (Bonner and Harris, 90). Age changes in hormones mean that drugs have a stronger impact on us. The elderly are more likely to develop drug-induced hypoglycemia (Lamy, 1986, 123). If poor diet causes protein deficiency, the impact of a drug may be intensified (Beizer, 14).

Adverse Drug Reactions

Each year 100,000 Americans or more die of adverse drug reactions, 1 million are severely injured, and 2 million are harmed while they are hospitalized, making ill effects from drugs one of the greatest dangers in modern society and one of the leading causes of death, according to Thomas J. Moore, an authority on prescription drugs (1998, 15). The incidence of adverse drug reactions is estimated to be twice to three times greater among the elderly (Gomberg, 95). For them, the physiologic response to drugs is "much more scattered and the predictability of drug action is much less certain than in younger people" (Lamy, 1986, 122). Approximately 17 percent of hospital admissions of people over seventy are caused by adverse reactions to drugs.

Not all of these reactions are caused by overmedication, but gerontologists surmise that it is the most common cause. Overprescribing psychotropic (mood altering) drugs is a leading cause of adverse reactions (Arluke and Peterson, 282). Robert Butler cites the findings of a 1998 study that 35 percent of Americans over sixty-five have an adverse drug reaction every year (2001).

Cough suppressants can cause drowsiness, unsteadiness, and constipation in the old. Prolonged use of antacids causes constipation and can weaken bones (Bonner and Harris, 95). Analgesics containing codeine can cause dizziness and fatigue and can increase the effect of most other drugs (Bonner and Harris, 99). Other common reactions to overmedication include: impaired movements, memory loss, confusion, anxiety, palpitations, restlessness, insomnia, blocked thyroid function, mood swings or other emotional imbalances, blurred vision, urinary retention, potassium depletion, gastrointestinal pain or bleeding, involuntary movements of the arms and legs, and lessening capacity to smell and taste. In addition, overuse of drugs can cause nutritional depletion resulting in such problems as hearing loss, anemia, breathlessness, and weakness. Among nutrients lost are vitamins A and C and beta carotene, all thought likely to help immune systems ward off cancer. Dr. Steffi Woolhander and colleagues identified twenty drugs that should not be prescribed for people over sixty-five, including some tranquilizers and sedatives, antidepressants, arthritis drugs, diabetes drugs, pain relievers, dementia treatments, blood thinners, and muscle relaxants (JAMA, July 27, 1994). Depression as a side effect of drugs is not limited to tranquilizers and other mood-altering medications. Anti-inflammatory drugs, medications for high blood pressure and high cholesterol, antihistamines, and antibiotics may all cause depression. Milder forms of depression are easily dismissed as natural to aging (Moore, 1998, 201). Old women are especially at risk for having treatable symptoms attributed to aging itself.

Alcohol and tobacco interact with prescription drugs, increasing risk factors for the old who take multiple drugs. Some arthritis medicines, for example, interact with coffee and alcohol to damage the lining of the stomach. When sleeping pills mix with alcohol, breathing can be impaired to a dangerous degree. Many people over sixty-five use both alcohol and prescription drugs. Concurrent use of these two substances (even ten or more hours apart) can make drugs much more toxic (Lamy, 1988, 11–12).

Unrecognized drug interactions can lead to a false diagnosis of Alzheimer's disease. Although the extent of this problem is hard to determine, it is likely to increase as the aging population increases. Both prescription drugs and over-the-counter medications can impair mental function: steroids such as Prednisone; drugs used to treat heart problems and high blood pressure; drugs prescribed for stomach ailments; drugs prescribed by psychiatrists; Parkinson's drugs; and treatments for anxiety and insomnia.

Of all the adverse consequences of drugs, the effect on cell division is probably the danger most underestimated, according to Thomas J. Moore. It does not show up in routine tests of new drugs, and it may result in large numbers of bone marrow injuries (1998, 108). When cell birth and death are disrupted, cancer, birth defects, and blood disorders may result (1998, 92). Drug catastrophes are not dramatic like plane crashes, but tend rather to be "slow, insidious, and difficult to see" (53). Studies of potentially dangerous drugs that should not have been prescribed for the elderly are summarized by Moore. In a nationwide sample of more than 6,000 people, 23 percent received drugs that were inappropriate. Using Medicare data, the General Accounting Office found that 17 percent of the drugs prescribed for the old were the wrong ones (Moore, 1998, 121). These figures probably only hint at the risks run by people over sixty-five who use prescription drugs. Unforeseen side effects not apparent during testing come to light only after the drug is in widespread use, and even more alarming, deaths and injuries from drugs are "vastly underreported" (Stolberg, Boom, 1999, A18). Since the old use so many drugs, they suffer disproportionately from unforeseen side effects and from the underreporting of deaths and injuries. For them, a wise precaution would be to avoid any drug on the market for less than a year.

Are women more at risk than men? They appear to metabolize some drugs differently, especially psychotropic ones. A report by CASA (the National Center on Addiction and Abuse at Columbia University) states that women over fifty-nine get addicted to alcohol and prescription drugs faster and on smaller amounts than other people, that women are much more likely than men to be given a prescription for a tranquilizer by their physician, and that the use of sedatives and sedating anti-depressants doubles the risk of falls and fractures among older women (Report, 2–3). For either sex, taking more than four prescription drugs is a risk factor for falls. Common sense suggests that women's smaller body size and hormone changes mean that standard doses of medications are too high, but the susceptibility of older women to side effects has not been studied. "Either no one thinks it's important, or if they do, they don't have funding," according to Katherine Sherif. It would be useful to know, for example, if drug prescribing should take hormone replacement therapy into account. Dr. Sherif points out that the F.D.A. now requires that women be included in clinical trials but does not require that study results be broken down by gender. Particularly frustrating is the fact that women must be included in research only if there is evidence of gender difference, but the evidence comes from research.[1]

Although adverse drug reactions affect the old who live independently or with families as well as those who are institutionalized, the problem is especially serious among nursing home residents. Since this population is largely female, the problem of overmedicating nursing home residents is a women's issue. Major problems are that: 1) Some drugs have very similar names, resulting in mix-ups; 2) many falls in nursing homes result from overmedication; and 3) nursing home residents are often given psychotropic drugs, 50 percent according to some estimates and 80 percent according to others. Geriatricians are concerned that in many cases, no precise diagnosis indicates a need for these powerful drugs and that residents are often overdosed with medications marked "as needed." They do not have the benefit of "comprehensive assessment, documentation of diagnosis, and consistent follow-up" (Agronin, 389). Even when a diagnosis of dementia is accurate, a very serious problem remains: psychotropic drugs have not "demonstrated efficacy for most of the behavioral symptoms" shown by nursing home residents who suffer from dementia (Sherman, 36). In other words, they don't work. Psychotropics are now so common that the American nursing home at the beginning of the twenty-first century is more like a psychiatric institution than a medical one (Agronin, 389). Women who live long enough to be placed in nursing homes may thus be transformed into psychiatric patients, not because of their individual needs or conditions but because they are a captive market for the drug industry. Those with mild dementia may need one or two drugs, but they are almost certain to be given several.

Sedating is a chemical restraint for out-of-control patients, but it is often unnecessary for the majority of nursing home residents. Cultural devaluing of the frail and dependent elderly and the convenience of often underpaid staff may play a larger role in medication decisions than the particular health needs of individual residents.

Gerontologists who write about prescription drugs sometimes use the word "polypharmacy" to refer to multiple drug use. While this term has an authoritatively scientific and neutral sound to it, polypharmacy can also be defined as a situation in which a person is given too many drugs, is kept on drugs for too long, or is given "exceedingly high doses" (Michocki and Lamy, 441). The precise extent of overmedication remains uncertain. The acknowledgement by geriatric pharmacologists that many drugs prescribed for the old are probably unnecessary or ineffective is somewhat misleading because drugs are powerful agents that alter body chemistry and thus they are not "ineffective" in the usual meaning of having no effect.[2]

Nonbiological factors contributing to adverse reactions are drug swapping by the old, poor doctor-patient communication, and noncompliance on the part of the drug user. Some elderly patients obtain prescriptions from various doctors so that no single doctor or pharmacist sees the complete picture of their drug consumption. Patients may not tell their doctor what over-the-counter medicines they take. They may not understand, for example, that long-term use of laxatives for constipation can damage their intestines. Others may neglect to mention herbal medications they are on, anticipating the doctor's disapproval. Latinas may not discuss remedies they obtain from a local botanical shop. Limited English, hearing loss, extreme deference to doctors, and a sense of powerlessness on the part of the patient are also factors in incomplete drug assessment.

Doctors who know most about adverse drug reactions in the old, geriatricians, seem to be the most cautious about prescribing drugs. The majority of old women and men are not treated by these specialists, however. One solution to the problem of overmedication is an increase in the number of geriatricians. Their wise prescribing advice is, "Start low, go slow" (Winker, 56).

Periodic re-evaluation of drugs is crucially important for the old. Drugs should have standard labels giving clear and precise information about how to use them. They now come with inserts that are intended to describe side effects, but inserts typically omit information about the most severe ones (Stolberg, FDA, 1999, A23). Armed with the full story of their medications' risks, consumers might balk at taking them. It would also be helpful if inserts clearly specified "geriatric dosage." More research is needed to define these doses (Beizer, 16). Another needed reform is include systematic collection of information about prescribing through computers to eliminate mistakes from illegible handwriting and to allow easier doctor-pharmacist cross checking of medications (Moore, 1998, 170).

Juxtaposing the bodily changes with age and adverse drug reactions and taking into account the high cost of medication, an impartial person might conclude that the old should take *fewer* drugs than others, not more.

The Drug Industry

Americans pay 38 percent more for drugs than Europeans (Trager, A13) and wholesale drug price differences between the U.S. and countries such as Canada and Australia range from 25% to 68% higher (Researchers, 8A). After

U.S. House Representative Tom Allen of Maine introduced legislation that would require drug companies to sell to pharmacies at the same lower prices given to the government and HMOs, the industry predictably launched a fervent defense of the escalating cost of drugs, claiming that research on new drugs would be threatened if elders paid less for their drugs. Allen replied in plain language: "Here you have the most profitable industry charging the highest prices in the world to senior citizens who don't have prescription drug coverage at all." (Campbell, 1A).

Drug company propagandists do not mention either that industry research is heavily subsidized by taxpayers or that the "me too" drugs flooding the market are designed not to create new medical knowledge but to increase their profits. New drugs to fight malaria and other tropical diseases are needed but the industry spends virtually nothing on them (Buell, A11). In response to the Clinton proposal for a prescription drug benefit in Medicare, the drug companies created an elderly character named Flo as their mouthpiece. Shown in a bowling alley, Flo says that she doesn't want big government in her medicine cabinet. She doesn't mention that Big Pharma is already there. The use of a working-class setting for the television ads was also misleading, because the exorbitant cost of prescription drugs did not become newsworthy until the middle-class old were hurt.

In May 2000, Maine became the first state to pass a law lowering the price of prescription drugs for 325,000 of its residents who have no drug coverage and for 200,000 people on Medicaid. Sponsored by State Senate Majority Leader Chellie Pingree, the Maine Rx program seeks voluntary price reductions from drug companies and after three years *requires* lower prices. It also imposes profiteering penalties. Maine Rx survived a challenge in federal court from the drug industry in May 2001.

Aggressive promotion of drugs meant for long-term use is much more common than it was a decade ago, especially now that pharmaceuticals are allowed to advertise on television. The industry spends $10 billion dollars a year marketing drugs (Buell, A11). Smart marketing transformed Claritin, a "moderately effective medication that had difficulty getting approved" into a blockbuster drug (Hall, 40). When pills are sold like potato chips or Pepsi, artificial needs for medicine are created to a degree that suggests brainwashing. Page after page of drug ads litter the front sections of many magazines today. False or misleading claims in drug ads have been documented, and they are most likely to occur in the drugs most heavily promoted (Adams, A24). Doctors are deluged with free samples, and often their only knowledge of a new drug comes from salespeople, who are unlikely to discuss side effects.

Several years ago, Kaiser Permanente of northern California banished drug companies for six months for offenses that included offering doctors $100 to attend company-sponsored dinners and filling out forms for them to sign in order to get their pharmacies to stock a drug. Vacations in the Caribbean and lecture fees are other forms of bribery that influence doctors and greatly increase the cost of prescriptions. Another unethical practice is buying lunch for doctors and nurses who attend presentations by drug representatives at hospitals and clinics. Flo couldn't say that the "free" supplies, dinners, and vacations provided for doctors by drug companies are not free at all, but paid for by their elderly patients.

Other abuses have come to light as a multi-billion-dollar industry has sprung up to take over the testing that drug companies used to do themselves. A ten-month investigation by the *New York Times* found that doctors conducting drug research often have limited experience and run tests unrelated to their medical specialties. They receive a bounty for getting patients into drug trials (unbeknownst to the patients), and those who recruit the greatest number get a special reward: they are listed as the authors of drug studies even though the real authors are ghostwriters using information provided by the companies themselves (Eichenwald and Kolada, A1, A28).

A series of articles in *The Washington Post*, the *New York Times*, and *The Boston Globe* called attention to the dangers of new drugs, suppressed competition by colluding companies, payment of doctors with free trips and lecture fees to use costly new drugs, the unnecessary proliferation of drugs, and inadequate F.D.A regulation.[3] A drug company that bribed doctors to prescribe its products will pay the government $875 million, the largest health care fraud settlement in U.S. history (*Boston Globe*, October 7, 2001, B1).

Patents on drugs are monopolies that let pharmaceutical companies raise prices higher than free market levels (Sager and Socolar, 29). Elderly consumers are especially harmed when pharmaceuticals pay manufacturers of generic drugs to keep the drugs off the market, so that their more expensive version is the only one available. The cost of these payoffs (and the unavailability of generics) contribute greatly to the dramatic increase in the cost of medications. The ugliest example of drug industry greed appeared early in 2001 when thirty-nine pharmaceuticals sued to prevent South Africa from providing generic drugs to people with AIDS, an outrage that public opinion stopped. This was a rare instance of the industry experiencing a check of any sort. Their interests are promoted by an army of federal lobbyists, six hundred and twenty five, according to a *Public Citizen* report issued July 2001, more than one for every member of Congress.

A company marketing a new form of estrogen sent representatives to a conference on women's health in May 1998 at New England University in Portland. Since women were supposed to take this drug for the rest of their lives, I asked the average age of women on whom it was tested. The answer, fifty-four years, revealed a common problem: drugs are not adequately tested on the old.

The economic and political dimensions of overdrugging are complex but may be reduced to a single inference: safety is too costly. When patients' right to be protected from harm collides with drug companies' drive for profit, "safety loses," Thomas J. Moore concludes. In his view, the current system is organized to promote maximum drug sales, not consumer safety (1998, 162). Those who take the most drugs risk the greatest harm. When problems with a drug turn up, as in the case of Halcion, pharmaceuticals have the power to go to court, lobby Congress, petition the F.D.A., "bombard the news media, pressure medical journals, and influence doctors," regardless of the facts of the case. Most of the information known about drugs is controlled by the industry. This is too much power to be concentrated in a global business (1998, 162).

Problems with prescription drugs are likely to increase because the integrity of medical research and medical journals has been compromised by their ties to the drug industry. The former editor of the *New England Journal of Medicine* acknowledged that researchers are swayed toward more favorable findings on products of companies who pay them (Associated Press, May 18, 2000), and the *Journal* apologized for violating its own conflict of interest policy by publishing nineteen articles on drugs whose authors had financial ties to drug companies (*New York Times*, February 24, 2000, A15). A recent issue of the *New England Journal of Medicine* ran ads for twenty-eight different drugs, making it look like a trade publication. The drug industry is attempting "the deliberate seduction of the medical profession, country by country, worldwide [and soon] unbought medical opinion will be hard to find" (LeCarre, 12). The implications of this judgment for elders who use prescription drugs are ominous.

A closely related problem that has not drawn journalists' attention is that the integrity of gerontology has also been compromised because its conferences and publications are subsidized by pharmaceuticals and therefore papers challenging drug industry hegemony will not be found. Silence about the link between the giant pharmaceuticals and gerontology prevents a critical examination of drugged aging either as a philosophy or as a practice. Journals read by gerontologists and geriatricians feature ads in which dreamy-looking old women (never men) smile out at the reader to show the benefits of tranquilizers. For the first time in 2001, *The Gerontologist* ran a full-page ad for a multinational drug company, a discouraging sign of increasing corporate influence on intellectual work. Gerontologists can admit that adverse drug reactions cause thousands of hip fractures each year and other problems causing billions of dollars annually, that one-third of nursing home residents take more than eight drugs a day, and that research on the effects of multiple prescription drug use is lacking (Lyder et al., 55–56); and geriatric nurses can suggest that because of the large number of deaths from adverse drug reactions, noncompliance (failure to take medicines) is sometimes the best choice (Fulmer et al., 47); but no one can name the present system a public health disaster for old women.

At gerontology conferences, alternative medical practitioners are not invited to lecture on what they have learned from the drug-free treatment of elders. The suppression of this knowledge is indefensible, for it limits public discussion of healthy aging to corporate voices and their echoes in gerontology. When I wrote to the president of a national aging organization to ask what percentage of her budget comes from the drug industry, I did not really expect an answer, but I strongly believe such information should be made public. How else can elders determine whether the organizations and publications focused on their issues can claim any degree of objectivity? How can they learn about alternatives to drugged aging if the industry's point of view is the only one allowed into print or into conferences? What is the real cost of this stultifying orthodoxy?

Doctors, Pharmacists, and the F.D.A.

An underlying cause of chemically dependent aging is that mainstream doctors are not trained to be healers of the whole person. Theoretically, with each patient a doctor has a choice: non-drug remedies or drug treatment, but the doctor usually sees the choice more narrowly, which drug to prescribe.[4] Only three U.S. medical schools have full departments of geriatrics, in contrast to *every* medical school in Great Britain, and geriatrics is not a popular specialty. HMO pressures on doctors to see as many patients as possible lessens the quality of care for all, but especially for the old, who may have several different ailments requiring a combination of individually-tailored treatments. Few doctors have time for a thorough review of a patient's drug-use history in relation to current symptoms. In an office visit that may be as short as fifteen minutes, they cannot perform a physical examination, determine whether to change medications, and adequately educate patients about them (Knight and Avorn, 111). In addition, doctors may not know the age appropriate dose of a drug or the information may not be available, making the choice of a medication a trial and error process in which undetected mistakes outnumber corrected ones (Atchley, 363). Doctors sometimes do not change their prescribing habits when the F.D.A. notifies them that a drug now in widespread use has been found to have adverse side effects that did not show up in clinical trials.

Medical training may reinforce rather than challenge ageist stereotypes. Even when a doctor consciously acknowledges these stereotypes and avoids patronizing behavior, he or she may not be aware of subtle changes in elderly patients caused by medication or may attribute observed changes to the aging process itself rather than to multiple drug use. As a result of all of these factors, establishing the right dosage, guarding against drug interactions, and monitoring use carefully are "beyond the capacity of medicine as it is currently organized" (Atchley, 371).

If adequate safeguards against overdrugging do not exist at the doctor's office, the risk to the old is compounded by changes in pharmacies. Harried pharmacists now sometimes work twelve-hour days, increasing the likelihood of error, and they have little time to advise customers about appropriate use of medications, as they used to do (Stolberg, Boom, A18). Managed care pressures on pharmacists result in drug switching to save money. The drugs treat the same disorder but differ chemically and have different side effects. Drug switching has been condemned as an "evil practice" by former Ohio senator Howard Metzenbaum (Stolberg, Drug Switching, 1999, 3).

Equally disturbing is the huge gap between the small F.D.A. budget and the "deep pockets of the industry it is supposed to regulate" (Mann). Twenty-one safety evaluators at F.D.A. monitor the 3,200 drugs in current use. An additional ten pharmacists monitor medication errors, and ten epidemiologists research safety reports and drug use patterns.[5] Ideally, the number of F.D.A. workers protecting consumers ought at least to equal the number of lobbyists who represent pharmaceuticals. Although the F.D.A. screens new drugs, a big loophole creates safety risks: testing periods are short, typically a few weeks or months for drugs meant to be taken for the rest of a person's life. Clinical trials for Prozac, Paxil, and Zoloft, for example, lasted only six weeks despite the fact that they are recommended for long-term use (Moore, 1998, 177–78). In the 1980s, approval of new drugs took three years, a process that offered consumers some protection. Other problems are that the F.D.A. is not required to collect data on deaths and injuries from prescription drugs, a serious impediment to protecting the public (Moore, 1998, 46, 175), and that it does not require drug companies to test for interactions before a new product is approved (Eastman, 16). Safe use would increase if approval of drugs were not permanent but were re-evaluated every five years to determine if safer alternatives had become available (184). Finally, the F.D.A. cannot prevent the development of "me too" drugs that are far more costly than those already on the market.

Related Social and Cultural Issues

Americans are well known for liking quick fixes, and taking a drug for a medical problem is certainly easier than changing diet, increasing exercise, or reducing stress. This cultural preference for a fast solution may predispose elders to expect doctors to prescribe drugs for them and to feel disregarded if they are given none. If they believe they need more drugs than before because they are old, an accumulation of drugs will not prompt questions, especially if their friends who are old also take several a day. A recent commercial for a hotel chain booms "more is better," another American cultural value that encourages overdrugging.

The more frequently old women and men see mainstream doctors, the more often they get prescriptions for drugs, and the more likely they are to get sick from side effects if they take several drugs. Thus heavy consumption of medical services by the old perpetuates itself. Ivan Illich exaggerated the problem when he wrote that "Doctors work increasingly with two groups of addicts: those for whom they prescribe drugs, and those who suffer from their consequences" (72–73), but he succinctly described the encapsulated world of medicalized aging.

Are the old sedated *because* they are old? "It may well be that in the minds of legislators and the public, keeping older people sedated is an acceptable idea" (Gomberg, 94). How much social control, especially of the frail and dependent old, is appropriate? Do racial and ethnic differences affect drug prescribing and monitoring? Do they affect drug impact? Stanford gerontologist Gwen Yeo cites a study suggesting that old Asian Americans may need only one-half of the drug dose prescribed for whites (76). Will baby boomers demand more careful drug prescribing as they age? Is drug coverage through Medicare an adequate solution to high prescription costs for low- and middle-income families? Will old citizens be scapegoated if their consumption of expensive drugs is blamed for driving up health care costs?

Prescription drugs have been in use only since World War II and heavy medication of the old is a fairly recent phenomenon. Thus people now in their eighties have been exposed to drugs for only part of their lives. In twenty years, however, most people will have been in the drug culture all of their lives. Heavy drug use by the old is now so embedded in American culture that a booklet titled *Using Your Medicines Wisely: A Guide for the Elderly*, published by the Department of Health and Human Services, provides space for eleven different drugs to be recorded in an attractive insert with the remarkably misleading title "Passport to Good Health Care." This official publication sends a subtle but powerful message: taking eleven different drugs a day is usual and acceptable.

Given the extent and seriousness of adverse drug reactions among people over sixty-five and considering their heavy drug consumption, it is logical to suppose that some of what we call aging is actually a cumulative reaction to prescription drugs, especially to multiple drugs taken over a long period. Those who live with the elderly and the elderly themselves may well believe that problems they experience result from a slowing down usual for their age. While some decline is normal for many women and men, drug-induced decline is not, but the two may be hard to separate in America. The only published work I have found that expresses doubts about drug use *per se* among the elderly is by a British pharmacologist and gerontologist who believes ginseng is more effective than prescription drugs for the physical complaints of aging.[6] Americans have paid too much attention to drug benefits and not enough to their risk (Moore, 1998, 29). Clearly the overdrugging of the old is related to the large number of children now on Ritalin. Both trends signal a "large-scale chemical control of human behavior" (Moore, 1998, 22) whose implications are both profound and unstudied.

Alternatives

If all of the alternative healers in the U.S.—chiropractors, homeopathic doctors, acupuncturists, herbalists, massage therapists, ayurvedic doctors, and naturopaths—profiled five patients over seventy whom they had treated for ten years, we could get a glimpse of drug-free aging that is currently unavailable. Indeed, drug-free aging is unthinkable to most Americans. Drugs keep alive some elders who would not have survived earlier, but we do not know how others would fare if they were relatively drug-free or if 75 percent of them were treated by complementary medicine. Having no basis of comparison to drugged aging, we cannot be confident that drugs are the universally and necessarily beneficent products that their makers would have us believe.

We must take this on faith. Individuals over sixty-five who have chosen alternative medicine do have a basis of comparison, however, and their decision to end prescription drug dependency frees them from conventional, corporate-sponsored belief. Elders who have left drugged aging must tell their stories. Those killed by inadvertent overdrugging unfortunately cannot tell theirs.

The drug industry relies on arguments from authority, its own authority, to persuade elders that multiple drug use is safe for them. If drug-free aging were studied systemically through longitudinal studies of a large number of diverse people, preferably two-thirds female, aged 65 to 100, we could eventually distinguish between the late-life conditions that can be treated effectively only by drugs and the ailments and illnesses best treated by other means. If most health plans covered a wide range of alternative care, the playing field would be more level. A truly free market would allow drug treatments to compete with non-drug treatments.

In a comprehensive and illuminating article on the placebo effect, Margaret Talbot notes that because illnesses are treated aggressively in this society, "[W]e know less about their natural history—what would happen if we did nothing" (38). This viewpoint has an intriguing application to aging: what if in some cases nothing was done to treat chronic illness? It is such an article of faith that the old need a great deal of medical care that this suggestion seems heretical. If Talbot is correct in stating that a placebo "probably works through a certain kind of expectation, generated by empathic care" (58), then expectation of improvement and empathy are powerful healing forces.

In England and Germany, where homeopathy is widely practiced, non-drug treatment of the old is more prevalent than it is in the U.S. In Japan, western drugs are available but an elderly person would usually not be on as many as four drugs and doctors prescribe traditional Asian remedies as well as drugs.[7]

Imagine a drug free-nursing home. Impossible from the viewpoint of medicalized aging but neither an oxymoron nor a utopian vision. In such a home, alternative doctors would show what their methods have to offer the old, and they would work together. If a resident's health problems were not helped, a drug would be considered and very carefully monitored. The remaining life energy of residents would not be sapped by multiple drugs. Many would be able to dress themselves, and food choices would not be regimented. If residents wished to express their sexuality, staff would not interfere except in cases of harassment. The prudish monitoring of sexual behavior in nursing homes has been called "iatrogenic loneliness" by doctors who envision more humane settings for end-of-life care (Miles and Parker, 40). Off drugs, nursing home residents would be more likely to express their intimacy needs and staff would be encouraged to understand sexuality as a basic human need for connection (Miles and Parker, 38). Drug-free residents might not value or be capable of sexual expression, but they would be more like their former selves when not heavily sedated.

Conclusion

As long ago as 1975, Robert Butler warned Americans about the high cost of drugs, deaths from adverse drug reactions (30,000 annually then, 100,000 now), the "far too cosy relationship" between doctors and drug companies, and the conflation of natural aging with slowing down from sedatives (1975, 200). Elders are the citizens most harmed by these trends; it is they who suffer when "health" and "care" are stripped from health care for the sake of profit. If they take multiple drugs for chronic conditions, their lives may be shortened or made more difficult by drug-induced illness created and maintained to benefit the pharmaceutical industry. The cost of overmedication is likely to increase because the fastest-growing segment of the elderly population, people over eighty-five, is most likely to be institutionalized and given multiple drugs.

In a sense, women and men on multiple drugs squander their health allotment because these powerful substances interfere with the body's healing powers, but the old who suffer side effects from prescription drugs should not be blamed for their plight. Many, especially old women, are denied the experience of aging—whatever it might be for them—because the chemicals in their bodies are literally changing who they are. And their doctors have unwittingly taken control of their aging.

Although complementary (alternative) medicine is reaching more elders, especially those who are white and middle-class, and the folk remedies that some people of color and some whites rely on are better understood, mainstream medicine has a near monopoly on the health care of elders. An insidious feature of this monopoly is that the most profitable businesses in America promote the myth that aging is a disease for which their product is the appropriate remedy. Pharmaceuticals have joined the tobacco industry as a high-profile threat to the public good. Their practices deserve far more scrutiny, the suppression of generic drugs, for example.

In a recent review essay on drugs and the elderly, two medical school professors acknowledge that the science underlying current prescription practice is "distressingly thin, especially considering the central roles that medications play in the care of elderly adults and the much reduced margin for error that makes prescribing for them such a challenge" (Knight and Avorn, 111). Pondering this candid assessment might prompt one to ask how drugs became so central to aging without an adequate science base. The answer I propose is that culture and the profit motive, more than biology or health, dictate heavy drug use by people over sixty-five. The primary reason many elders take six or eight drugs a day is not that their health will benefit but that the drug companies need new markets. An aging population offers more territory for their expanding empires.

The two parts of the statement quoted above, thin science and central roles, collide. What is missing is an admission that the old risk being harmed, perhaps greatly harmed, by current prescribing practice. What is missing is the recognition that drug-induced aging may now pass for normal aging. Older people on medications need to know that the combination of the "thin science" behind the drugs they take and the fat purses of Pfizer et al. leaves them open to exploitation and danger. Learning to be old requires keen skepticism about the widespread use of multiple prescription drugs. It may mean questioning one's trust in medical authority for the first time. And families of elders must balance their solicitude for their loved one's well-being with knowledge of the potential dangers of drugs and consider that their parent or grandparent may need far fewer drugs than she is on or no drugs at all.

Many older women, and especially women over eighty, are needlessly and dangerously overmedicated. In the absence of drug tests designed specifically for old bodies and able to differentiate old women from old men, prescribing multiple drugs for them is a custom that rests more on belief than on evidence. The overdrugging of the old is a tragedy of unfathomable proportions. It cries out for a scientist/writer like Rachael Carson to sound the alarm that will wake up Americans of all ages.

Notes

1. Katherine Sherif, M.D., Medical College of Pennsylvania, quoted in "Drugs and the Older Woman," 6. Wyeth-Ayerst Global Pharmaceuticals has a research unit on women's health, and Pfizer observes women's reactions to its drugs for diabetes and lung cancer. A drug that Glaxo Wellcome found ineffective for treating irritable bowel syndrome in men was recently found to work only in women. See David J. Morrow, "Women's Drugs: Big in Profits, Narrow in Scope," *New York Times* (June 13, 1999): 15:9.

2. In 1986, for example, Peter Lamy wrote that 25 percent of drugs prescribed for the elderly were unnecessary or ineffective; the percentage must be much higher now because of the great increase in the number of drugs and demand increased by television advertising. "Geriatric Drug Therapy," *American Family Physician* 34, no. 6 (1986). Although this article is dated, I cite it because of Lamy's eminence in the field of geriatric pharmacology. "Pharmacology and Older People," an issue of *Generations* edited by William Simonson, is dedicated to Lamy, 18, no. 2 (1994).

3. See, for example, Alice Dembner, "Drug Firms Woo Doctors with Perks," *Boston Globe* (May 20, 2001): 1; and Sheryl Gay Stolberg and Jeff Gerth, "High Tech Stealth Being Used to Sway Doctor Prescriptions," *New York Times* (November 16, 2000): A1.

4. I thank Matile Rothschild for pointing this out to me.

5. Information from Paul Seligman, M.D., Director, Office of Pharmacoepidemiology and Statistical Science, Center for Drug Evaluation and Research, F.D.A.

6. Stephen Fulder, *An End to Ageing? Remedies for Life Extension* (New York: Destiny Books, 1983). Fulder tested ginseng in his lab, and his book provides an excellent antidote to the drug bias of American doctors.

7. Personal communication with Tami Kurashimo.

CHAPTER FIVE

Healthy Physical Aging

Three decades of research on healthy aging indicates that much of what we call "aging" results from lack of exercise, smoking, other addictions, poor nutrition, falls, and stress. How much of the decline seen as normal aging is due to preventable chronic illness? Perhaps as much as half. Thus the challenge is to distinguish the late-life conditions that truly are unavoidable from those caused by disuse and lack of movement. But this distinction is often lost in mainstream health care for elders, and age denial keeps many who are under sixty from realistically assessing their chances of reaching eighty intact.

Increased susceptibility to disease often accompanies aging. Age-dependent conditions (those which rise steadily with age) include vision and hearing loss, Type 2 diabetes, hip fracture, Parkinson's disease, dementia, pneumonia, incontinence, and constipation. Measurements of health and ability to function show gradual rather than precipitous changes with age, however, according to the Baltimore Longitudinal Study of Aging.

Robert Schmidt defines healthy aging as "minimal interruption of usual function, although minimal signs and symptoms of chronic disease may be present," and lists its components as exercise, nutrition, stress management, support from family and friends, and spirituality (35). This is a good definition because it does not sharply separate health from impairment or disability.

Homeostasis, a state of equilibrium in different but interconnected parts, is a useful concept for healthy aging. When people say they are "fighting" cancer, they speak as if confronting an external enemy instead of an imbalance in their bodies. If old women and men think of aging simply as decay, they overlook a fundamental life characteristic, our capacity for self-repair (Bortz, 1991, 41).

These views are fairly comprehensive if the focus is on individuals but as soon as it shifts to social structures, the notion that we are responsible for our health in old age, repeated for example in Rowe and Kahn's *Successful Aging,* The MacArthur Study of Aging in America, seems questionable. Healthy aging has great relevance for women because they live longer than men and experience more chronic illness and disability as they age. Although the problems they face are created partly by the health care system itself, women are encouraged to see their health status only in individual terms and expected to find solutions on their own.

Chapters 5 and 6 offer a highly selective look at the complex subject of healthy aging. Chapter 5 discusses the elements of healthy physical aging and chapter 6 considers its political dimensions. In few subjects are the hopeful aspects so intertwined with the grim.

Exercise

In the midst of many unanswered questions about aging and contradictory health research reports in the mainstream media, it is reassuring to know that scientific evidence definitively proves the benefits of exercise for older people, not only for those already fit but also for those who have led sedentary lives before beginning to exercise and for frail elders as well. Moreover, relatively modest exertions can lead to significant improvements. It is not necessary to exercise heroically like Doris Haddock of Dublin, New Hampshire, who spent thirteen months walking across the country, ten miles a day, to call attention to campaign finance reform. Haddock was 90 at the time she completed her walk in February 2000, a remarkable feat for a woman who has both emphysema and arthritis.[1]

Exercise prolongs life, even for people who have chronic illness and disability (Kaplan, 42). It improves all bodily functions, including our immune system, and improves mood, cognition, and memory (Bortz, 1991, 191). Exercise protects against adult onset diabetes, and strength training (resistance training) enlarges muscle fiber in older women and men, improves balance, and burns calories (Rowe and Kahn, 105–106). It can also lessen arthritic pain.[2] The MacArthur Study of Aging found that people with higher mental function were also more likely to be physically fit and, surprisingly perhaps, the level of emotional support a person received strongly predicted his or her chances of staying fit over time (Rowe and Kahn, 123).

In "Aging and Activity," a fascinating essay that combines evolutionary biology, anthropology, and medicine, Walter Bortz notes that our bodies are designed to keep moving to find food. What is normal bone, he asks, "our own crumbly type or that of our ancestors, which could outlive a sledgehammer that assaulted it?" (199). Lack of exercise leads to heart disease, muscle weakness, weakened immunity, obesity and depression (200). Our present inactive life, which Bortz calls "zoolike," finds many of us, especially women, "languishing on the orthopedic floors of hospitals with fractured hips, spines, and pelvises, neither as a result of age nor of calcium or estrogen lack, but because of our cultural disuse. There are no broken hips in the jungles of Borneo" (1991, 130). Here the social construction of aging is succinctly stated. The Industrial Revolution made us more sedentary than our agricultural ancestors, but Bortz observes that cultivating land requires less physical movement than hunting and gathering. The recommendation that vigorous exercise be undertaken on alternate days rather than daily derives from the optimal hunting frequency for hunter-gatherers (1991, 195). A male model slips in here but the idea is intriguing. Ideally, women and men over sixty should get four kinds of exercise: aerobic, muscle-strengthening, flexibility, and balance training (1999, 211). A big benefit of exercise is cutting the risk of falls (Rowe and Kahn, 111). More generally, regular exercise decreases the chances of a prolonged dying process (Bortz, 1999, 219).

Walking to Wellness, a fitness education program for minority women that began in 1990, has motivated 10,000 women to walk. It is sponsored by the National Black Women's Health Project, founded by Byllye Avery of Provincetown, whose work is motivated by a racial gap: black women are more likely to die of heart disease and breast cancer than white women, and their diabetes rate is 50 percent higher. They are also more likely to have high blood pressure (Flaherty, 3).

Yoga, Tai Chi, and Qi Gong

Because it builds strength and flexibility, yoga is particularly conducive to healthy aging. Older women who have lost some mobility benefit from gentle yoga postures, and stretches help them maintain balance and prevent falls. Yoga's development of the breath is an important health asset, since lung capacity diminishes with age. Enhanced self-esteem and zest for life often result from the regular practice of yoga. Two devotees who lived past 100 were Sadie and Bessie Delany, authors of *Having Our Say*, who attributed their longevity to two other factors: never marrying and eating many vegetables each day.

Tai Chi is an ancient form of exercise using slow movements in precise patterns to stimulate energy pathways, improve balance, and reduce pain (Peck and Peck, 1). Simplified versions are suitable for people who are not very strong or flexible at the beginning of their practice. It is an excellent exercise for fall prevention.

Qi Gong, another ancient Chinese form of disciplined movements, is very beneficial for older people. The version called Falun Gong is now a mass movement with a strong supernatural element that threatens the authority of the Chinese government.

Dance therapy, movement for physical, mental, and emotional benefits, strengthens elders who cannot do yoga, tai chi, or qi gong. Classes for those with physical or psychological problems are held in clinics, psychiatric hospitals, prisons, nursing homes, and rehab centers. People in wheelchairs can move rhythmically and enjoyably through dance therapy.

Nutrition

In a nutshell, as people age, "the obstacles to good nutrition multiply even while eating properly becomes increasingly important to optimal health" (Brody, 1990, B7). Declining sense of taste and smell, difficulty shopping, reluctance to cook for one, dental problems, and attachment to lifelong eating habits all interfere with healthy eating. Malnutrition may afflict as many as 40 percent of the old who see doctors (Bennett, 10). Less dire but nonetheless serious signs of nutritional problems common in the elderly are diminished immunity, slower wound healing, and more fragile tissue (Bortz, 1991, 206). The familiar notion that the old need fewer calories has been questioned as an ageist myth, but bodies that shrink need less fuel. On the other hand, the caloric needs of vigorous old women and men "remain largely unchanged" (Bortz, 1991, 206). Bodily changes impact nutritional needs.[3] The capacity of the kidneys to conserve water declines with age, for example, and our sensation of thirst diminishes. At greater risk for dehydration, older women and men should drink 1½–2 quarts of fluid a day (Rowe and Kahn, 112).

As most women over fifty have discovered, weight gain seems to accompany menopause. For those who are mostly sedentary, declining energy needs are not matched by reduced food intake, which leads to abdominal fat, which in turn leads to a greater risk of diabetes (Evans and Cyr-Campbell, 632).

Because women live longer than men and have less money, nutritional deficits are likely to have a more adverse affect on them and thus nutrition is an
older women's issue.[4] When Boston activist Anna Morgan was ninety-four,
she volunteered for a study of elders and diet and was told the cut-off age was
seventy-nine. Presumably, her nutritional needs differ from those of a sixty-
year-old.[5]

A diet including fruits, vegetables, whole grains, legumes, seeds, and nuts
is healthy at any age but especially for women and men over sixty-five whose
digestive systems may be overtaxed by the usual American diet high in
refined carbohydrates and saturated fats. Many Chinese Buddhists believe
that age sixty is the time to give up red meat (Sankar, 267), a practice that
helps the body maintain homeostasis. Meat eaters excrete more calcium in
urine than vegetarians (Gannon, 158), and thus older women at risk for
osteoporosis should consider a vegetarian diet. Over a lifetime, women lose
nearly twice as much calcium as men.

When oxygen is metabolized, cells form by-products called free radicals.
"Great white sharks in the biochemical sea, these short-lived but voracious
agents oxidize and damage tissue, especially cell membranes" (Walford, 87).
Free radical damage has been linked to heart disease, cancer, Parkinson's disease, inflammations and cataracts. Antioxidants—vitamin C, vitamin E,
selenium, and beta-carotene—protect cells by scavenging free radicals, bind-
ing to them, and carrying them out of the body (Calbom and Keane, 13).
Air pollution, ultraviolet light, and smoking are also sources of free radicals,
and the older we are, the more exposure we have had to them. Theoretically,
then, the best diet for an older person is one that minimizes their impact.
Light eating, for example, creates fewer opportunities for oxygen to be
metabolized.[6]

A perennially interesting question in gerontology is whether caloric
restriction extends life. It may reduce free radical damage and preserve the
capacity of cells to proliferate (In Search, 28). Experiments in the 1930s by
Clive McKay showed that mice live longer when underfed. Similar experiments were conducted in the 1960s by Roy Walford. Current research studies
caloric restriction in primates. For many years, Walford has restricted his own
diet to see if that will increase his longevity. Few would give up 30 percent
of their caloric intake to live longer, but the implications of caloric restriction are important, if only to suggest that light eating promotes healthy
aging. It may be possible to mimic the effects of caloric restriction through
some natural substances while avoiding the hardship of a 30–40 percent cut
in calories.

The role of vitamins and other supplements in warding off disease is increasingly acknowledged by mainstream medicine. Older adults deficient in vitamin B6 or B12 show symptoms that may be mistaken for dementia. Vitamin D helps the body process calcium and D deficiency is thought to be a key factor in hip fractures (*Aging News Alert*, Vitamin D, 1999, 10). Aside from its benefits for bones, calcium enhances nerve function, blood clotting, and muscle contraction, and it may protect against colon cancer and stroke (Nutrition, 6). The protective effect of vitamin E against cancer has been demonstrated.

Herbal medicines are used by one-third of American adults; sales increased dramatically in the 1990s, reaching $4 billion by the end of the decade (Brody, 1999, D1). The advantage of herbs over drugs is that they cause many fewer side effects. Ginkgo biloba improves blood flow in the brain and appears to improve cognitive function in people with mild dementia (Haber, 179). St. John's wort is now used to treat depression. On the other hand, exaggerated claims are made for herbs, they are poorly regulated in the U.S., and sometimes they do not contain the ingredients listed on the label (Brody, 1999, D7). Faddish consumption of herbs probably wastes money of older Americans, if health concerns increase their susceptibility to unproven advertising claims. In Germany, the growing, harvesting, and processing of herbs is monitored by the government (Grady, 2000, D1). Thus German elders who use herbs are better protected than their American counterparts.[7]

Addiction to coffee, especially over a lifetime, is a liability many Americans carry into old age. Because of physical changes with age, caffeine has more impact on old bodies than on young ones, a fact that should lead gerontologists and writers on healthy aging to regard it as "an addictive psychotropic drug" (Zuess, 93). Coffee addiction does its harm slowly and silently. Research on the possible link between lifelong coffee drinking and late-life illness will not be conducted because the question is not interesting to gerontologists, many of whom, like most other Americans, drink coffee daily. Coffee consumption is a given to them, part of the natural landscape, not something to question.

A few doctors have begun to explore the health implications of widespread coffee consumption in the U.S. In *Eat for Health*, William Manahan, M.D., lists some of the effects of caffeine that may not be recognized: it stimulates the nervous system, stimulates excessive gastric acid secretion, relaxes the bladder, stimulates heart muscle, increases urine production, raises the level of fatty acids in the blood, and raises sugar levels (9). Of particular importance for old women is the finding that calcium loss from urine doubles after consumption of caffeine (Manahan, 19). Studies show a correlation between drinking two cups of coffee a day or more and suffering bone density loss (Gannon, 64). Thus anyone with osteoporosis or at risk for developing it should consider eliminating coffee.

The heavy use of coffee in the U.S. chiefly benefits multinational corporations. Coffee tastes bitter. The appetite for it is acquired as we are socialized in coffee-drinking families. It is served everywhere, including senior centers and nursing homes. Because of the spread of corporate chain coffeehouses, baby boomers are drinking much stronger coffee than Americans used to drink. Our social mythology brands heroin and cocaine addicts as bad but places no such harsh judgment on caffeine addicts.

Sugar is another source of addiction. Added sugar consumption has risen 20 percent since 1986, and Americans use an average of 152 pounds of sugar a year (Sugar, 5). The Agriculture Department recommends using no more than ten teaspoons a day, but many people average twice that amount. The 43 percent increase in soft drink consumption since 1985 (especially dangerous for teenagers, who now drink far more soft drinks than milk at a time when they are building bone mass), the increase in sugar consumption by people who eat fat-free foods, and the increased use of artificial sweeteners may eventually lead to an epidemic of osteoporosis (Brody, 1998, D7). The link between excessive sugar consumption and bone loss is particularly relevant to women, as is the strong connection between sugar and depression. Sugar addiction is comparable to alcoholism (Manahan, 77). Reducing consumption increases energy and strengthens immune function (Zuess, 145). With a few exceptions such as Kathleen DesMaisons, researchers are not interested in the damage sugar causes.[8] We have no studies of the cumulative effect of caffeine and sugar addiction, or studies of people over sixty who use little of either substance.

The Brain

Brains of healthy old women and men remain intact, although the part that controls memory shrinks slightly. The ability to do more than one thing at a time declines. Older people tend to take in new information more slowly than the young, but they retain it as well. Both physical and mental exercise help stimulate brain function. Research by Marian Diamond on old rats placed in an enriched environment showed brain growth (Bortz, 1991, 173–74), the first evidence that the structure and chemistry of the brain could be influenced by environment (Ebersole and Hess, 794). More recent work by Diamond has shown increases in neuron size and in the number of neuron branches that transmit information to other cells; nerve cells shrink in an unstimulating environment (Ebersole and Hess, 794). Current thinking is that the brain develops and maintains itself by adding new cells, a reversal of the long-held belief that the old had to expect gradual mental deterioration as cells died off (Blakeslee, D1). Thus the buzzword in current brain research is "plasticity" (Bortz, 1991, 163), and researchers are beginning to "explore development, as opposed to deterioration" in middle-aged and older people (Gannon, 39).

Paul Baltes and his colleagues theorize that the old have untested "reserve capacity" that enables them to perform at higher levels than their test scores indicate (Whitebourne, 268). Another plausible hypothesis is that old people may use different parts of the brain than young people use to accomplish the same task. Studies of cognitive ability, developed on young men, are probably not applicable to middle-aged and old women (Gannon, 39). Moreover, perceived decline in cognitive functioning "may reflect performance measurement rather than defects in competence" (Bortz, 1991, 175). This is an important caution, given the cultural bias of intelligence tests. Intelligence measures that favor a quick response put old test takers at a disadvantage and often contain material not relevant to their lives. On a test of practical information, older adults outscored the young (Gaylord, 79).

In a longitudinal study in Seattle, K. Warner Schaie and his colleagues studied 5,000 people aged twenty to ninety to see what happens to intellectual ability. Decline was found to vary greatly. Those who sustained a high level of mental functioning had several things in common: a high standard of living marked by above average education and income; lack of chronic disease; active engagement in reading, travel, cultural events, or professional associations; willingness to change; an intelligent partner; the ability to grasp new ideas quickly; and satisfaction with accomplishments (Thompson, 8). Of these seven characteristics, three directly reflect class privilege (income, health and travel), while another (life satisfaction) is probably related as well. Intellectual competence may improve in old age (Schaie, 281). Elders in the MacArthur Study of Aging who showed a decline in inductive reasoning not only demonstrated marked improvement after only five training sessions but also maintained their improvement (Rowe and Kahn, 136). If cognitive function is thought of as functions, plural, "even moderate decline in some areas of mental functioning does not necessarily interfere" with preserving independence (Rowe and Kahn, 136). Data from 2,380 people in

Amsterdam aged fifty-five to eighty-five showed those with high scores on cognitive tests tended to live longer than people with lower scores. Information processing speed was the strongest predictor of mortality (Sison, 1).

Emotions

Emotions and illness are clearly linked, as folk wisdom has long held and mainstream medicine is belatedly acknowledging. Emotions change with age, according to speculative work in neurobiology, and one day chemical manipulations may be able to turn off negative emotions such as anger and loneliness and turn on "playfulness, nurturance, and intimacy," a prospect that raises ethical questions for the psychology of aging (Manheimer, 1998, 263). Very little psychological theory is based on the actual experience of older people, as Betty Friedan notes in *The Fountain of Age*, although she quotes Jungian analysts who believe a root cause of psychological problems in the elderly is an insistence on seeing themselves as young (461–62). This suggests that psychological strength in late life depends partly on acceptance of one's life stage and on self-esteem, and those characteristics in turn depend on freedom from internalized ageism. Friedan believes that decreased resistance to disease in elders may be caused partly by low self-esteem, a sense of powerlessness, and few opportunities for meaningful participation in society. Individual psychology is linked to social contexts.

The irascible woman or man who is not afraid to say no or to insist on his or her own way probably has a strong sense of self. One may be outspoken and contrary when a situation demands it but serene in one's usual disposition and able to let anger pass when it arises. Older women have been socialized to repress their anger, and it will be interesting to see if this traditional female socialization fades with future generations. Some older women express anger indirectly through querulousness. Repression of negative emotion tamps down the life force and narrows emotional range. Being unconventional may be advantageous for old women if it leads them to express freely what they feel.

Despite charges of "false memory syndrome," many health care workers understand that large numbers of children, especially girls, experience incest. David Finklehor, director of the Crimes Against Children Research Center at the University of New Hampshire, estimates that 20–25 percent of all women, and 33 percent of women on welfare, were abused as children (DeParle, 1). Sexual violence against children is a "silent epidemic in a society fascinated by violent crime" (M. Gould, 6). Our bodies store memories of what happens to us early in life, and if those events are traumatic, aches and pains, chronic tension spots, or blocked areas may be relieved or cured by recovering memories. When oral sex is forced on children too young to protest or escape, for example, interruptions in their normal breathing patterns may have long-lasting consequences such as shallow breathing rather than diaphragm breathing. One root of adult psychological problems such as addictions or relationship failures is sexual assault occurring during childhood.

What does this have to do with aging? An estimated 3.5 million women over sixty-five survived childhood rape and incest, yet little is known about their experience (Faris and Gibson, 31). I believe that one of the best preparations for healthy aging is confronting memories of childhood sexual assault if they arise. This is a risky process that may trigger old feelings of shame, worthlessness, and terror. Survivors of incest and early rape often feel powerlessness throughout their adult lives, even if to outward appearances they are high achievers. Their self-esteem is often low. If they escape the damage of obvious addictions to drugs and alcohol, they may be compulsive overeaters or exhibit patterns such as workaholism, perfectionism, or an extreme need to be in control. As they age, the accumulation of stresses on them can produce illness. Since the illness is rooted in a profound psychological disturbance that remains hidden, it is not likely to be considered by a doctor making a diagnosis.

An example of ageist bias is the belief that therapy is wasted on the old, who are thought to be incapable of growth. Clearly this is fallacious. A woman in her sixties or older who comes to understand hidden parts of her past may find that mysterious pieces of her life are now explained. If she can re-experience early traumas and integrate them into her current self, she will almost certainly become healthier emotionally and physically. Tense places in her body will relax. Breathwork is often a key to this transformative process, which is more often circular than linear. A woman who knows what was done to her may feel a new sense of power. Her anger may channel itself into creative paths. Her pride in having survived something horrible may embolden her to take risks.

With incest, the past lives on, cruelly in some instances, as it does with survivors of torture. To be free of inner feelings of worthlessness and uncontrollable rage is an invaluable asset as we age. To be sure, therapy cannot always accomplish such healing changes, but in most cases, women who grapple with past abuse and identify behavior patterns directly related to it are much better off than if they continue living oblivious to a truth about their childhood or living in the shadow of recurrent depression.

Some gerontologists believe that depression is the most serious disorder of late life, but few studies differentiate between depression occurring for the first time after sixty-five and this affliction experienced throughout life. Clinical depression appears to be less common among elders than among younger people, but when measured by indicators such as sluggishness, feeling sad, feeling lonely, and difficulty concentrating, depression occurs frequently (Quadagno, 1999, 156). According to research surveyed by Betty Friedan for *The Fountain of Age*, all physical symptoms found in older people, including symptoms of Alzheimer's, in the absence of a defined disease, may mask depression "or somatic equivalents of depression, even without depressed mood" (429). Depression among older women may be caused by prescription drug interaction.

At all ages women report depression more frequently than men, and the gap is greatest for women over eighty (Quadagno, 1999, 156–57). Depression may go undiagnosed in the elderly because models for detecting it were developed for the young. The deficit model of aging in the mental health system—elders are not portrayed as coping, adapting, and demonstrating psychological strength—especially harms old women. They are missing from major research on depression (Rodeheaver and Datan, 651). Predictably, nursing home residents have high rates of depression (I. Katz, 270).

Compared to others, old women and men more frequently have depressing experiences such as loss of a partner, illness, or relocation to a relative's house or nursing home. It may be hard to distinguish between situational depression and depression originating in chemical imbalances in the brain. Depression leads to decreased physical activity and to increased social isolation. Social isolation may lead to inactivity and greater likelihood of depression (Kaplan and Strawbridge, 71), a sign of the complex interplay of social and biological factors.

In 2020, the middle of the baby boom cohort, 55 million strong, reaches sixty-five. Since present mental health systems are inadequate, baby boomers will overwhelm them, and those who suffer most will be elders with chronic mental illness (Koenig et al., 674–675). A recent Department of Human Services report in Maine, for example, shows that 86 percent of older adults with a mental health diagnosis receive psychotropic drugs without counseling or other support services.

Physical and psychological health are connected for everyone, but their "mutually interacting association seems to accelerate with age" (Gannon,

47). Thus an old woman who has lost some ability to move about freely may be at risk for depression. The stigma of mental illness may prevent some in their seventies or older from saying they are depressed; instead, they may say dismissively that they are just a little "blue" or "down" and not see getting help as an option. Doctors may be afraid of inquiring into the emotional states of older patients for fear of opening Pandora's box (Koenig et al., 235), a tendency certainly exacerbated by shortened office visits. In a materialist culture, doctors usually do not ask their patients about the state of their souls, although they may know intuitively that much illness begins in the psyche. How can the psychological health of the old be improved? This is a key question for healthy aging.

The notion that healing emotions bolster the immune system, long understood in alternative medicine, is slowly coming to be accepted by the mainstream medical community as well. Since decreased immune function is common in late life, whatever we do to strengthen it is good. Immune function varies greatly, but people over seventy-five or eighty usually need longer to recover from a cold or from wounds, and their infections tend to be more serious than those of younger people. Since we cannot see our immune system or locate it in our imaginations as we can our heart, it is difficult to think of strengthening it in a way comparable to strengthening our hearts by walking three miles a day. Nonetheless, the mysterious processes of getting sick and recovering can be modified somewhat by our own actions.

What are healing emotions and what does it mean to encourage them? It may simply mean awareness: if I know a certain emotion is beneficial, that awareness may help me, if only because I have shifted from acting without thought to acting consciously and deliberately. Three good examples of healing emotions are serenity, gratitude, and reverence. A common way serenity is cultivated by the old is gardening. Nurturing new growth is calming, and gardeners seem to thrive in old age. The ability to feel and express gratitude is an important part of healthy aging. In the lives of most people there are at least a few things to be grateful for. Sometimes this is just a matter of mindfulness. "I'm grateful that it is a clear night and I can see the stars." Speaking of herself when old, Colette expressed gratitude for each flower she passed as she walked slowly by. Gratitude for old friends must be one of the deepest pleasures of old age.

Reverence seems more abstract than gratitude or serenity. The old who only grumble and air grievances have lost, or perhaps never had, a sense of reverence. It may grow out of the healing following a serious illness or life-threatening operation. The hard breathing that accompanies strenuous exertion or exercise can induce feelings of reverence. This emotion acknowledges the life force greater than our individual sparks of life. It may make us feel puny or exalted. A group experience may evoke it, or it may be solitary. Reverence may come from a flash of understanding that all beings are interconnected. In "Tintern Abbey" Wordsworth expresses reverence for nature and also for himself.

To be old without a sense of reverence is an unenviable lot. If we lack the power to transcend our personal concerns, the stiffening and slowing down of our bodies signals the end of meaning. To survive into old age capable of feeling reverence requires some freedom from the prevailing materialism of our culture. Looking over one's past life as well as looking at a mountain may inspire reverence for the sheer doggedness of humans who live to be old.

Alternative Medicine

Conventional medicine has little to offer people dealing with chronic health problems or with the complex and interconnected conditions that sometimes accompany aging. Alternative or complementary medicine is safer and more effective. Its benefits deserve to be far better known, but little attention is paid to alternative medicine by gerontologists, their texts, or the media. At aging conventions, no exhibits extolling homeopathy or herbal remedies will be found alongside the booths of the drug companies that fund the events. Typically, alternative practitioners spend far more time with patients than mainstream doctors are able to, getting emotional information as well as hearing about specific symptoms. Thus they are more likely than mainstream doctors to develop a healing relationship with the people they treat. In this way, they resemble healers in other cultures. Their holistic approach to health equips them to work especially well with older people.

The rise of alternative medicine represents a growing awareness that while allopathic medicine is good for diagnosing and treating major illness, it is not very good for keeping us well. In 1997, an estimated 46 percent of Americans saw an alternative practitioner, up from 30 percent in 1990. Of those choosing complementary treatment, 54 percent saw a chiropractor; 25 percent, massage therapists; 14 percent, acupuncturists; 2 percent, homeopathic doctors; 2 percent, naturopaths and 3 percent, other alternative practitioners (Stolberg, 2000, A1). The budget of the National Center for Complementary and Alternative Medicine in the National Institute of Health increased from 2 million in 1993 to 68 million in 2000 (A1). The implications of the growth in alternative medicine for healthy aging are both profound and unexplored. For the middle class, this development may well lead to improved health in old age.

Attacks on alternative medicine have become increasingly heated as it grows more competitive with mainstream medicine, and usually health insurance covers only the latter. Some plans now cover chiropractic care, however, and many Americans choose it for health maintenance. If homeopathy, acupuncture, massage, herbal medicine, naturopathy, and ayurvedic medicine were also covered, their use would increase and their effectiveness would be more widely known.

Chiropractic

Chiropractors treat back pain and many other conditions by manipulating the spine. Poor alignment causes a number of short- and long-term problems. The traditional method of forceful correction has been supplemented by the activator, a device that allows doctors to move bones without force. The space between our vertebrae narrows as we age, reducing movement. Since spinal mobility is a key to healthy aging, chiropractic care is especially important for the health of middle-aged and older people.

Homeopathy

This healing system was synthesized early in the nineteenth century by Samuel Hahnemann. It uses extremely diluted solutions of active substances to cure disease, following the principle of "like cures like," that is, the same substance that causes symptoms of a disease in a healthy person will cure the disease in an ill person. Homeopathy is enjoying a resurgence in the U.S., where it has not been as widely accepted as in Europe. Like other alternative medical systems, homeopathy pays close attention to emotional states, stimulates the body's own healing capacity, and looks for underlying causes of disease.

Acupuncture

Acupuncture is a Chinese medical system that is 5,000 years old. Extremely thin needles are inserted into the body along pathways called meridians to ease pain, stimulate organs, and release blocked energy. Since acupuncture corrects imbalances in the body and restores vital energy, it is especially suited to easing the process of aging. It can help people accept the slowing down they experience in their bodies.[9]

Ayurveda

Ayurveda is an ancient Indian healing system that uses dietary change, herbs, meditation, and massage to relieve the body of toxins and restore balance. It makes use of whole plants, believing that plants contain material that counteract side effects from the curative element. *Ayu* means life in Sanskrit, and *veda* means knowledge.

Clinical Ecology

Clinical ecologists, usually allergists trained in U.S. medical schools, treat environmental illness (multiple chemical sensitivity). Typical patients are middle-aged women with a history of vaguely-defined health problems undetected by lab tests and frequently mistaken for mental illness. Exposure to pesticides, sealed buildings, or formaldehyde in furniture and carpeting can trigger chemical reactions that are sometimes disabling. Thyroid disease or other endocrine problems may be an underlying cause of immune system breakdown, along with exposure to chemicals. Some endocrinologists therefore recommend that all women over sixty be tested for underactive thyroid (Kelley, 146).

Massage

Massage involves both touch and movement. It focuses not only on problems in the body but also on maximum development of the person. Because older women are so accustomed to giving to others, the receiving of massage encourages balance in their lives. Massage is one of the best aids to comfortable aging because it is gentle, non-invasive, and benefits the whole body.[10] It helps relieve inflammation and stiffness of the joints. It releases muscle tension, lessens anxiety, and induces feelings of relaxation and well-being. Massage stimulates the flow of blood throughout the body. It may alleviate depression and chronic pain. It bolsters immunity by improving lymph flow, and it increases tissue elasticity (Tappan and Benjamin, 338). A form of massage that uses acupressure points is practiced by Chinese American doctors. Massage is a form of passive exercise. It is especially beneficial for old women and men because they are often touch deprived and feel "skin hunger."[11] Massage helps counteract the dehumanizing impact of institutional health care, according to a study by two Canadian nursing professors. Being touched is particularly important for elders who have diminished sight and hearing (Fraser and Kerr, 238–242).

Massage is so beneficial for older people, in fact, that Medicare should cover it. Imagine a bi-weekly massage for anyone over seventy who wanted one. A reasonable expense? The results would be shorter recovery periods after surgery and illness; stress reduction; delayed onset of serious illness and disability; safer treatment of depression; decreased falls, leading to prolonged independent living; and tonic effects resistant to quantifying.

Most Americans over seventy have not experienced massage, but as a therapeutic practice it is growing increasingly popular and is now used in some hospitals. How to extend its benefits to more working-class elders and people of color remains a challenge for healthy aging.

Rolfing

Rolfing, developed by biochemist and physiologist Ida Rolf, increases balance within the body by working on muscles and connective tissue. Stretching fascia (the tissue surrounding a muscle) allows bones to become properly aligned so that bodies move in gravity with less strain. Rolfing improves posture and range of motion and alleviates chronic pain.[12] It is an excellent method for correcting tension and stresses that accumulate with age or result from injury or surgery.

Body Mechanics

Whatever the condition of our health, the ability to be comfortable in our bodies may be a reward for living to be old, but by the time we reach sixty, we have characteristic ways of moving that are so habitual that they are unconscious. Often these movements unnecessarily strain backs, hips, shoulders, and necks. Thus an important aspect of healthy aging is becoming aware of body movements that may cause tension. Alternative practitioners are more likely than mainstream doctors to notice when a person's way of walking or holding her shoulders puts stress on other parts of the body. A worker who carries a briefcase in the same hand for forty years or who drives clenching the steering wheel with both hands may experience pain seemingly unrelated to the habitual movement. By changing customary patterns, we wake up dormant neural pathways. The bodily pleasure of easy movement can be experienced by many older women and men who have not been physically active earlier in life, by people recovering from strokes and injuries, and by those labeled frail. When long-held muscle tensions, including those caused by past trauma, are released by body work, therapy, or breathing exercises, older people may be able to experience their bodies more directly than was possible before. Discovering new movements may bring emotional and psychological benefits inseparable from the physical change. All gentle bodywork systems hold great promise for healthy aging. Experiencing many of them would be ideal.[13]

Feldenkrais Method

A movement philosophy and practice especially well suited to older people is Feldenkrais. Dancers and athletes use it to improve performance, and it works equally well for people with a limited range of movement. It emphasizes finding comfortable and easy ways to move and encourages pleasure in movement. Moshe Feldenkrais (1904–1984) was an Israeli physicist and judo master who originally developed his system of movement education by healing a knee injury. He watched babies crawl and synthesized what he knew from science, body mechanics, and the martial arts, refining his ideas over several decades. In the 1970s he trained many people in the U.S. in his method, which has two formats: 1) Awareness through Movement group classes and 2) Functional Integration, one-on-one sessions in which a practitioner gently touches and moves parts of the body. Feldenkrais believed that very early in life we develop habitual ways of functioning which we repeat "compulsively to the exclusion of other patterns" that might be easier and more efficient, and that we use only about 5 percent of the movements we are capable of making (Claire, 101–102). His method reprograms the brain by substituting conscious and deliberate movements for ones that cause strain. This "sensory motor re-education" can occur at either the unconscious level or the level of conscious awareness (Claire, 105).

Unlike other systems, Feldenkrais places authority within students to decide for themselves what is beneficial rather than to fit a standardized model. This is one reason it is so effective with older adults. Another is that Feldenkrais does not envision an ideal body type, which in our culture is often the athletic twenty-year-old "without blemish or trauma who is not yet visibly marked by life experiences." This method stresses moving "more efficiently, not more forcefully," with less stress on joints and muscles, and thus it is an excellent practice for older women and men, who may have accepted weakness or stiffness as natural to aging.[14] Another advantage is that Feldenkrais is not goal-oriented; you don't have to do your best.[15] The attentiveness required to make the very small movements characteristic of Feldenkrais allows students to re-evaluate the high-speed, high-stress lives many Americans now live. Moving slowly can be a revelation, especially to people who have been on fast forward for decades, not thinking of their bodies unless they felt pain.

Using excessive energy to move is a hard habit to break; it overrides our body's sense of knowing. Feldenkrais is not exercise. It consists of "tiny little noticings," and even imagined movements can cause microscopic muscular responses.[16] Some movements are quite easy and familiar, such as turning the head slowly, while other movements are ones we would not make in daily life, bringing a knee close to the opposite elbow, for example. Movements having several parts are challenging. I have observed Feldenkrais classes in which all participants were over eighty and several hampered by strokes or disabilities. It is unusual for people this age to find pleasure in their bodily movements. Very slow, gradual, repeated movements give people with impairments a chance to feel physically competent and unself-conscious. The particular relevance of Feldenkrais to healthy aging is that our "nervous and muscular systems are so flexible that we can reverse previously learned patterns" (Claire, 102).

Healthy Aging Programs

Over the past two decades, numerous healthy aging programs have been developed for senior centers, YWCAs and YMCAs, schools, and other community sites. Examples are the Wallingford Wellness Project, sponsored by King County, Washington, and The University of Washington School of Social Work, and Health Promotion in Older Adults, a collaboration between Group Health of Puget Sound and the University of Washington. Programs typically focus on exercise, nutrition, alcohol and drug use, stress management, and home safety. Wallingford offered assertiveness training in preparation for visits to doctors. Another innovative Seattle program developed for frail elders, The Senior Wellness Program of King County, includes evaluations by nurses that cover psychological as well as physical aspects of health and a seven-session course that teaches pain management (Aging News Alert, Program, 1999, 7).

Health Watch, a longitudinal healthy aging study of 2,200 San Francisco residents, measures general well-being, psychological health, physical activity, nutrition, and use of alcohol and tobacco. Data accumulated over time allows participants to determine what is normal *for them*. Early danger signs are detected before illness develops. The Health Watch model has been used to study elderly Hawaiians of various ancestries and Sun City, Arizona, residents (Schmidt, 37).

Gerontologists in New Orleans who developed longevity therapy for nursing home residents, based on a belief that growth can occur at any age, encourage residents to participate in their own health care, practice gentle stretches, explore breathing and relaxation techniques, and express themselves through art (Graubarth-Szyller).

Some health promotion programs are called "It's Never Too Late," which sounds glib but is literally true. If more elders could be persuaded of this, perhaps more would slowly change their habits. My neighbor Meda Benoit walks a quarter-mile twice each day, a more meaningful fact about her than her chronological age of ninety-two. The best exemplar of the never-too-late philosophy is Jeanne Calmont, the French woman who died at age 122. She stopped smoking at age 117.

Healthy aging programs have demonstrated the benefits of conscious aging by showing for example that loss of function is sometimes reversible, even in the very old. These programs have not reached many Americans, however, particularly low-income elders and people of color, and often they last only a few weeks or months until a grant runs out. Until they are permanent and available to all who wish to take part, the health potential of American elders will not be known.

Related Issues

The interconnecting issues of healthy aging lead to a question of particular relevance to old women. Is it possible to be severely impaired or immobile and at the same time to be healthy? Traditional gerontology, opposing health to frailty, would answer no, thereby consigning many women over eighty-five to an undesirable category. But as more women live to be very old, the paradoxical coexistence in some of major impairments and vitality may encourage broader definitions of health relative to old women. University of Maine social work professor Nancy Webster, for example, has interviewed a bedridden woman who would not be judged healthy by conventional norms. Yet she writes poetry, publishes books on theology, and keeps in touch with a wide circle of friends. Surely she is healthy.

Decline and loss of some function can coexist with good health. Adequate late-life health is a reasonable expectation for most white, middle-class Americans. Furthermore, improved health, in some cases dramatically improved health, is a realistic hope for some women and men over sixty-five. Learning to be old means being aware that we have been so conditioned to expect decline that our late-life health expectations may be too low, and we may unthinkingly attribute to aging ailments or problems that can be successfully treated.

The conventional images of healthy aging in the media focus only on bodies, not on the power of the breath to create mind-body harmony. This may suit the tennis-playing seventy-five-year-old but eventually she, too, will live past the ability to perform and will need other ways of conceiving of healthy aging, perhaps as a vital force not dependent upon physical vigor or as a quality that transcends good habits and the various components of well-being considered here. Neither a woman who will never exercise again nor a woman who exercises one month but is too weak to do much the next should be made to feel guilty by the preachments of healthy aging.

Gerontologists debate whether longer lives will mean more or less late-life disability. A reasonable hunch is that these trends will occur simultaneously: an increasing number of older people remaining healthy until the end of their lives and an increasing number having prolonged, severe illness or disability (Lamphere-Thorpe and Blendon, 78). Arizona doctors followed a group of healthy elders for five years. Those who died during this period were sick an average of 4.9 months before their deaths.[17] The fear of a long, slow descent toward death is so strong that most people would probably accept a short illness at the end of a healthy life. But how can Americans be persuaded that the choices they make in their fifties and sixties will affect their condition at eighty?

Conclusion

Some signs bode ill for healthy aging, the rising obesity rates, for example, and the increase in drug-resistant bacteria. The number of Americans with brain cancer has doubled since the mid-1980s, according to *New York Times* columnist Jane Brody (Oct. 19, 1999, D7). This is due partly to better detection but also to environmental causes: more people have been exposed to more chemicals for longer periods. The current epidemic of asthma among children, especially those who are poor or black, is a troubling public health development (Stolberg, "Gasping," 1999). World Health Organization statistics project a slight increase in breast cancer for American women over sixty between 1990 and 2020 (Caselli, 260).

HMOs are leaving rural areas. In 1999, for example, Arizona was a model for rural health care options, but in 2000, elders in only four counties there had access to HMOs (West, 1). By early 2002, many of the nation's largest HMOs had dropped or cut back prescription drug coverage for Medicare recipients, creating a particular hardship for cancer patients. Dental school enrollment has dropped 50 percent in the past decade, creating a shortage of dentists in rural areas at the same time that population aging is increasing the need for dental work.

Future cohorts of old Americans will be better educated than those now in their eighties, a change that may lead to healthier habits and lower disability rates. Data from the 1990s suggests a reduction in arthritis, hypertension, stroke, emphysema, and dementia but also more Parkinson's disease, heart disease, bronchitis, pneumonia, and hip fractures (Crimmins, 10). The health benefits of better education may be partially offset by heavy use of prescription drugs, the high stress of longer work hours and harried family life, and by poor nutrition, especially if it is true that one-fourth of all American breakfasts are now eaten at McDonalds. On the other hand, the percentage of people unable to care for themselves is declining. Medical advances such as hip replacements and lens replacements for cataracts significantly ease aging. A cure for macular degeneration would improve late life for many Americans.

Stem cell research holds promise for organ regeneration. Developments in the field of psychoneuroimmunology, the study of interactions of the mind, stress, and the immune system, may lead to new knowledge about aging. Hardiness, for example, formerly thought of as a manifestation of physical health, now appears to have an important psychological dimension as well (Friedan, 442–43). And yet a study of patient interactions with mainstream physicians found that only 17 percent said that psychosocial issues were discussed with their doctors (Innes et al., 43). Other studies have shown that doctors spend less time with old patients than with others.

Finally, there are telomeres. "Bits of simple repetitive DNA sequences at the end of chromosomes . . . formerly thought to be biological 'junk,' have been shown to prolong the longevity of cells. The longer the telomere, the longer the cell life. The longer our cells live, the longer we live" (Weisstein, 4). Experiments with a naturally occurring enzyme, telomerase, that synthesizes new caps on chromosomes, may lead to a better understanding of life extension (Schwartz, 152).

Signs of unusual physical capacity among a few hearty people over seventy, the snowboarders jocularly called "Grays on Trays," for example, should not be used to denigrate elders who experience the more common slow decline and gradual loss of function associated with advanced age. We may be approaching a time in which large numbers of white, middle-class older adults exhibit a level of health that would have seemed remarkable to their grandparents or even to their parents. But that promise will not extend to all of their fellow citizens.

Notes

1. For an excellent discussion of exercise and aging that interprets research findings, see Linda Gannon, *Women and Aging: Transcending the Myths* (New York: Routledge, 1999), 55–67, 140–141, 159–162.

2. "Don't Take it Easy, Exercise," National Institute on Aging Page: www.aoa/ddhs/gov/aoa/pages/agepages/exercise.html (accessed 2–20–2000).

3. For age-related bodily changes, see Priscilla Ebersole and Patricia Hess, *Toward Healthy Aging*, 5th ed. (St. Louis: Mosby, 1998), chapter 4. The authors discuss psychotropic drug management in chapter 23.

4. Stephanie Ross, unpublished paper, "Older Women and Nutrition," Women and Aging, WST 235, University of Southern Maine, Fall, 1999.

5. Anna Morgan, "Just Keep Breathing," in *Fierce with Reality: An Anthology of Literature about Aging,* ed. Margaret Cruikshank (St. Cloud, Minn.: North Star Press, 1995), 91.

6. For more on free radicals, see Brian J. Merry and Anne M. Holohan, "Effects of Diet on Aging," in *Physiological Basis of Aging and Geriatrics*, 2nd ed., ed. Paola S. Timiras (Boca Raton, Fla.: CRC Press, 1994); Walter Bortz, *We Live Too Short and Die Too Long* (New York: Bantam, 1991), 37–40; Roy Walford, *Maximum Life Span* (New York: Norton, 1983), chapter 5; and Richard A. Passwater, *The Longevity Factor: Chromium Picolinate* (New Canaan: Keats Publishing, 1933), chapter 3.

7. For an analysis of vitamins and dietary supplements in relation to aging, see David Haber, *Health Promotion and Aging,* 2nd ed. (New York: Springer, 1999). Research on herbs by Purdue University Professor Emeritus Varro E. Tyler is widely respected because he has no financial ties to herb manufacturers. With Steven Foster he wrote *Tyler's Honest Herbals: A Sensible Guide to The Use of Herbs and Related Products* (New York: Haworth, 1999).

8. Kathleen DesMaisons wrote *The Sugar Addict's Total Recovery Program* (New York: Ballantine, 2000). For a detailed discussion of sugar addiction, see William Manahan, M.D., *Eat for Health* (Tiburon, Calif.: H.J. Kramer, 1988), chapters 6–9.

9. Information from Vicki Cohn Pollard, acupuncturist, Blue Hill, Maine.

10. These perspectives are from massage therapist Donna Murphy, Corea, Maine.

11. Massage as passive exercise and "skin hunger" are observations of massage therapist Theresa Hart of Bangor, Maine.

12. Information from Annie Wyman, certified Rolfer, Belfast, Maine.

13. These include Reiki, Trager, Lomi, Rosen Method, Alexander Technique, and Rolfing. A comprehensive survey of these and other systems can be found in Thomas Claire's *Bodywork*. Although she left behind no method named for her, Magda Proskauer was an important figure in the development of bodywork healing and teaching, in the early days of Esalen and later. A Jungian analyst and physical therapist, she taught breathing classes for many years in San Francisco. Proskauer wrote an essay about her work in Herbert Otto, ed., *Ways of Growth* (New York: Viking, 1968).

14. Feldenkrais practitioner Nancy Werth, Blue Hill, Maine, personal communication, April 5, 2000.

15. Nancy Werth, discussion of Feldenkrais with Bella Johnson, host of "Alternative Currents," WERU radio, Blue Hill, Maine, April 7, 2000.

16. Jane Burdick, presentation on Feldenkrais, Downeast School of Massage, Waldoboro, Maine, April 17, 2000.

17. James Goodwin, Paula. D. Thomas and Philip Garry, "Morbidity and Mortality in an Initially Healthy Elderly Sample: Findings After Five Years of Follow-up," *Age and Aging* 15 (1996): 105–110. Five year follow-up studies of healthy old blacks, Latinas/os, Asian Pacific Islanders, and Indians could be done to see if they, too, have relatively short periods of illness before their deaths.

CHAPTER SIX

⌇

The Politics of Healthy Aging

Despite positive developments in science and medicine, the only way to make healthy aging a realistic possibility for *most* Americans is to eradicate poverty. That would not eliminate all self-destructive behavior, obviously, but even a decrease in poverty would lead to healthier aging. National health care might mitigate some of the damage to health caused by poverty, but even that modest reform eludes us. "The new longevity" is a popular slogan now in gerontology. The question is, for whom?

An egalitarian spirit might prompt one to say that age levels differences. In certain instances this may be true, as for example when a retired CEO and a retired laborer are both ignored at the hardware store on Saturday morning or when a receptionist calls a famous author by her first name as she does any old woman patient. But inequalities in money, status, and power matter greatly where healthy aging is concerned, except perhaps in an Alzheimer's ward. Until we have more accurate measures of late-life health, especially for people of color and for women, the extent and meaning of difference may not be knowable. Decades of experiencing prejudice and discrimination based on class, ethnicity, or gender, or all three, exacts a serious toll on health. That is a political judgment. A spiritual or psychological perspective would emphasize wholeness and recovery from oppression.

The class bias and individualist bias inherent in successful aging were noted earlier. Gerontologists also urge "responsible aging," a phrase that suggests not costing taxpayers too much. Responsible aging puts the burden on me of making wise choices without inquiring as to my capacity to make them. When a stigmatized group is told to behave responsibly (like the "deserving" poor), unjust distribution of resources is conveniently ignored. Thus the theme of this chapter is inequality.

The complete elimination of differences in health care, a goal of Healthy People 2010, is unrealistic, given the difficulty of achieving the more modest goal of *narrowing* the race and class gap. In 1997, The National Institute on Aging and the National Institute of Nursing Research funded six resource centers for minority aging whose goals are to reduce health care disparities.[1] A racial difference in pain treatment has been documented, for example, for both blacks and Latinas/os (Glaser, D8). Even if such injustices can be remedied, a larger structural problem remains: the rapid growth in the numbers of minority elders means that current policies "designed for a homogenous population are increasingly obsolete" (Wray, 357).

Class

Low-income elders are far more likely than others to have restricted physical functioning or disabilities (G. Kaplan, 45). Low socioeconomic status, as measured by occupation, income, and education, and the conditions associated with it, is a more fundamental cause of both unhealthy lifestyles and poor health than individual behavior (Robert and House, 268). This hard truth is seldom acknowledged in gerontology, even though recent epidemiological research clearly indicates that "countries with less income disparity have longer life expectancies and lower rates of mortality from specific diseases" (Wallack, A22). Class difference means not only that the wealthy live longer in better health but also that poor health threatens the economic resources accumulated over a lifetime (Smith, 282). Aside from determining who has adequate health care and health insurance, class determines who will feel entitled to good care. In noting the link between class and late-life health, two public health authorities observe that poverty by itself is disabling (Kennedy and Minkler, 95).

A problem inherent in healthy aging, often overlooked, is that healthy choices and habits are to some degree middle-class luxuries. To state the problem differently, the ideas about health promulgated by gerontologists reveal middle-class assumptions about personal responsibility. To make choices that the middle class regards as healthy requires a sense of control over one's circumstances. It requires belief that planning for the future is worthwhile or even possible. To be poor or working-class often means that others control the conditions under which we live and that long-term planning or deferred gratification are meaningless. Maine, for example, has many poor residents and the highest adult smoking rate in the country. Self-destructive behavior among people of color may often be "a response to recalcitrant racism" that dehumanizes them and deprives them of hope (Bayne-Smith, 14). Making these connections does not absolve people of responsibility for their actions, but it highlights the impact of race and class. Careful eating, exercise, and moderate drinking are choices of people whose self-esteem and relative freedom from addiction result in part from their social and economic niche. People who are just getting by, who lack education, who face prejudice at work or in housing cannot be expected to place the same value on healthy habits as middle-class people. Many do, in spite of the obstacles, but organic food, alternative medicine, long vacations, and workshops on self-care all lie beyond their means.

Ethnicity

Generalizations about minorities may be unreliable, given the diversity of people under that umbrella term, both between groups and within groups. Elderly black women, for example, include those who did not reach eighth grade and those who have earned graduate and professional degrees (Jackson, 1988, 35). It is clear, nonetheless, that inadequate health care in childhood and middle age has a big impact on the late-life health of many blacks, Latinas/os, Asian Pacific Islanders, and American Indians. A report by the Institute of Medicine concluded that minority Americans use fewer health services than whites but need them more (Fleming, 28). When they do enter the system, they tend to get poorer care. The Women of Color Health Data Handbook issued by the National Institute of Health documented significant disparities in every category studied, including access to insurance (Reed, 46). A related problem is that the number of minority nurses and doctors has declined since the 1980s (Fleming, 24). In emergency rooms, where many people of color get the only care available to them, 85 percent of the doctors are white.

Racism at school, at work, and in housing has life-course consequences not only in poorer health but also in lower life expectancy (Quadagno, 1999, 270) for blacks, Latinas/os, and American Indians. Cumulative disadvantage is the pattern by which those who begin life with few advantages fall farther behind as they age. Unfortunately, the inequities that suppress vitality in many people of color are not a central concern of gerontology.

Ethnogerontology gathers data not only about social inequality but also about age changes affected by ethnicity, nationality, and culture (Jackson, Race, 291). Ethnogerontology and ethnogeriatrics, the integration of aging, health, and ethnicity, are particularly important because by 2030, 25 percent of all elders will be minority elders (Wadsworth and FallCreek, 254). The number of old Latinas/os will triple by 2050, and the number of blacks will double (Binstock, 5). By 2050, old Asian Pacific Islanders could number seven million, or 16 percent of their total population (Scharlach et al., Module 2, 10). By the same year, 500,000 American Indian elders will constitute 12 percent of all Indians (Scharlach et al., 22). Besides sheer numbers, another reason that minority concerns should take up a much larger space in healthy aging studies is that cultural patterns affect the way people define illness, how an ill person is perceived by his or her group, and what health-seeking strategies are appropriate (Tripp-Reimer, 236).

Compared to whites, blacks' hypertension is more prevalent, more severe, and more likely to lead to disease and death (Svetkey, 64). A study of Navajo showed that hypertension increased with age and weight. Greater exposure to the dominant culture since the 1930s may be a factor in the high incidence of hypertension among Indians. Asian Pacific Islanders in California also have high rates (Stavig et al., 677). This problem is worse for Filipino Americans than for the more prosperous Japanese Americans, an instance of class as well as ethnicity affecting health.

Minority elders are underrepresented in clinical trials; they may react to medication differently from whites on whom the drugs were tested; they often lack health insurance; they may be unaware of programs they qualify for; and limited access to long-term care burdens their economically vulnerable families (Harper, 12). Lack of money keeps elderly people of color out of nursing homes, but discrimination is probably another factor accounting for low nursing home use across all minority groups (Kiyak and Hooyman, 305). Minority elders lack a voice in formulating health care policy, "bilingual and bicultural barriers abound," and most doctors will not understand their traditional customs and beliefs or the folk medicine they may be using (Harper, 12). In addition, their pensions are decreasing in value (Villa, 213), and many seek supplementary income from work (E. Percil Stanford, quoted in Scharlach et al., Module 1, p. 14). There is a great need for more minority health care professionals trained in geriatrics (Jackson, 1988, 42).

A problem for researchers is that past and present studies take whites as the standard measure, so that dimensions of aging or of a disease particular to a minority group are overlooked (Miles, 119). While comparative studies may be useful, conditions common to whites should not be the "explicit or implicit standard for black health conditions" (Jackson and Perry, 172). A good alternative is to focus on a specific problem, disease, or issue in one population (Miles, 119). Heterogeneity within ethnic groups must be studied from the perspective that factors accounting for variability between groups do not necessarily affect variability within groups (Whitfield and Baker-Thomas, 75).

Emphasis on the fundamental unfairness built into our social structure should not obscure the fact that minority elders act in their own behalf, bringing strengths and resources to the aging process that may be invisible to white, middle-class professionals. The advantages of membership in minority communities, racial or ethnic solidarity, for example, or interdependence, are significant, as are the unique personal histories that shape health and illness. Black elders tend to see friends as family members to whom they can look for help and encouragement, thus extending their support network (Charlotte Perry, quoted in Scharlach et al., Module 1, p. 23). The suicide rate among elderly blacks is very low, and black women have greater bone density and greater bone mass than whites (Gannon, 155). Strong religious belief often characterizes elderly Latinas/os and blacks, and the reverent world view of American Indians smoothes their passage into old age. Indian elders have been called "unifiers" of their families (RedHorse, 491). Perhaps the greatest advantage for older Asian Pacific Islanders, Latinas/os and blacks is the respect given them in their communities. This attitude is so uncharacteristic of the dominant culture that it may be hard for many whites to imagine what it would be like to be old and deeply valued in the community.

Blacks

Racism has damaged the self-esteem of older black Americans and very little discussion or research tries to understand its impact (Stanford, 1999, 164, 169). Over a lifetime, blacks absorb physical, mental, and emotional abuse, and to survive they stifle anger at unjust treatment (176). Misdiagnosis, over-drugging, and cultural insensitivity have marked the mental health system's dealings with black patients (170–171). Older black women and men have learned to "present themselves and their outward actions in ways that will be most acceptable" to the dominant group, but these adaptations may not be compatible with their own beliefs, needs, or circumstances (Stanford, 175). The health of older black women is affected not only by discriminatory experiences in their current lives, but also by "the aftermath of dealing with housing discrimination and daily racist acts" (Lawson et al., 287).

Older blacks have high rates of stroke, diabetes, obesity, and chronic illness (Harper, 17) and a higher incidence of cervical, colon, and lung cancer than whites (K. Gould, 208). At every income level, black women over fifty-four are only half as likely as white women to have a mammogram ordered for them by a doctor, even if they see a primary care doctor just as often (Lisa Cool, 17). Thus their breast cancer is detected later, and only one-half of elderly black women diagnosed with breast cancer are alive five years later, compared to three-fourths of white women. In addition, the death rate from heart disease in black women aged 65–74 is double that of white women of the same age (Fahs, 115–16). Hypertension is a bigger problem for black women than for black men (Taylor, 112).

Compared to whites, blacks are more likely to live in cities where they are exposed to air pollution and crime. They are more likely to have hazardous jobs and greater exposure to workplace toxins. Black women are sicker than whites when they see a doctor, perhaps because of low income, trouble getting child care, fear of hospitals, or fear of becoming a guinea pig (Edmonds, 208–09). Feeling a need to work regardless of health, they may overestimate their health as a way of coping, or they may believe that illness is their cross to bear (Edmonds, 213–15). Older blacks are 2–3 times as likely as whites to give health problems as their reason for not working (Wallace, 260).

A study led by Dr. Peter Bach of Sloan-Kettering Cancer Center, based on records of 11,000 patients and reported in the *New England Journal of Medicine*, concluded that blacks over sixty-five were less likely than white patients to get surgery for early stage lung cancer and as a result were "more likely to die from a potentially curable disease" (Grady, 1999, 1).

Shortcomings of existing research are the inadequate size of black samples and the lack of longitudinal studies that would shed light on the process of aging among blacks (Jackson and Perry, 121, 143). It has been thought that blacks who reach sixty-five are more likely than whites to survive to seventy-five, either because of a lower incidence of heart disease or because they must be hardy to reach their mid-sixties, but this apparent advantage may be based on faulty data (Jackson and Perry, 142).

Latinas/os

Stressors that may affect Latino/a health include limited education, low income, and difficult transitions from rural to urban life (Torres, 213). This transition is especially hard for elders driven out of Central America by war who speak only Spanish. Their American-born grandchildren may speak only English. Those who are illegal aliens may fear getting help when they are sick. More than 20 percent of Latina/o elders have incomes below the poverty level, compared to less than 10 percent of Anglos (Scharlach et al., Module 2, 1). Most older Latinas/os have no pension and do not receive Social Security (Sotomayor, 459). The systems developed by the dominant culture to manage health may be alienating to Latinas/os, who respond better to surrogate family approaches to services (Ramon Valle, quoted in Scharlach et al., Module 2, 7).

Chronic health problems are found in 85 percent of older Latinas/os (Kiyak and Hooyman, 304), and nearly three-fourths have some health impairment that restricts their activities (Scharlach et al., Module 1, 8). Latinas have higher rates of cervical and uterine cancer than whites and get these diseases at earlier ages. Diabetes is a major health problem (Markides, Southwestern, 1989, 194), and Latinas/os are more likely than whites to die from infections, flu, pneumonia, and accidents (197). They also tend to have high cholesterol (Harper, 17). Problems among Mexican Americans include lack of awareness of hypertension and the stress of poverty leading to depression (Markides, Aging, 1989, 82, 84). On the other hand, they have less osteoporosis and arthritis than non-Hispanic whites (74). The Sacramento Area Longitudinal Study in Aging will follow 2,000 Latinas/os to determine whether heart disease risk is related to dementia.

Asian Pacific Islanders

Asian Pacific Islanders are the most diverse minority group in language, in the culture of their country of origin, and in the circumstances of their arrival in the U.S. (Louie, 147). Little is known about their health status because national surveys inadequately sample them (D. Yee, 43). Health care needs of recent arrivals from Laos, Cambodia, Korea, and the Philippines differ from those of Chinese American and Japanese American elders born here (D. Yee, 46–7). Nearly three-fourths of Asian Pacific Islanders live in California, Hawaii, and New York. Although they are healthier in late life than members of other minority groups, they have higher rates of tuberculosis, hepatitis, anemia, and hypertension than whites (Yee and Weaver, 41). They have high rates of cancer—stomach cancer for Japanese Americans, lung and breast cancer for Hawaiians, and pancreatic cancer for Chinese American women (Harper, 17). Among older Filipino Americans, diabetes is common (Yeo and Hikoyeda, 94). The late-life health problems of Asian Pacific Islanders result from low income, lack of adequate health care throughout life, likelihood of working at physically demanding jobs, language barriers, and "distrust of services from the dominant culture which has historically discriminated against them" (Scharlach et al., Module 2, 13).

Sixty-five percent of Korean American women have never had a Pap smear (Lisa Cool, 17). Asian Pacific Islanders are more at risk for osteoporosis than are other people of color, but they are less likely to die of heart disease than blacks, Latinas/os, American Indians, or whites. Adapting to the high sodium American diet appears to have increased their susceptibility to high blood pressure. They may take herbs that interfere with drugs and cause serious side effects (Yee and Weaver, 41). Chinese Americans typically believe that health is maintained by balancing opposite forces in the body, yin and yang. Vietnamese immigrants explain many illnesses by bad wind in the body, released by rubbing the back (Yeo, 75), a belief that will not be understood by most white doctors.

A mental health issue is that standardized psychological tests are unreliable for diagnosing problems of Asian Pacific Islanders. Because of the stigma attached to mental illness in their communities, they may express psychological problems through physical symptoms such as stomach upset or fatigue (Louie, 151). Older Chinese American women have three times the suicide rate of white women (Yeo and Hikoyeda, 94). High levels of stress and anxiety among Korean Americans living in big cities have been linked to racial discrimination (Louie, 152). Refugees from Southeast Asia experience relocation depression and post traumatic stress disorder (Yeo and Hikoyeda, 82). A strength in the Asian Pacific Islander communities is the traditional high status of the elder but "declining expectations of filial piety" are also characteristic (Yeo and Hikoyeda, 80). Unlike other minorities, Asian Pacific Islanders have longer life expectancies than whites (Scharlach et al., Module 2, 13). It is not clear if this greater longevity results from some genetic protection or from factors such as exercise, diet, and stress level (Barbara W. K. Yee, quoted in Scharlach, 18).

American Indians

A major difference between Indians and other minorities is that a far greater proportion of them, 53 percent, live in nonmetropolitan areas (A Portrait, 7). Unlike whites, they consider aging "a natural process to be embraced," and they readily define themselves as elders (Robert John, quoted in Scharlach et al., Module 2, 26). The number of Indian elders increased 52 percent between 1980 and 1990 (A Portrait, 8). They have the poorest health of all minorities and the shortest life expectancy. Those fifty-five and older who live on reservations have impairments comparable to those of non-Indians over sixty-five. The Indian Health Service, difficult for Indians living in cities to use, focuses on young people and families rather than elders (Kiyak and Hooyman, 305). In addition, the IHS is better equipped to treat life-threatening problems than chronic ones, to the detriment of the 20 percent of Indians over fifty-five for whom arthritis is the leading cause of impairment

(John, Hennessy, and Denny, 68). Fourteen percent of the elders not registered in a tribe have no access to the IHS (Scharlach et al., Module 2, 23).

Compared to whites, American Indians have higher death rates from car accidents, alcoholism, and pneumonia, and they are ten times more likely than whites to have diabetes (Harper, 17). These problems are exacerbated by poverty, overcrowding, malnutrition, and distance from hospitals. Men are sicker than women, having three times as much emphysema, twice as much cancer, and 1.5 times the heart disease (John, Hennessy, and Denny, 54, 57). Indian women are less likely than whites to get breast exams, mammograms, and Pap tests. Because little is known about the chronic health problems among Indians (54), an especially important goal of the Native Elder Research Center at the University of Colorado is to train Indians to do aging research.

The diabetes epidemic in their communities seriously threatens their health. The Pima of Arizona, for example, have the world's highest diabetes rates. Their traditional low-fat diet protected them but their current diet is 40 percent fat. Native Seeds, a group promoting preservation of ancient crops, collaborated with nutritionists and conservationists from the Seri, Papago, and Pima tribes and from the Sonora Desert Museum to determine that native foods dramatically reduce blood sugar levels and improve insulin production (Montgomery, E4).

American Indians use vapor baths to treat disease, for example in sweat lodges. One consequence of drug companies' support of U.S. medical schools is a turning away from water therapy, which remains widely used in Europe (Nikola, 5).

The study of Indian aging did not begin until the 1970s. Before then, work on elders was based on an anthropological model which in turn was based on assumptions about "primitive" cultures (John, quoted in Scharlach, et al., Module 2, p.26). Research has not adequately considered diversity within the Indian population or the specifics of Indian women's aging (John, Blanchard, and Hennessy, 309–10). Moreover, health research on old Indian women is limited by small sample size, narrow focus, and the selection of only a few tribes, precluding valid generalization (300). Today, a great need of Indian elders is a comprehensive, culturally competent, long-term care system made up primarily of community-based services rather than institutional care (John, quoted in Scharlach et al., Module 2, 28). Ethnogerontologists use "culturally competent" to indicate health workers' responsibility to learn and adapt rather than simply have good feelings and intentions, as the earlier phrase "culturally sensitive" suggested.

Gender

For a woman, learning to be old means learning to cope with medical professionals who may be unresponsive to her needs and uncomfortable with assertive old women. Most older women can expect to be treated by doctors who have no specialized knowledge of aging and little time to take the medical histories that would distinguish disease from normal aging. In the U.S., women are twice as likely as men to seek preventative help, but this leaves them open to being dismissed as "whiners, complainers, and hypochondriacs" (Gannon, 51).

Heart disease is the leading cause of death or disability among older women. Their heart attack symptoms may be back pain rather than the more familiar signs of chest and arm pain, and thus they may not be diagnosed as readily as men are. They are less likely than men to be given clot-dissolving drugs during a heart attack and are referred less often for carotid surgery to prevent strokes (Our Mothers, 196). Other instances of age and gender bias in health care have been well documented. Data from 4,000 breast cancer patients showed for example that older women were "significantly less likely" than younger ones to receive a two-step surgical procedure, first biopsy and then tumor removal (Hynes, 336). When these two steps are combined, little time is spent evaluating the results of biopsy (336). Elderly women with breast cancer are less likely than young women to undergo lymph node dissection, regarded as essential to treatment (Our Mothers, 195).

Compared to old men, old women suffer more chronic illness, including hypertension, arthritis, gall bladder conditions, thyroid problems, and intestinal diverticula. They have higher rates of restricted activity and spend more days in bed (Verbrugge and Wingard, 115–117). Women have more vision problems but better hearing (189). They use more medication both prescribed and over-the-counter and take more psychotropic drugs (194). They adjust to health problems "earlier and better than do older men," however (190).

Why, then, are old women sicker than men their age? This question, which seems logically to be one of the most important in gerontology, has not attracted much attention. Women's "greater survival at every impairment level" (Ory and Warner, xxix) is a plausible biological explanation. Since women are more likely to perceive health problems than men, more apt to discuss symptoms with others and more likely to see doctors, their poorer late-life health may reflect more reporting of illness than more actual illness (Verbrugge and Wingard, 135). On the other hand, it is conceivable that women are sicker in old age than men because their lives have been more stressful. Before becoming old, they juggled multiple roles and often worked in unchallenging jobs (Verbrugge and Wingard, 123). Another explanation that gets at the cultural roots of the problem is that the health care system is geared to women of child-bearing age, not to older women. If social causes of their late-life illness were reduced so that women felt more productive, experienced less stress and got aerobic exercise, they would be likely to have fewer chronic health conditions (Verbrugge, 1990, 184). But the social causes of older women's health problems may increase rather than decrease as the health care system further deteriorates and more women take on the stressful job of caring for aged parents.

Social conditions such as poverty, widowhood, and caregiving place a woman at risk psychologically, and if she enters the mental health system, "her vulnerability continues" (Rodeheaver and Datan, 649). A false diagnosis of psychosomatic illness is more likely to be given women than men, especially poor women, immigrants, and those with an earlier psychiatric diagnosis. Age may be a factor as well, because older women's health is not well understood and thus a doctor may disregard or underrate physical symptoms by considering them psychosomatic. In addition, older women's low social status may lead to "low believability and authority, which, in Western medical settings, puts a person at risk for receiving a psychosomatic diagnosis" (Wendell, 143).

Chronic pain among older women is a neglected area of research (Roberto, 5). Non-drug treatments such as heat and cold applications, relaxation exercises, ergonomics, and transcutaneous electrical nerve stimulation (TENS) are effective, but information about their specific application to older adults is limited (5). When research priorities that ignore the needs of millions of older women are juxtaposed to the heavy marketing of painkilling drugs, the politics of healthy aging comes into focus.

The problem of death or injury from falls is most serious for people over seventy-five. Each year, 300,000 people break their hip and 500,000 suffer vertebral fractures, leading to annual medical costs of $14 billion (McDonald, A16). Another estimate is $60 billion, not counting the indirect costs to family and friends of the injured person (Fahs, 124). Many nursing home admissions result from falls, and hip fractures are increasing faster than can be explained by population aging (Pousada, 456). Although weak bones are blamed for falls, a more likely cause is weak muscles from disuse (Bortz, 1999, 201). Poor balance or unsteady gait also causes falls. Gait measuring devices that analyze walking patterns in elderly women and men may play a role in reducing falls. A study outside of the office of a healthy aging researcher showed that women over eighty could walk only half way across the street before the light changed (Kaplan and Strawbridge, 69), a fall risk created by the environment. Traffic lights should be timed to accommodate old women, not harry them.

The decision to take estrogen is one of the most difficult and frustrating decisions confronting women over fifty, and the difficulty is increased by the refusal of many health plans to cover the bone density test that would let a woman gauge her risk of osteoporosis. Bone density tests should be considered a routine part of older women's health care. Studies published early in 2000 that found no link between estrogen and lowered risk of heart disease among older women, and in its journal *Circulation*, the American Heart Association recommends that women should not take hormones to prevent heart disease (July 24, 2001). The observational studies suggesting a benefit may have overlooked a possible link between affluence, leading to better health and more exercise, and estrogen use. The idea that women should protect themselves against heart disease and osteoporosis by taking a costly drug fits in well with medicalized aging. These diseases have been "reconceptualized as being *caused* by menopause without adequate scientific research to support this conclusion" (Gannon, 137). We need a large body of data from long-term studies, in which women of color are well represented, to reevaluate the hypothesis that a sound diet and regular exercise offer sufficient protection against heart disease and osteoporosis.[2]

The estrogen issue was to be clarified in 2005 when results of the hormone replacement therapy trial of the Women's Health Initiative were scheduled to be released. This national study of middle-aged and old women was examining the impact of diet and estrogen on heart disease, colon and breast cancer, and osteoporosis.[3] In April 2000, researchers told 25,000 women in the trial that estrogen may slightly *increase* rather than decrease their risk of heart attack and stroke (Kolata, A1). In the same month, a study published in JAMA found that estrogen had not improved cognitive function in women with Alzheimer's Disease (Mulhard et al., 1013). As this book was going to press, the Women's Health Initiative announced that the estrogen-progestin study would be ended because of evidence of increased risk of breast cancer, heart attack, and stroke in women taking the drugs. These findings should make women skeptical of claims made for estrogen and more aware that drugs are not "systematically tested long enough to be sure (presumed) health benefits truly exist" (Moore, Estrogen, 2000, E1). The myth that aging requires drugs for routine management has led to the neglect of diet and lifestyle as the primary means to achieve healthy aging (Willett et al., 535).

Complete regeneration may not be possible for most ill older women, but Americans are so conditioned to expect deterioration with age that restoration of function is not aggressively pursued. The powerful, often insidious side effects of drugs, especially multiple drugs, noted in chapter 4, keep women from discovering what natural aging might be for them. Some new drugs may benefit them, but generally speaking, the healthiest aging is drug-free or nearly drug-free.

Drugs can suppress sexual desire and cause sexual dysfunction, for example. The sexuality of old women, a subject of mirth in classical literature and in popular culture today, deserves far more attention. The sex drive of healthy old women remains fairly constant, although lack of partners is a problem for heterosexual women, two-thirds of whom over sixty-five are single, compared to one-fourth of their male peers (Porcino, 117). The obvious importance of masturbation for women in this age group is a taboo topic in gerontology. For some women, thinning of the vaginal walls and decreased lubrication cause discomfort during sex. Orgasms are shorter than those experienced by younger women (Neuhaus and Neuhaus, 76). For some postmenopausal women, testosterone cream increases libido. Whatever her age, an older woman is entitled to "the freedom to explore and expand her sensual, sexual self" as long as she lives (Weg, 220). For many old women, touch deprivation is potentially threatening to health, an issue that neither feminists nor gerontologists have begun to address. Commenting on the sexuality chapter of her book *Growing Older, Getting Better,* Jane Porcino laments the few options for intimacy for older heterosexual women. "We should do more touching of each other. I think it's as important as any other facet of life for us after fifty" (quoted in Downes, 33). A key to healthy sexuality in late life is a rejection of cultural images that portray old women as ugly and asexual. When Viagra was in the news, a television station looking for a gerontologist to comment called me. I said that the topic of masturbation among old women interested me more. "You can't say that on television," the reporter hissed. Older men's sexual needs are front-page news, while older women's are draped in silence.

Combined loss of companionship and the income drop that accompanies widowhood creates health risks for heterosexual women over sixty-five, some of whom will be widows for thirty years or more. Increasing the longevity of men, not usually thought of as a women's health issue, is nonetheless relevant. In 1900, women outlived men by only three years, compared to eight years today. If men's deaths could be postponed even an average of one year, the economic gains (and indirectly the health gains) for heterosexual women would be significant. Increased male longevity would be especially beneficial for black women, whose husbands die earlier than the husbands of white women.

Although lesbians have an advantage in partner life expectancy, their bereavement is more likely to be hidden. Lesbians in long-term relationships are often denied the right to make decisions for a critically ill partner. A newsletter of the Center for Lesbian Health Research at the University of California San Francisco identifies other issues: differences and similarities between lesbians and heterosexual women in breast cancer treatment and disclosure of sexual orientation to health care providers (Fall-Winter 2000, 2).

A study of health care experiences of older lesbians in rural Maine found that 29 percent of those interviewed lacked health insurance and that their doctors or alternative medical practitioners were often far way. Women who had previously lived in cities felt freer and safer in the country (Butler and Hope, 2). Like urban lesbians, they fear eventual isolation from other lesbians in a nursing home. Alternatives being planned within the gay/lesbian community so far are residences for the well elderly rather than long-term care facilities.

Medicare is increasingly inadequate. Today people over sixty-five spend an average of 20 percent of their annual income on health care, for example on insurance to fill the large gaps in Medicare coverage and on exorbitantly priced medications (Drugs, 8). The health care costs of single, older women consume more than a third of their annual income (Estes and Close, 324). Thus Medicare has lost its original purpose of providing comprehensive health care coverage, and after January 2002, some doctors stopped taking Medicare patients. The budget was balanced in 1997 not by reductions in corporate welfare but by Medicare cuts that harmed home health care agencies and the frail, homebound elders they serve. Between 1997 and 1998, federal payments for home health care dropped 45 percent, forcing many Medicare patients to stay longer in hospitals and nursing homes (Pear, A1). Agencies have turned away the most disabled, fearing their care would cost more than agencies could be reimbursed (Pear, A18). This dramatic slashing of benefits shows how relatively powerless the elderly in America really are: a potent "gray lobby" would have beaten back this assault on its constituents. Budget cuts drove some health care agencies out of business; others faced revenue shortfalls of 30 percent. Nurses were forced to make more home care visits per week. The National Association for Home Care reports that the total number of visits has been cut 55 percent since 1997.

These cuts have had especially bad consequences for minority elders and their families (Binstock, 17). Most of their oldest old live outside of nursing homes and thus have a special need for home care (Wallace and Villa, 413). Lack of home health care endangers blacks, Indians, and Latinas/os, who are twice as likely as middle-income whites to have chronic diseases that limit their activities (Kiyak and Hooyman, 303–04).

Medicare is a prime example of the male model of aging in the U.S. According to the Older Women's League (OWL), it covers more health expenses for elderly unmarried males than for unmarried females, for example (Steckenrider, 247). Medicare is based on the "traditional illness model, an acute-phase model, grafted onto a time of life when chronic problems predominate" (Bortz, 1991, 267). Since men tend to get the acute diseases and women the disabling chronic conditions, Medicare is more aligned with men's needs, and thus it does not sufficiently protect women from preventable health problems (Steckenrider, 246–47). Many more women than men require home care, but Medicare covers intermittent nursing care rather than the expenses of food preparation, bathing, dressing, or transferring out of bed (Steckenrider, 251). The failure of Medicare to cover health maintenance results in "specific discrimination against minority and poor women" (Healey, 7). Because Medicare reimburses elders for very few preventative measures, it pays much more later on for serious illnesses, an example of wastefulness and of unfairness to women because it is they who would benefit most from early disease detection or prevention (Steckenrider, 254), not only in longer but healthier lives.[4]

Imagine a reform that required Medicare to give every American over sixty-five $5,000 a year for preventative health care. Very costly in the short term, it would be a bargain within ten years because Medicare spending on serious illness would probably be cut dramatically. Illness and disability would still strike many older people, but if the onset of illness could be pushed back even a year or two, the savings would be significant. Women would be the chief beneficiaries. Such a reform has little chance of being enacted because a system organized by illness and disease rather than prevention needs illness and disease to maintain itself. If old women could choose among a variety of alternative medical systems to stay well, many fewer would choose conventional medicine for chronic health problems.

Because of laziness, inertia, or lack of time, many of us will not exercise as we age, and the structures that might encourage that on a large scale are not likely to appear in the decades ahead, healthy aging centers like those in Japanese villages, for example. We will be subtly coerced by the ethos of rugged individualism into seeing our health concerns as personal and to looking out for ourselves. But as old women and middle-aged women increasingly understand how little we can expect from mainstream medicine or from government, and as we recognize that we are now chiefly valued as a big market for prescription drugs, we may see the disadvantages of confronting old age health challenges on our own.

The creation of healthy aging circles like the consciousness raising groups of the 1970s might be a good strategy. Some would evolve from already existing friendship networks, while others could be started with the express purpose of helping members age comfortably. If a woman got sick, her support system would be in place. If she needed advice about prevention and health promotion, circle members would help her gather and evaluate information. When a grass roots response directly connects an ill woman to a support group, the providers of help benefit as well as the woman being helped (Stoller, 17). Self-help is not a very satisfactory response to the magnitude of the structural problems that beset American health care, but it is better than accepting the passive victimization encouraged by the status quo. The self-help groups envisioned here might also advocate reforms that would benefit older women, federally-funded fall prevention programs, for example, nutrition programs geared to low-income women, and more respectful treatment of old women by doctors.

Neglect of preventative care and health promotion is the biggest problem of the current system. The health care dollar is divided as follows: 97 cents for disease, less than 3 cents for prevention, and half a penny for health promotion (Haber, 21). Increasingly, older women may see this resource allocation as irrational and dangerous to their interests. Are citizens entitled to good health in old age? The present answer is a resounding no. If we were, half of the health care dollar would go to health rather than disease, and drug-free care would be available to all. The nearly total neglect of health promotion in this country is a women's issue yet to be discovered by feminists and an aging issue that concerns too few gerontologists.

Doctors may cover up their ignorance of aging or lack of interest in the complicated problems an old woman often presents by saying, "It's old age." When hearing this, a woman in her eighties who has been socialized to treat doctors with extreme deference may find it hard to challenge the interpretation or get a second opinion. Urinary incontinence, for example, is twice as prevalent among women as among men. Despite the opinion of doctors who think aging inevitably brings incontinence, it can be alleviated or cured (Sharpe, 15). When women now in their fifties reach old age, they will probably be less inclined than their mothers to defer to doctors, but what may not change is their doctors' limited understanding of the aging process, of ageism, or of gender and racial differences in late-life health and health care. On the other hand, women now fifty have a good chance of being treated by a woman doctor when they are seventy-five, and it is possible that geriatric knowledge will become more integrated into medical practice than is now the case.

A persistent problem is the near invisibility of older women's health concerns in widely-used texts. In *Annual Editions Women's Health 1999–2000*, for example, three articles out of fifty examine old women's issues and two are devoted to mid-life. The previous edition of the text, 1998–1999, has a unit called "Special Issues for Older Women," in which the focus is disease. It offers nothing on differences among old women, diet, alternative medicine, or fall prevention. Slight attention is paid to exercise. These editorial choices show how healthy aging has been narrowly construed as a medical topic.

Changes in journalism as well as medicine and textbooks are needed. A large-scale content analysis of mass media by the National Council on Aging (NCOA) found that one in four news stories about older women's health omitted crucial information such as sample size, other research on the same topic, or control of variables. Breast cancer was overemphasized relative to its incidence and heart disease underemphasized.[5] Clearly, women need more reliable sources of health information, for example from newsletters published by the Brandeis Center for Women's Aging and by the Center for Women's Healthcare at Cornell and from articles and books created by older women themselves such as the 500-page resource book *Ourselves, Growing Older* by the Boston Women's Health Collective and *The New Ourselves, Growing Older* (Doress-Worters).

In research and in practice, health promotion has been slow to recognize how significantly class, ethnicity, and gender influence the health of older women. Furthermore, it tends to accept "current social structures and power relationships as functional for society and for women" (Ward-Griffin and Ploeg, 284). Ideally, health promotion research would make its assumptions explicit and involve older women in research design. Such changes would begin to address the problem of research subjects' relative powerlessness to account for their experience in their own way. As Sally Gadow notes, an ethical issue as important as access to health care is "access to meanings that establish the woman at the center of her own health" (Whose Body?, 295). It would be illuminating, for example, if old women investigators interviewed 100,000 women over seventy with health problems. As corporate control over health care tightens, it is all the more urgent that older women interpret their own experiences. When a false dementia diagnosis is given an old woman who takes six different medications a day, or when depression is over-looked because the doctor thinks an old woman has much to be sad about, ignoring women's stories becomes oppressive.

Older women are more diverse than any other group in their health status, and many are psychologically strong despite all the obstacles to good health that they face (Rodeheaver and Datan, 652). Compared to men, they exhibit "greater intrinsic (genetic or hormonal) robustness" (Verbrugge, 1990, 35). The life expectancy gap between women and men has narrowed slightly, however, because more women are dying of lung cancer (Verbrugge and Wingard, 108–09).

The health of older women in the future will depend on many factors including disease patterns, environmental risks, new technologies, and "society's conception of the value of life" (Lamphere-Thorpe and Blendon, 79). A hopeful sign is that feminists are looking closely at the ways women's health is conceptualized by researchers. It is now obvious that just as blacks' aging or the aging of American Indians deserves to be studied in and of itself, not only in comparison to whites, the health of older women and especially of women over seventy-five must be studied apart from men's health and younger women's health.

Conclusion

To a large extent, aging was something that just happened to our mothers and grandmothers. Often its attendant problems were denied and its possibilities unnoticed. Women now young and middle-aged have an opportunity to age more deliberately and mindfully, with a sense of options and strategies for self preservation. This will be easier for white, middle-class women than for poor women and women of color.

The possibility of greatly improved health in old age through alternative medicine, health promotion programs, and bodywork is exciting. But the blitzkrieg of prescription drugs nearly obliterates creative thought about this prospect. Nowhere are the limits of Western thinking and Western medicine more starkly revealed than in attitudes toward the health of elderly people. Alternative medicine and bodywork, influenced by Eastern philosophy, have much more to offer. Full use of them and comprehensive healthy aging programs in every community would not only eliminate the need for multiple prescription drugs, it would radically alter our conception of aging.

The challenge for policymakers now is "to give as much serious attention to living as to dying, to the nonfatal conditions and difficulties in doing desired activities that compromise life's value in later life, especially for women" (Verbrugge, 1990, 70). If health and research priorities focused on delaying the onset of chronic conditions such as arthritis or lessening their severity, American elders could "gain precious years of comfortable aging" (Jacob Brody, 1995, 30). The economic consequences of not postponing illness or dysfunction are "staggering" (Butler, 1995, 3). More importantly, the damage done to women—the cost that is not quantifiable—remains hidden. If health care continues to emphasize disease, health problems will be redistributed so that conditions that "bother and disable but do not kill" increasingly mark individual lives (Verbrugge, 1994, 93). This prediction is ominous for women.

Policies that "address the deficits of old age without attending to opportunities" are fundamentally wrong (Moody, 1988, 2). This is manifestly the case with health care because nearly all of the resources are devoted to disease (deficits) rather than health promotion (opportunities). A society that spends virtually nothing for preventative care in effect creates illness for its older citizens, and the frailty and dependency that often accompany late-life illness appear to be natural rather than partly the result of health care policy. The current incidence of illness among old women and men, far from being inevitable, is more determined by culture than biology. Without this understanding, our expectations of late-life health will be too low.

But the situation is more complicated than misdirected priorities. The ideology of individualism that determines the priorities is hidden in directives to eat carefully and exercise regularly, etc. When the individual is the "basic unit of social analysis," then the focus is individual behavior rather than structural patterns such as the distribution of wealth and power, and health education is assumed to be the best way to prevent disease (Tesh, 161). The assumption that health is controlled by the individual runs counter to the "interdependence and collective responsibility valued by many ethnic minority elders" (Yee and Weaver, 43). Individualist philosophy shields corporations and government from responsibility for their major roles in creating illness (environmental pollution) and sustaining it (inadequate regulation of polluters and drug companies). The older we are, the greater the cumulative impact on us of corporate and governmental action or inaction.

Whatever our personal characteristics or individual choices, therefore, our late-life health may be determined or greatly influenced by forces beyond our control, even if class privilege benefits us. As the distinguished geriatrician Christine Cassel has said, the social and economic challenges of aging are greater than "unlocking the biological mysteries" (Ethics, 63). Now that we have the knowledge to maintain and in some cases improve the health of older women and men, we lack both the regard for elders that would lead to wise health care policy and a collective commitment to our own future well-being.

Notes

1. Resource Centers for Minority Aging Research locations include the University of Michigan, University of North Carolina, University of California San Francisco, and the University of North Dakota Grand Forks. Minority aging is the focus of the National Resource Center on Native American Aging, National Caucus and Center on Black Aged, National Hispanic Council on Aging, National Indian Council on Aging, and the Pacific Asian Resource Center on Aging. *Closing the Gap* is a newsletter published by the Office of Minority Health, Public Health Service, U.S. Department of Health and Human Services. The American Society on Aging publishes *Diversity Currents*, the quarterly newsletter of its Multicultural Aging Network.

2. For feminist interpretations of menopause, see V. F. Meyer, "Medicalized Menopause: Critique and Consequences," *International Journal of Health Services* 31 (2001): 769–92; Margaret Lock, "Anomalous Women and Political Strategies for Aging Societies," in *The Politics of Women's Health*, ed. The Feminist Health Care Ethics Research Network (Philadelphia: Temple, 1998); Margaret Lock, *Encounters with Aging* (Berkeley: University of California, 1993); Joan C. Callahan, "Menopause: Taking the Cure or Cursing the Takes," in *Mother Time*, ed. Margaret Urban Walker (Lanham, Md.: Rowman & Littlefield, 1999); Betty Friedan, *The Fountain of Age* (New York: Simon and Schuster, 1993), chapter 15; Linda Gannon, *Women and Aging: Transcending the Myths* (New York: Routledge, 1999), chapter 4; Anne Fausto-Sterling, "Menopause: The Storm before the Calm," in *Feminist Theory and the Body*, ed. Janet Price and Margrit Shildrick (New York: Routledge, 1999); and Jacqueline Zita, "Heresy in the Female Body: The Rhetoric of Menopause," in *The Other Within*, ed. Marilyn Pearsall (Boulder, Colo.: Westview, 1997).

3. For an analysis of the claim that estrogen protects women against heart disease, see Joan C. Callahan, "Menopause: Taking the Cure or Cursing the Takes," in *Mother Time*, ed. Margaret Urban Walker (Lanham, Md.: Rowman & Littlefield, 1999). Many women have chosen hormone replacement, believing the benefits outweigh the risks.

4. Jane Brody, "Adding Zest to the Golden Years," *New York Times*, (January 18, 2000), D8. Brody reports that the following preventative measures are partly or fully funded by Medicare but underused by the elderly: flu vaccine, pneumonia vaccine, mammogram, Pap smear, pelvic exam, and screening for cancer of the colon, rectum, and prostate.

5. National Council on Aging, "Women Must Look Beyond Medical Headlines, NCOA Study Indicates," (October 18, 1999): 1–3. Also online at www.womenshealth-aging.org/media/look_beyond.htm (accessed 1–8–2000). See also Noeleen O'Beirne, "The 'Docile Useful' Body of the Older Woman," in *Envisioning Aging*, eds. Jenny Onyx, Rosemary Leonard, and Rosslyn Reed (New York: Peter Lang, 1999).

⌐⌐

CHAPTER SEVEN

Gender, Class, and Ethnicity

Gender, class, and ethnicity strongly determine how well Americans age. Class may be the most important of these intersecting factors. While not the whole story of aging, economic determinism is often ignored because it does not fit the middle-class worldview of most gerontologists, advocacy groups such as AARP, or the mainstream media. The strong impact of class and ethnicity on American aging is powerfully illustrated by a 2000 World Health Organization (WHO) report on "healthy life expectancy" that measures life expectancy by factoring in diseases and disabilities. In the WHO ranking, Japan comes first and the United States twenty-fourth. Rich Americans are judged the world's healthiest people, but our overall ranking is lowered by the relatively poor health of people of color and poor Americans, and by cancer, heart disease, and violence. According to a UN official, the poorest 2.5 percent of Americans have health life expectancies comparable to those of sub-Saharan Africa in the 1950s (Moulson, A2).

This chapter considers class, ethnicity, sexual orientation and gender in relation to aging and then examines caregiving and retirement as institutions that show their convergence especially well.[1]

Class and Gender

Ethnicity and class give gender specific meanings and at the same time class and ethnicity acquire specific meanings through gender (Calasanti and Zajicek, 121–22).[2] While it is true, for example, that older women are far more likely to be poor than older men (a gender difference ignored when gerontologists say that Social Security and Medicare have reduced poverty among "the elderly"), older women of color are more likely to be poor than white women. The meanings of designated family caregiver for a female will depend on her class and ethnicity. Gender in itself is significant, however, for as Amanda Barusch notes in *Older Women in Poverty*, longevity increases women's risk of old-age poverty, a gender difference that cuts across all groups of women (xxxiii).[3]

At the same time, ethnicity and class are also strong predictors of late-life poverty (Barusch, xxxiii). In Europe the poverty rate of old women living alone is negligible, but it is high in the U.S.: Germany, 2.4 percent; Sweden, 1.7 percent; France, 0.8 percent; the Netherlands, 0.0 percent; and the U.S., 17.6 percent (Barusch, xx). While approximately one-third of all older women in the U.S. are poor or near poor, this designation applies to 58 percent of black women and 47 percent of Latinas (Malveaux, 1993, 172). Those most likely to be poor are women of color over eighty-five who live alone (Davis, Grant, and Rowland, 81). By 2020, the number of elderly living alone will be 13.3 million, of whom 11 million will be women (80). Widowhood increases an older woman's poverty risk (Barusch, xxxiii); half of the widows who are poor today were not poor before the death of their husband (Davis, Grant, and Rowland, 82). Another estimate is three-fourths (Steckenrider, 239).

Poverty statistics do not reveal the extent of hardship. If they were calculated on the basis of income left over after medical expenses are deducted, the proportion of elderly poor would greatly increase (Davis, Grant, and Rowland, 85). Another factor not taken into account is the differences in the cost of living across the country.

The long-term consequences of class difference can be illustrated by simple examples. A middle-class professional woman in her twenties can afford to buy an IRA each year, but the woman her age who cleans her office cannot. Forty-five years later, the former may have accumulated several hundred thousand dollars, the latter nothing. To acquire this wealth, all the first woman has to do is to keep breathing. Very likely, her husband has a secure job that, like hers, will provide a pension. Their childcare expenses take a smaller percentage of their salary than of the office cleaner's wage. Moreover, the working-class woman's parents will probably need her caregiving help sooner than the parents of the middle-class woman. If the working-class woman and her husband manage to save enough for a down payment on a house, they may be denied a mortgage because of redlining, a form of discrimination that will never impede the upward mobility of the middle-class couple. In late life, home ownership is often the key to financial security, but when working-class people of color own a home, it may have declining value in an inner-city neighborhood (Malveaux, 1993, 188).

Class, ethnicity, and gender play a large role in determining not only access to education and jobs but also to "the opportunities those jobs allow or the limitations they impose" (Atchley, 451). A major limitation lies in earnings: a black woman earns 65 cents, and Latinas 57 cents, for a dollar earned by a man (Hooyman and Gonyea, 1999, 155). The more familiar figure, 74 cents, masks racial and ethnic disadvantage and does not apply to women over 55. They earn 66 cents for a dollar earned by a man, and the gap widens as they age (Older Women's League, 300).

White women frequently fare better than blacks or Latinas, and white families are better off than minority families, in part because they are more likely to have pension income (Dressel, 116–17). Elderly minority women should be differentiated from the men in their communities, however, as well as from older white women (K. Gould, 212).

The economic status of older women is a "map or mirror of their past lives" (Malveaux, 1993, 168). Unemployment levels for black women, for example, tend to be twice those of whites or Latinas (Malveaux, 1990, 230). While numerous women work in sex-segregated jobs, many black women work in jobs segregated by race as well; they are chambermaids, cleaners, nurses' aides and welfare service aides (231). Many black women who work in private homes do not receive Social Security benefits. Besides the labor market disadvantage of sex and race, a black woman shares in the disadvantage of her spouse or family members, giving her a triple burden (Malveaux, 1990, 233). Moreover, when black men are unfairly treated by the criminal justice system, their retirement is jeopardized and the future financial well-being of the women in their families is undermined as well (235).

Gerontologists allude to the "cumulative disadvantage" of older Americans whose lives have been characterized by physically demanding jobs or unemployment, poor housing, inadequate health care, and low levels of education, but they rarely examine the other side of the coin, middle-class cumulative *advantage*. A good education, white-collar jobs that do not cause bodily harm, health insurance, sufficient money for a healthy diet, and control over many life circumstances do not guarantee good health in old age, but they make it likely rather than exceptional, unless a person's genes or bad luck interfere. Middle-class privilege operates in less obvious ways, too. When I speak to a doctor or a banker from this class position, I am taken seriously. In an emergency, I probably have a friend or a relative with enough disposable income to help me out. I carry an invisible sense of entitlement that may be reflected in my gait and demeanor as well as in confident speech. Being middle-class gives me the privilege of being oblivious to class. I can believe that my favorable circumstances result from my own individual effort.[4]

Ethnicity and Gender

Current trends that work against all of the elderly are especially onerous for minority elders, the increase in out-of-pocket medical expenses, for example, and Medicare cuts in home health care. A plausible scenario is that any future health care changes will "protect corporate profits and existing medical care enterprises at the expense of adequate access to health care for minority elderly" (Wallace and Villa, 251). The development of ethnogerontology may encourage advocacy through organizations such as the National Asian Pacific Center on Aging, the National Caucus and Center on Black Aged, the National Hispanic Council on Aging, and the National Indian Council on Aging, but no single national organization advocates for all minority elders.

Ethnicity and class come into sharp relief in studies of life expectancy. Many people of color do not live long enough to collect their Social Security benefits. Christopher Murray of the Harvard Center for Population and Development has found that Indian men on two South Dakota reservations live to an average of only 61 years, while the figure for black men in Washington, D.C., is even worse, 57.9 years. Women in predominantly white Stearns County, Minnesota, on the other hand, have a life expectancy of 83 years. Murray also found that Asian American men in affluent counties in New York and Massachusetts live to nearly ninety and Asian American women into their mid-nineties. These life expectancy differences are comparable to differences between impoverished Sierra Leone and affluent Japan (*New York Times*, December 4, 1997, A9).

Much work on minority aging focuses on families. Gerontologists have suggested, for example, that closely-knit communities may not survive for future generations of Pacific Asian elders because of the increasing social and geographic mobility of younger community members (Kiyak and Hooyman, 309). Elderly Pacific Asians feel conflict between traditional communal family values and the American emphasis on self-reliance, "making them loath to ask others for support" (309). Is the role of honored elder declining in some communities? It is reinforced where the oral tradition remains strong (Long, 18). The aging experiences of urban Indians differ from their counterparts on reservations. Elderly blacks are known to adopt "fictive kin" by turn-ing friends into family. Although great diversity exists within families considered "minority," they have more in common with each other than with white middle-class families, particularly their shared experience of rac-ism (B. Yee, 75).[5]

Recently ethnogerontologists have begun to look beyond families. A life-course perspective emphasizing aging as a process should encourage future researchers to view Chicano or Latino elderly in relation to their earlier lives (Wallace and Facio, 345), not simply in relation to whites. Big economic gaps exist within groups: Japanese Americans are better off than Korean Americans or Vietnamese Americans, for example. Moreover, "gender and class dominance transcends the family and continues into old age" (Wallace and Facio, 348). Qualitative research may be better suited to discovering sub-tleties of ethnicity than survey research (C. Johnson, 308), for ethnicity is both subjective and flexible (Cool, 1987, 265). When Chicano aging is stud-ied through the family, women appear only as wives, mothers, and grand-mothers (Facio, 339). Many older Chicanas would like to be seen not only as grandmothers but also as cultural teachers (342). Another theme in ethno-gerontology is that too heavy an emphasis on social inequality overlooks peo-ple's strengths. Gerontologists need to know not only how Chicanos are disadvantaged, for example, but also how they fashion meaningful lives (Wallace and Facio, 347). If quality of life is examined through many lenses, strengths inhering in social networks and spirituality will be seen (Kiyak and Hooyman, 311). In the face of "social and political imprisonment," Blacks have shown a powerful will to survive, and their elders deserve to be under-stood through their own history without being compared to others whose circumstances are far more favorable (Stanford, 1995, 117). Ethnicity pro-vides "continuing self-identification and communal belonging at a time when the older person begins to experience the diminution of his or her con-ventional identities formed on age, sex, or occupation" (Linda Cool, 1986, 267).

Problems with studies comparing people of color with whites were noted in chapter 6. Whites become the norm, gender disappears, and an implicit judgment is that people of color need to "catch up" to whites. The few stud-ies that have looked at differences within groups are seen as interesting only to minority researchers (Stanford and Yee, 17). Comparative work assumes that gender, ethnicity, and age are "fixed, immutable, biologically based indi-vidual properties with predictable (if as yet undetermined) behavioral and social consequences" (Dressel, Minkler, and Yen, 276–77). Studies of adjustment to old age based on whites have not considered the meanings of this concept for blacks, Latinos, Asian Pacific Americans, or Indians. For them, aging may more likely signify a process of survival, and the struggle to survive "in fact may mean that an individual has developed strategies to keep from adjusting" (Burton, Dilworth-Anderson, and Bengtson, 132).

Will the incipient growth of ethnogerontology encourage white, middle-class gerontologists to rethink the meanings of "minority"? This question became less theoretical with the release of 2000 census figures showing that minorities are now the majority in forty-eight of the nation's 100 largest cities. By the year 2030, 25 percent of those over sixty-five will be people of color (Angel, 503). Could Asian Pacific women, Indians, Latinas, and black women be imagined as central actors in aging America, not as "special"? To themselves, after all, they are not special, only to the dominant group.

The usual rationale for studying Latino, black, Asian Pacific, and Indian elders is to serve them better, but this could happen without changing their marginal status. Mainstream gerontology could absorb ethnogerontology without being transformed itself. Or, new thinking about diversity could become "an energizing force for understanding the aged and aging in this country" (Stanford and Yee, 20), not only the aging of particular groups. For a conservative field like gerontology, however, adopting multicultural perspectives may be a slow process.

The discipline would be enlivened by the application of theoretical writing by women of color to aging. Aida Hurtado explores the meanings of multiple identities, for example, through "shifting consciousness," the ability of many women of color to move from "one perception of social reality to another, and, at times, to be able simultaneously to perceive multiple social realities without losing their sense of self-coherence" (384). Shifting consciousness would be valuable for old women who can see with ironic detachment the ways others project "old" onto them, without internalizing ageist attitudes. Surviving the dominant culture's influence requires, in the words of Paula Gunn Allen, "an uncompromising commitment to multiplicity" (1998, 78). The theory arising from an understanding of multiplicity may not conform to Western notions of logic and abstraction for, as Barbara Christian writes, "our theorizing (and I intentionally use the verb rather than the noun) is often in narrative forms, in the stories we create, in riddles and proverbs, in the play with language, since dynamic rather than fixed ideas seem more to our liking. How else have we managed to survive with such spiritedness the assault on our bodies, social institutions, countries, our very humanity?" (336). Rarely in professional settings are gerontologists encouraged to think of women of color in these terms, or to reflect on the meanings of whiteness for individuals or for the organization and perpetuation of geron-tology itself.

Gloria Anzaldúa and others formulate "marginal" theories, partly outside and partly inside Western frameworks, seeking out the "in-between, Border-land worlds" (xxvi). This stance responds to colonization and social invisi-bility but is far more than defensive, for it makes space for subjectivity and declares intellectual freedom from an either-or, dominant-subordinate para-digm. What are the "in-between worlds" within aging? María Lugones observes that the Anglo world may construct her, a Latina, in ways she does not understand or would not accept, "and yet I may be *animating* such a con-struction, even though I may not intend my moves, gestures, acts in that way" (631). Something similar must occur when people who have many identities are perceived only as old.

Sexual Orientation

Like women of color, lesbians are "special" and unlikely to be seen as norms for aging. Nearly all published work on women's aging assumes heterosexual-ity; a few studies mention lesbians. Media images of lesbians exclude those who are old. Paradoxically, old women in general are seen stereotypically as asexual, while old lesbians, when they are noticed at all, are perceived only through their sexuality (Fullmer, Shenk, and Eastland, 137). They differ in ethnicity, class, education, income, and degree of identification with the gay and lesbian community. Some older women who would be regarded by others as lesbians because of lifelong emotional attachments to women and an absence of heterosexual partnerships do not identify themselves as lesbians. Because of slowly growing acceptance of lesbian and gay identity, future cohorts of old lesbians will include many more who have been out of the closet for most of their lives, and it is likely that in the future, increasing numbers of women will come out in their sixties and seventies. Lesbians who were once married often have supportive children and grandchildren, although others have been rejected by their families. Some have speculated that the resilience needed to cope with a stigmatized identity helps older lesbians adapt to aging, but it may also be true that the special stresses of their lives, especially if they have been fired from jobs, lost custody of chil-dren, or otherwise harmed because of their sexual orientation, have long-lasting consequences.

Lesbians have the same concerns as heterosexual women as well as partic-ular concerns, a desire to live in a retirement setting where they can be open about their lives, for example, fear that a partner's role might not be acknowledged by medical workers, and fear of confinement in a nursing home where being gay is not acceptable. Bereavement leave is a benefit heterosexual women can take for granted and most lesbians cannot. Pension plan benefits and Social Security benefits are unjustly denied survivors of lesbian and gay partnerships. Some advantages enjoyed by many old lesbians are a life history of self-reliance and high status within lesbian communities. Having been free to de-emphasize or entirely disregard conventional notions of female attractiveness, many seem to accept their aging bodies with equanimity. Those who were tomboys when young tend to retain their physical competence.[6]

Old Lesbians Organizing for Change (OLOC) has raised consciousness about ageism within the lesbian feminist community. Other groups include New Leaf Outreach to Elders in San Francisco and Seniors Active in a Gay Environment (SAGE) in New York. The Lesbian and Gay Aging Issues Network of the American Society in Aging publishes the newsletter *Outward*. Research on older lesbians, gay men, bisexuals, and transgendered people raises some of the same issues as research on people of color: will the concerns of the group be distorted as they are filtered through the lens of the dominant group? Are the interests of the group served by this research? How will it be used?

Gender Gaps

The best examples of gender gaps in aging are caregiving and retirement. Class and ethnicity interweave with gender in the examples that follow.

Caregiving

Caregiving covers everything from occasional help for a relative who lives on her own to 24-hour total care for a person in the same home. Although some men provide care, most caregivers and recipients of care are older women. Women provide 70–80 percent of home care for elders (some estimates 90–95 percent). Daughters-in-law are more likely to be caregivers than sons and sisters more likely than brothers. Thus the commonly used term "family care" is a euphemism for women's work.

The productivity of older women is largely invisible, yet if all women caregivers were paid the minimum wage for their work, its annual value would be an estimated $87 billion (Wood, 12). Caring for older family members is low status, "emotionally binding work" (Hooyman, 1990, 229). Ninety-five percent of paid caregivers are women (McLeod and Roszak, 12). They number more than 500,000, mostly poor, predominantly black women or recent immigrants who receive the minimum wage and no benefits (Holstein, What, 1999, 3).

Several trends have significantly altered the caregiving landscape, including longer lives, smaller families, delayed childbirth, higher divorce rates, and growing numbers of blended families. Today many families have two or more generations over sixty-five, and thus a woman in her sixties or seventies may be caring for an aged parent. The biggest difference between caring today and in earlier times, however, is the large increase in the number of women in the labor force. But business and government still operate as if "an unpaid army of caregivers" were available at home (Toner, 29).

The added duties of caregiving are "obscured by their seemingly common-place nature" (Holstein, Home, 1999, 236). The assumption that women are naturally suited to caregiving rests on a belief in separate spheres for women and men that blocks women's access to economic benefits and "thereby perpetuates their powerlessness" (Hooyman, 1990, 221–22). This issue is complicated for feminists because many have attributed a special caring capacity to women and have seen women's customary caregiving role in a positive light. The emotional and psychological benefits possible in the role can be acknowledged at the same time that substantial and sometimes hidden costs to care providers are identified.

Not only is the hard work of caregiving unpaid labor, performing it actually penalizes women because it often takes them from the workforce entirely or forces them to cut back on their hours or turn down promotions. Not all caregiving is performed by women who also work outside the home but those who do often find that home duties negatively effect job performance and evaluation. In a study by the Coalition of Labor Union Women and the National Policy and Resource Center on Women and Aging, among women who lost time at work, 31 percent used sick leave to cover caregiving duties and 69 percent took unpaid leave (Alcon and Bernstein, 47). Another study found that Latina and Asian American caregivers were more likely than whites to have taken a leave of absence from work to provide home care (Family Caregiving, 33).

A less immediate but potentially catastrophic problem is that caregivers who work outside the home suffer long-term economic losses by having lower incomes, smaller pensions, and lower Social Security benefits than they would otherwise have had. A study by the National Alliance for Caregivers and the National Center on Women and Aging at Brandeis estimated that the total loss in wage wealth of the caregivers in their survey was $566,443. Lost Social Security benefits totalled $25,494 (Rimer, A8). The loss is even greater if money not contributed to accounts that use pre-tax wages to accumulate retirement funds is considered. Thus women caregivers who are coerced into self-reliance by government policies not only sacrifice their time and energy (often willingly) but their future financial security as well. This huge sacrifice is taken for granted. Its magnitude is analyzed neither by feminists nor by gerontologists. This particular exploitation of women is not as dramatic as unequal pay or domestic violence, but it contributes to their subjugation.

Men have the advantage of doing one job, while many women do two, one paid and the other unpaid. As long as women's position in the labor market is subordinate to men's, "strong economic pressures reinforce the traditional assignment of unpaid caregiving work to women" (J. Allen, 223).

Women of color and working-class women suffer disproportionately because they are clustered in low-paying jobs that are not waiting for them after a caregiving period, jobs that offer fewer benefits than middle-class women receive. Poor women do not have husbands with professional jobs whose income can ease the financial strain of caregiving. Assuming that an elderly Chicana will automatically take on a caregiving role reinforces her subordinate status and assumes that family is the only significant part of her life (Facio, 338). According to the National Alliance for Caregiving, Asian American and Latina caregivers were significantly younger than whites and were more likely to have out-of-pocket expenses for caregiving (Family Caregiving, 8, 24). Women's financial sacrifice to provide care is a major cause of their late-life vulnerability to poverty (J. Allen, 224).

A theme of *Age Through Ethnic Lenses: Caring for the Elderly in a Multicultural Society*, edited by Laura Katz Olson, is that the traditional value of great respect for elders, leading to caregiving within families, is in flux. It is affected by differences between native born and immigrant elderly, social mobility of younger family members, language differences, outmigration from rural areas, intermarriage, and generational differences heightened by assimilation. The cultural emphasis on filial duty does not eliminate the need for public programs and services. Many elderly immigrants share the experience of Polish immigrants: old women and men have a place of honor in the family, but they may not have family members here in the U.S. who can help them. Moreover, they are shut out of the formal care system because they do not know about it, they wish to conceal their undocumented status, or because the services "represent a shameful failure of the family system of care" (Berdes and Erdman, 184).

Compared to white, middle-class women, poor women and women of color have more chronic illness and disability. Even though they are the old who most need care, they are the least likely to have access to services (Hooyman and Gonyea, 1999, 153). A review of studies since the mid-1980s on race and ethnicity as influencing care for a person with dementia showed that blacks and Latinos as compared to whites reported less depression and stress; had less sense of care being burdensome; and were more likely to cope through faith or prayer (Conell and Gibson, 355). Future studies of differences within the black community and among Latinos will give a more nuanced view of caregiving experiences and attitudes. An issue for some Asian Americans is that dementia tends to take away a second language, and often the only available adult day care is for English speakers (Goodman, 111).

Caregiving studies have documented a wide range of physical and psychological illnesses experienced by care providers. Despite these problems, they are motivated by emotional bonds, a need to help others, reluctance to turn to community resources or institutions, and the unavailability of other family members. Women provide care because their family role "leads them to see few alternatives" (Rizza, 68). In interviews, caregivers express satisfaction in closer relationships with parents as well as a rewarding sense of discovering new strengths and abilities (Rizza, 70). The experience of working at a paid job while caregiving is "not as uniformly negative as it is sometimes portrayed." Work provides a welcome break from all-encompassing home responsibilities, for example (Scharlach, 1994, 383).

When noting that family care of the elderly is unpaid, it is important to remember that caregivers do emotional work as well as chores and tasks. If forced to leave a paid job to provide home care, women feel cut off from opportunities and even from their aspirations (Healy). When external resources such as respite care and affordable home health care are limited, and the elderly parent suffers as a result, the caregiver may blame herself and not the current caregiving system. Her sense of inadequacy and the parent's experience of insufficient care may cause family conflicts that seem private but also reflect large social problems (Healy).

Caregiving opens up other emotional issues as well: it tends to be lonely work; a caregiver may lose a sense of control over her life (Abel, 1989, 75); and caring for a dependent parent may trigger unresolved resentments (76). A major difficulty for caregivers is the "chasm between their overriding sense of responsibility and their ultimate powerlessness" (Abel, 1991, 76). They also find it hard to exert authority over a parent (105). Focus on the care recipient may entail less time and attention for other family members. One study reported that mother-daughter conflict was heightened by the increased dependence of the mother, and that both mothers and daughters felt a tension between the daughter's social needs and her filial responsibilities (Brandler, 50, 53). A study of urban white women caring for a chronically ill older parent found that feelings of resentment, anger, and frustration were "so threatening that they were not dealt with directly, except in the most secure families. Seemingly small issues became the targets permitting expressions of feeling" (Archbold, 43).

Psychological explanations of caregiving are limited because women are not "uniformly nurturing and expressive." In addition, psychological explanations take the nuclear family as the ideal and overlook a structural problem: the current system overvalues masculine traits in the public arena and undervalues feminine values expressed in the home, and thus caregiving is seen as a personal issue (Hooyman and Gonyea, 1995, 22–24). In this framework, caregiver stress is emphasized rather than the social reorganization that would make caregiving more equitable and humane (Abel, 1991, 66).

Chapter 2 linked the socially constructed fear of an aging population to conservatives' goal of shrinking federal government. Increased emotional burdens on women have resulted from the "increasing devolution of responsibility from the federal to local levels along with cutbacks in federal funding and the privatization of care," and as public agencies that have traditionally served poor women have cut services, the reduction in public support has intensified gender and racial inequalities (Hooyman and Gonyea, 1999, 164). Caregivers' right to public support has not been recognized (Hooyman and Gonyea, 1999, 162; Quinn-Musgrove, 106).

Another issue is the neglect of old women and men without family members to provide care. In the future, many more elders will have no children to care for them (Abel, 1991, 177).

A problem at the heart of caregiving is the dichotomy between dependency and autonomy, noted in earlier chapters, an example of either-or thinking that undermines the self respect of older Americans. How can dependency be disassociated from failure? How can overrated (and partly illusory) autonomy be seen as a relative rather than an absolute value? Instead of apologizing for no longer being totally self-sufficient, could an old woman say to her daughter or son, "I need help and you have an opportunity to provide it"? This sounds ludicrous but only because we are conditioned to believe autonomy means self-reliant separation from others.

Wanting to be self-reliant and not wanting to be a burden, older women will "often ask for less help than they need, even at their own peril" (Holstein, What, 1999, 3). The overused phrase "the burden of care" deflects attention from the ways in which caregiving can be mutually beneficial or positive, as well as a source of difficulties. The general term "burden" does not identify particular problems or distinguish between economic and psychological hardships. If I feel I *am* a burden, that differs from feeling that my situation creates challenges for my caregiver. The unreflective use of "the caregiving burden" objectifies older people and fuels alarmism over the growing size of the elder population (Arber and Ginn, 1991, 130). Furthermore, emphasis on burden "devalues the act of caring—caring about as well as caring for" (Wenger, 374). When caregiving is defined as a burden, its "structural and cultural roots" become invisible (Holstein, Home, 1999, 235). Caregiving is understood not so much as a duty or a burden among many Chinese, Filipinos, and Vietnamese who have settled in the U.S. A common saying among them is, "When I was young and helpless, my parent cared for me. Now that my parent is old, it is my turn to help them."

The term "eldercare" reinforces the stereotype that old women and men are inherently dependent, like children. It also fails to acknowledge the presence of reciprocity in intergenerational relationships (Matthew and Campbell, 131). Similarly, the sharp split between caregiver and care recipient overlooks the effort the receiver may expend in taking care of herself (Ray, 1996, 677).

Proposed reforms to the present system include reimbursement for family caregivers, Social Security credit for years spent caregiving, greater involvement of men, and a more family-sensitive workplace. Pay equity should be seen as a caregiving issue because wage inequality reinforces the tendency for women to be the ones to leave paid work in order to provide care at home (Foster and Brizius, 70). Other proposals are the creation of caregiving accounts for every adult through Social Security, which could be used to pay for services (Foster and Brizius, 68–69) and a Caregiving Corps modeled on the Peace Corps (McLeod and Roszak, 12). Imaginative planners envision "carebots," robots that roam around the house making sure that a person with dementia has not wandered away or that an elder has not fallen (Emerman, 12).

While significant, these changes would not get at the underlying problem that the U.S., alone among industrialized nations, relies on an ethic of individualism to abdicate its responsibility for the care of elderly citizens. As long as caregiving is seen as a private duty rather than a public value, the economic disadvantage suffered by women who do the work will limit their participation in society (Hooyman, 1990, 234–37). Caregiving is both a "profound personal experience and an oppressive social institution" (Hooyman and Gonyea, 1995, 24). Whether women give care or receive it, whether they are unpaid in the home or underpaid outside the home, gender prescribes their role.[7]

Retirement

In the institution of retirement, male privilege, class privilege, and white privilege grandly converge, filling the stage of late life with operatic fullness. In comparison to other countries, the U.S. shows the greatest inequality among the elderly (O'Rand and Henretta, 2). Conditioned to seeing retirement only in personal terms, many Americans miss the big picture of socioeconomic advantage and disadvantage. Media images of affluent elders at play deflect attention from the many whose lives do not fit this picture.

Women's retirement income is lower than men's because of their lower pay, interrupted work histories, and workplace gender segregation. Other factors that increase their poverty risk relative to men are their greater likelihood of being retired a long time, of losing a spouse, and of having a chronic illness (Price, 9). Pensions are inadequate or reduced by discrimination (Barusch, 186). Fifty-five percent of men over sixty-five have pensions but only thirty-two percent of women, and women's pensions average one-half as much as men's (Tyson, 8). Working-class women and women of color fare worse than white women because their wages and the wages of their spouses and families are lower and because the good educations that lead to good jobs are frequently denied them.

Men spend an average of 1.3 years out of the labor force compared to 11.5 years for women (Davis, Grant, and Rowland, 82) or 14.7 years by the calculation of the Older Women's League (300). This gender difference is extremely significant: if a woman has fewer than thirty-five years of earnings, a zero is averaged into her Social Security calculation for each of those years, in effect reducing her benefits (Williamson and Rix, 47). Defining an older woman's caregiving years as "zero years" is blatant gender discrimination. Women are penalized for doing the work society expects of them. Social Security benefit losses for caregiving are greatest for workers with low and moderate earnings (O'Rand and Henretta, 93).

The system still operates with the outmoded assumption that retirees are male wage earners and stay-at-home spouses, and provides more benefits for them than for two-earner couples. Even worse, when the husband in a one-earner couple dies, his widow receives 67 percent of their total Social Security benefit, compared to 50 percent for the survivor of a two-earner couple. Thus Social Security clearly favors traditional marriages (O'Rand and Henretta, 95). Often a woman who has worked for many years is entitled to higher Social Security benefits as the wife of a retired worker than as a retired worker herself; her benefits are no greater than if she had never worked. Moreover, the payroll taxes she contributed to the system decreased her disposable income (Dailey, 94).

Social Security accomplishes some income redistribution that benefits lower-income workers but in its present form, it "overdelivers retirement income to economically advantaged workers and underdelivers retirement income to low-income workers" (Atchley, 464). Two mechanisms that disadvantage the latter are the exemption of wage income over $80,400 from Social Security taxes and the exemption of income from interest and dividends (Bergman and Rush, 42). Eliminating these generous and unacknowledged gifts to the affluent would be fairer and fiscally sounder than "privatization," the stealth attack on Social Security in the guise of reform.[8]

Clinton proposed voluntary private plans in *addition* to Social Security, but the Bush proposal to "privatize" some payroll tax deductions creates risk in a secure system. Who would shoulder the greatest risk? Those whose retirement income depends most heavily on Social Security: women, people of color, and the working class. In addition, any of the changes needed to pay for "privatization" would disproportionately harm them: increased payroll taxes, decreased benefits, an increase in the eligibility age, or an increase from thirty-five to thirty-eight as the number of years used to calculate benefits. Privatization's welfare for Wall Street would be very costly for many Americans. The ghost of FDR still haunts conservatives. Privatization, the biggest proposed change in Social Security since its inception, would be their exorcism ritual.

Only recently has women's retirement been examined through the prism of their own life experiences.[9] "The particular mix of paid and unpaid work shifts constantly throughout our lifetime, and continues to do so whether we are officially retired or not" (Onyx and Benton, 100). Little is known about the impact of retirement on women's identities (Price, 10). A sense of identity for some seems to be maintained by expanding their roles after retirement (Price, 154). Thus researchers should not assume that home life is the focus of retired women's lives (156).

Retirement is not a meaningful concept for the many Americans who have to keep on working, mainly people of color and low-income workers. Blacks do not fit the norms by which retirement has traditionally been marked: age sixty-five, sharp distinction between work and non-work, income from sources besides Social Security, and self-identification as retired (R. Gibson, 120). For black women and men alike, work is lifelong and discontinuous; they are the "unretired retired" (125, 122).

The conventional view of retirement does not fit middle-class white women very well, either. Retirement is a dubious proposition for those who began careers in midlife and do not wish to end them at sixty-five. Moreover, women do not retire from housework. Increasingly, women over sixty-five are working for pay, but it is not clear that they want to. "Women have multiple needs and priorities—not just for wages but for time spent on family, friends, community, and on themselves" (Johns, 42–43). An Australian study of professional women makes a similar point: retirement means not just a switch from active involvement in a job to leisure, but readjustments, "a finer balance of time and energy to allow a more creative and satisfying engagement with the many sides of life and self" (Onyx and Benton, 107). In the future then, retirement will not be as sharply differentiated from work as it is now, and will require multiple measures (Hatch, 136). It will be an unfolding process.

"Bridge jobs,"part-time, temporary paid work that spans work and retirement and offers the advantage of flexibility and income, disguise the compulsory nature of retirement under our economic system. Since full employment is impossible, some people must be kept out of the work force. Retirement is not simply leisure, the early bird special and senior discounts on Tuesday; it is a mechanism for income reduction. The mechanism is ageist but more importantly, to the extent that women, people of color, and the working class reach retirement with already lowered incomes, it reinforces discrimination.

A recent study finds that 17.3 percent of unmarried elderly women are poor (Anzick and Weaver, 1). Nearly four times as many widows live in poverty as do wives of the same age, according to the Older Women's League (301). Many women have limited savings and only 18 percent have pensions (299). Social Security, pensions, and savings or investments are considered the "three stools" of retirement, but because of the high poverty risk for unmarried women over sixty, husbands have been called the fourth stool for [heterosexual women] (Johns, 15).

Incomes of married women are increasing, but the incomes of widowed, separated, and divorced women are declining.[10] Pensions and Social Security are based on "a misperception that marriage is permanent" (Meyer, 1996, 472). Divorce will become more common among old women and with it will come an increased poverty risk (Hatch, 135). In addition, the marriage rate for older black women declined significantly from 1990 to 2000, so that linking Social Security benefits to marital status particularly disadvantages them (Meyer, 2001). Another danger sign is that the eligibility age for Social Security will increase to sixty-seven, and women who take retirement at sixty-two will get 75 percent of their total benefit compared to 80 percent today. Many black households will continue to be headed by women, some of whom will work "off the books" where they will not accumulate benefits (Malveaux, 1993, 177).

Women who do have pensions are likely to have the defined contribution kind, in which the value depends on fluctuating markets, rather than the traditional defined-benefits pension, which guarantees a fixed payment. In short, the present system is inadequate for many, for women caregivers, for workers in low-paying jobs with few benefits, "and for increasing numbers of workers, male as well as female, in a 'new economy' characterized by more frequent job changes and less paternalism on the part of employers" (Johns, 36). Uncertainties and risk will mark the retirement of baby boom women, fewer than 20 percent of whom should feel secure about it (Dailey, 8, 124).

Proposals to reduce inequities in the present system include using twenty-five years rather than thirty-five to determine Social Security benefits, to take caregiving years into account (Malveaux, 1993, 177); making widow's benefits a larger percentage of a couple's benefits (Anzick and Weaver, 12); encouraging men to share caregiving responsibilities equally; lifting the cap on wages taxed for Social Security; and ending the disadvantage for two-earner families. Their survivors would get the same benefits as survivors of one-earner families (Burkhauser and Smeeding, 13).

In 1981, a presidential panel recommended national pensions to supplement Social Security, an idea that seems unthinkably progressive today when a woman's marital status still plays such a large role in deciding her retirement income. Whatever her personal choices and individual circumstances, her late-life income is largely determined by family and workplace structures and by public policy (O'Rand and Henretta, 70), policy that favors the white middle class.

Conclusion

The dynamic interplay of class, ethnicity, and gender with aging is not yet well understood. It is obvious, however, that women's old-age poverty is "directly linked to a sexual division of labor," whereby much of their work earns neither wages nor credit for retirement (Meyer, 1996, 466–467). For many women, the seeds of late-life financial struggle are being sown today. Thus the connection between women's caregiving and their retirement needs more attention (Price, 150). As the aging population grows, inequality is likely to increase (O'Rand and Henretta, 207). The widening gap between classes in the U.S. today "causes pain far beyond economic suffering," concludes bell hooks, "denying us the wellbeing that comes from recognizing our need for community and interdependency" (158). These non-material values, embodied by caregivers and particularly relevant to aging, are our real source of wealth.

Whatever individual differences mark our experience of aging, this process is profoundly shaped by gender, class and ethnicity. Theoretically, this needn't be so. If advantages and disadvantages were more justly distributed, our aging differences might chiefly reflect our biological inheritance or the care we took of ourselves earlier in life. Most Americans become uneasy at the thought that individual effort counts for little. As long as the U.S. rank on the WHO healthy life expectancy scale is a shameful twenty-fourth, however, extolling individual effort will only disguise the many forces that determine how we age.

Notes

1. For a lively discussion of problems inherent in the terms "minority" and "race," see Atwood D. Gaines, "Culture, Aging, and Mental Health," in *Serving Minority Elders in the 21st Century*, eds. May L. Wykle and Amasa B. Ford (New York: Springer, 1999).

2. For other studies of ethnicity and aging, see Ronald J. Angel and Jacqueline Angel, *Who Will Care for Us? Aging and Long Term Care in Multicultural America* (New York University Press, 1997); M. Jocelyn Armstrong, "Ethnic Minority Women as They Age," in *Women as They Age*, 2nd ed., eds. J. Dianne Garner and Susan O. Mercer (Haworth, 2001); Marjorie Cantor and Mark Brennan, *Social Care of the Elderly: The Effects of Ethnicity, Class and Culture* (Springer, 2000); Melvin Delgado, ed., *Latino Elders and the Twenty-First Century* (Haworth, 1999); Donald E. Gelfand and Charles M. Barresi, eds. *Ethnic Dimensions of Aging* (Springer, 1987); Toni P. Miles, "Aging and the New Multicultural Reality," *Gerontologist* 39, no. 1(1999); *Minority Elders: Five Goals Toward Building a Public Policy Base*, 2nd ed. (Washington, D.C.: Gerontological Society of America, 1994);

Jay Sokolovsky, ed., *The Cultural Context of Aging*, 2nd ed. (South Hadley, Mass.: Bergin and Garvey, 1997); Eleanor Palo Stoller and Rose Campbell Gibson, *Worlds of Difference: Inequality in the Aging Experience*, 3rd ed. (Thousand Oaks, Calif.: Pine Forge, 2000); Sandra Torres, "A Postmodern Ethnogerontology . . . Why Not? . . . What For?" *Contemporary Gerontology* 6, no. 4 (2000): 114–17; Keith E. Whitfield and Tamara Baker-Thomas, "Individual Differences in Aging Minorities," *International Journal of Aging and Human Development* 48, no. 1 (1999): 73–79; and May L. Wykle and Amasa B. Ford, eds. *Serving Minority Elders in the 21st Century* (New York: Springer, 1999).

3. For gender issues, see Colette V. Brown, *Women, Feminism, and Aging* (New York: Springer, 1998); Margaret Urban Walker, ed., *Mother Time: Women, Aging, and Ethics* (Lanham, Md.: Rowman & Littlefield, 1999): Linda R. Gannon, *Women and Aging: Transcending the Myths* (London: Routledge, 1999); Toni M. Calasanti and Kathleen F. Slevin, *Gender, Social Inequalities, and Aging* (Lanham, Md.: Alta Mira, 2001) and "Women and Aging," in *A Sociology of Women*, 2nd ed., by Jane C. Ollenbergen and Helen F. Moore (Upper Saddle River, N.J.: Prentice-Hall, 1998).

4. Peggy McIntosh's influential essay "White Privilege: Unpacking the Invisible Knapsack" helped me think about middle-class privilege.

5. In the social gerontology text *Worlds of Difference: Inequality in the Aging Experience* (Thousand Oaks, Calif.: Pine Forge, 1994), edited by Eleanor Palo Stoller and Rose Campbell Gibson, working-class elders and people of color are central figures. The editors juxtapose literary texts and analytical essays.

6. Some of the earliest work on old lesbians was done by Sharon Rafael and Mina Robinson (Meyer). See "The Older Lesbian: Love Relationships and Friendship Patterns," *Alternative Lifestyles* 3, no. 2 (1980): 207–29. Matile Rothschild and Dottie Fowler led the first support group for older lesbians in San Francisco. See also Ken South, Sean Cahill, and Jane Spade, *Outing Age: Public Policy Issues Affecting Gay, Lesbian, Bisexual and Transgender Elders* (New York: National Gay and Lesbian Taskforce, 2000); Marcy Adelman, *Long Time Passing: Lives of Older Lesbians* (Boston: Alyson, 1987); Morgan P. Slusher, Carole J. Mayer, and Ruth E. Dunkle, "Gays and Lesbians Older and Wiser (GLOW): A Support Group for Older Gay People," *Gerontologist* 36, no. 1 (1996): 118–23; Jeannette A. Auger, "Living in the Margins: Lesbian Aging," *Aging and Society: A Canadian Reader*, ed. Mark Novak, (Toronto: Nelson Canada, 1995); Jacalyn A. Claes and Wayne Moore, "Caring for Gay and Lesbian Elderly," in *Age Through Ethnic Lenses: Caring for the Elderly in a Multicultural Society*, ed. Laura Katz-Olson (Lanham, Md.: Rowman & Littlefield, 2001); Tonda L. Hughes, and Gretchen E. LaGodna, "Aging Lesbians," in *A Reader's Guide to Lesbian and Gay Studies*, ed. Timothy F. Murphy (Chicago: Fitzroy, 2000); and Mary Meigs, "Memory is as Uncertain as Grace," in *Fierce with Reality. An Anthology of Literature on Aging*, ed. Margaret Cruikshank (St. Cloud, Minn.: North Star Press, 1995). Works by Barbara Macdonald and Cynthia Rich and by Baba Copper are cited in chapters 8 and 10. The work of photographer and artist Tee A. Corinne includes striking images of midlife and old lesbians. *Nitrate Kisses* is a Barbara Hammer film about a lesbian couple in their seventies. "Golden Threads," a video produced by

Lucy Weiner and Karen Eaton for the *Point of View* series on PBS, features Christine Burton, ninety-three, founder of a group for older lesbians.

7. For caregiving, see Emily K. Abel, *Hearts of Wisdom: Caring for Kin 1850–1940* (Cambridge: Harvard, 2001); Jean Oxendine, "Who is Helping the Caregivers," *Closing the Gap, Newsletter of the Office of Minority Health* (Washington, D.C.: HHS, May 2000): 4; Eleanor Palo Stoller, "Why Women Care: Gender and the Organization of Lay Care," in *Worlds of Difference*, 3rd ed., eds. Eleanor Palo Stoller and Rose Campbell Gibson (Thousand Oaks, Calif.: Pine Forge, 2000); Joanna K. Weinberg, "Caregiving, Age, and Class in the Skeleton of the Welfare State," in *Critical Gerontology*, eds. Meredith Minkler and Carroll L. Estes (Amityville, N.Y.: Baywood, 1999); Sally Bould, "Women and Caregivers for the Elderly," in *Handbook on Women and Aging*, ed. Jean M. Coyle (Westport, Conn.: Greenwood, 1997); and Katrina Hash, "Care-giving and Post-caregiving Experiences of Midlife and Older Gay Men and Lesbians," doctoral dissertation, Virginia Commonwealth University, 2001. U.S. Senator Olympia Snowe of Maine has introduced bills that would give a tax credit to caregivers of people with Alzheimer's and allow a deduction for home health care costs.

8. For analysis of privatization, see *ReSecuring Social Security and Medicare: Understanding Privatization and Risk*, ed. Judith G. Gonyea (Washington, D.C.: Gerontological Society of America, 1998); Laura Katz Olson, "Women and Old Age Income Security in the United States" in *Aging in a Gendered World* (Santo Domingo: INSTRAW, 1999); and Barbara Bergman and Jim Bush, *Is Social Security Broke?* (Ann Arbor, Mich.: University of Michigan, 2000).

9. For other work on women's retirement see Vanessa Wilson-Ford, "Poverty Among Elderly Black Women," *Journal of Women and Aging* 2, no. 4 (1990): 5–20; Virginia E. Richardson, "Women and Retirement," *Journal of Women and Aging* 11, nos. 2–3 (1999): 49–65; Kathleen F. Slevin and C. Ray Wingrove, "Women in Retirement: A Review and Critique of Empirical Research Since 1976," *Sociological Inquiry* 65, no. 1 (1995): 1–19; Jill Quadagno and Jennifer Reid, "The Political Economy Perspective in Aging," in *Handbook of Theories of Aging*, eds. Vern K. Bengtson and K. Warner Schaie (New York: Springer, 1999); and Miriam Bernard et al., "Gendered Work: Gendered Retirement," in *Connecting Aging and Gender*, eds. Sara Arber and Jay Ginn (Buckingham: Open University Press, 1995). See also Robert C. Atchley, "Critical Perspectives on Retirement," in *Voices and Visions of Aging*, eds. Thomas R. Cole et al. (New York: Springer, 1993).

10. Robert B. Hudson and Judith G. Gonyea, "A Perspective on Women in Politics: Political Mobilization and Older Women," in *Gender and Aging*, eds. Lou Glasse and Jon Hendricks (Amityville, N.Y.: Baywood, 1992), 135. The authors note that neither the women's movement nor the national aging organizations has made older women's issues a priority and that the heaviest caregiving responsibilities fall on women of color and lower-income women.

CHAPTER EIGHT

Ageism

Ageism is mentioned in litanies of social problems such as racism, sexism, and homophobia, but it is more often invoked than analyzed. Although the term "ageism" was first coined by Robert Butler in 1969, awareness of it as a social, political, economic and moral problem is still so low that the fields of health care, gerontology, and women's studies provide numerous examples. No credible public figure would condone sex or race discrimination, but the harmful impact of age discrimination has been denied or trivialized by Supreme Court justices.[1]

The tenacity of ageism is not surprising, given its deep roots in Western culture and the absence of a mass movement of the old, comparable to civil rights, women's rights or gay and lesbian liberation, to challenge it. People over forty are targets for an astonishing range of insults, including birthday card jibes, and the mass marketing of fear and ignorance of aging through these cards elicits few protests. The message that being old is funny or embarrassing is so ingrained that many old women and men take this view of themselves, at least in social groups. These biased attitudes reinforce discriminatory practices, such as firing older workers and maintaining an educational system focused on the young.

Fear of death is a major source of age bias. The limited use of hospice is one sign of powerful death denial in the U.S. To call our society youth-worshipping is an understatement. Fashion models who used to look sixteen now look eleven. When large numbers of women and men over sixty-five move to a community, their migration brands them a "gray peril," as feared and unwanted as the late nineteenth-century arrivals in California who were branded the "yellow peril" (Longino, 449).

Discussions of individuals' ageist attitudes and behaviors stress the psychology of stigma and prejudice, but understanding ageism requires looking beyond individuals to its structural roots, taking power relations into account (Thompson, 379). Two groundbreaking books of the 1980s, *Look Me in the Eye: Old Women, Aging, and Ageism* by Barbara Macdonald and Cynthia Rich, and Baba Copper's *Over the Hill: Reflections on Ageism between Women*, examine one structural root of ageism, women's subordination in the patriarchal family.[2] Their analysis shows that while women are victims of ageism, they may also be its perpetrators.

An ageism motif runs through preceding chapters, in the irrational fear of an aging population, the dominance of the sick role, the lack of programs designed to preserve the health of older citizens, and the exhortation to keep busy in order to prove one's worth. Ageism may coexist with other oppressive attitudes and actions. An elderly Latina in her seventies who receives inferior health care, for example, may experience three layers of prejudice simultaneously, based on her sex, her ethnicity, and her age; but in her own family, she may be highly regarded. While ageism intensifies negative treatment based on ethnicity, gender, or sexual preference, it deserves separate scrutiny. In this chapter, I consider sources of ageism—stereotypes, the focus on appearance, and overemphasis on "old" as a category—and the workings of internalized ageism.

Stereotypes

Robert Butler defined ageism as "a process of systematic stereotyping of and discrimination against people because they are old, just as racism and sexism accomplish this for skin color and gender" (243). The British gerontologist Alex Comfort, better known for *The Joy of Sex* than for *A Good Age*, defined ageism as the notion that "people cease to be people, cease to be the same people, or become people of distinct and inferior kind, by virtue of having lived a specified number of years" (A Good Age, 35).

In Butler's definition, the link to racism and sexism is a rhetorical device that highlights the damage caused by ageism, but the analogy falters by comparing lifelong identities to one we have for only a part of our lives. Secondly, ageism is unique because whites do not become victims of racism nor men victims of sexism, while a young or middle-aged person will probably live long enough to become a target of ageist stereotypes. A final important difference is that women and people of color accept those designations, whereas many people over seventy or eighty, perhaps most, spurn "old" as an identity. Age discrimination is just as irrational, arbitrary and unjust as race or sex discrimination and in all three cases, one's appearance determines the classification.

Men as well as women experience ageist bias, but men do not face the "primal loathing" that old women evoke merely by existing (Copper, 19). Women over sixty or seventy naturally do not want to think of themselves as objects of scorn, but "primal loathing" shapes the ways aging plays out for them. Although the taunt of "dirty old man" is cruel and nasty, it lacks the fierce contempt of "old hag." The terms "shrew" and "crone" are more intensely negative than terms for old men such as "geezer" and "old fart." Lately, "geezer" has appeared in newspapers and magazines to cover both women and men, and this contemptuous term appears even in the title of a recent *Scientific American* article, "From Baby Boom to Geezer Glut."[3]

Ageist stereotypes require dualistic thinking. Sharply differentiated pairs such as old/young, black/white, and feminine/masculine impart reassuring familiarity, with one valued over the other. In the past two decades, gender differences have become less rigid and black/white no longer frames our increasingly multicultural society, but old/young remains as fixed as ever, blurring the complexities of aging and defining the old as less worthy than others. "A cleaver-sharp binary between beauty and the so-called ravages of time, between health and disability, figured as old age, is encoded daily in the stories and advertisements in the mass media" (Woodward, 1999, xvi). A good example comes from "The Faces of Alice Neel," a *Boston Globe* article about the artist, illustrated by several reproductions, including one of a nude girl. The nude self-portrait Neel did at age eighty was not reproduced, merely described: "sagging breasts and belly are offset by a chin lifted so high her head grazes the top of the canvas. Inevitable defeat of the flesh is here, but not of the spirit" (Temin, C1). This equation sets off the bad flesh from the good spirit, although the chin, as flesh, complicates the effort to praise the artist and simultaneously present her as a victim. In this article, as almost everywhere in American culture, an old woman does not speak for herself but is spoken for. Old flesh can only be judged "defeated" through resolute youth worship. As long as the disdain for an aging female body expressed here is the dominant viewpoint, the individuality of old women will be obliterated. They will be typecast as carriers of pathos.

Older people are often thought to be incompetent, selfish, and a threat to the economic security of others. They are viewed as poor, disabled, and isolated from their families (Quadagno, 1999, 9), as the "culturally residual, the decrepit, the distorted, and finally, the alien in the new world to come" (Russo, 27). Old women are reviled as grumpy, frumpy, sexless, and uninteresting. Their prototypes are the wicked witch, the bad mother who is needy and neurotic, and the comical, powerless, little old lady (Copper, 14). A study of ageist and sexist stereotypes in Disney movies found old women depicted as ugly, evil, and power hungry, as well as devil-like, greedy, and crazy (Perry, 206, 208).

An old woman who fails to be cheerful will be thought "bitter, mean, complaining" (Healey, 1986, 61). When one of these labels is affixed, it may expand into an identity rather than mark a passing mood. Just as young women may be typecast as virgins or whores, old women face similarly restrictive and distorting stereotypes of grandmother, hag, or spinster.

A journalist covering an Elizabeth Dole campaign appearance in Iowa observed that the audience included many elderly women: "a blizzard of blue-grey permanent waves, they radiated the starched, sweet propriety of a Temperance Union meeting." (*New Yorker*, July 26, 1999, 30). The Iowa women are seen as monolithic and as relics of an innocent past, reduced to a mere part of themselves, their hair (of course). Judged out of place at a political rally, they are figures of fun. Like Kingfisher and Sapphire from the radio and TV show *Amos 'n' Andy*, they reflect an image the dominant group wishes to see.

Folklore is a rich source of negative attitudes towards the old, especially old women. In fairy tales, for example, an old woman who is kindly at first may turn out to be a witch. Meeting an old woman on the road brings bad luck, a folk belief epitomized by the saying, "If the devil can't come himself, he sends an old woman." In German fairy tales, the old draw vitality from the young, and those thought to have lived too long can be killed. A saga describing a tenth-century famine in Iceland tells of the old being thrown over cliffs. Danish tales describe the murder of a grandmother or great-grandmother (Ashliman).[4]

On his travels, Gulliver encounters the Struldbruggs, who are frozen in old age and can never die. They are "peevish, covetous, morose, vain, talkative," envious, impotent, incapable of friendship, "dead to all natural Affection . . . and cut off from all Possibility of Pleasure." Gulliver pronounces the Struldbruggs "the most horrifying sight I ever beheld; and the Women are more horrible than the Men" (Swift, 181–183). An examination of English cartoons revealed three predominant themes: failing eyesight, failing memory, and reduced sexual activity (Bytheway, 63). An analysis of drug ads in physicians' journals found that the old were depicted as "disruptive, apathetic, temperamental, and out of control" (Levin and Levin, 91). Behind many of these caricatures is the unconscious fear of a strong old woman.

An old woman bears the brunt of ageism because she is already devalued as female. If she is a woman of color, her ethnicity may play a greater role in her devaluation than her age. White women often lack cultural traditions in which old women are revered, but not all blacks, Latino/as, Asian Americans and Indians benefit from such traditions. An old woman whose culture favors elders may find her authority resisted or subverted within her family. In general, however, it appears that women of color may command more respectful and deferential treatment within their families than white women.

Accusations of witchcraft often targeted old women but the large body of scholarship on the witch-craze does not focus on the *age* of victims (Feinson, 437). Why were old women vulnerable? Scholars have noted that they were blamed for stillbirths, crop failure, and male impotence. In her book *The Crone*, Barbara Walker states that old women in particular were called witches because of the survival of an ancient archetype, the destructive Crone Mother (13). The old woman who could kill with her gaze could also cause death by curses (58). In addition, an accusation of witchcraft was a good way to get rid of poor women too weak to work and seen as economic drains (132). Any woman living outside of male control—a single woman, a widow—could be singled out. If a woman accumulated medical knowledge or gained a special understanding of the natural world or animals, or if she were suspected of reading philosophy or dispensing spiritual advice, she could be labeled a witch (141). It seems plausible that old women, who had the most time to acquire knowledge, would have been the most threatening. The witch-crone was a woman "who reserved her powers for herself" (Arber and Ginn, 1991, 38).

Women past childbearing age were seen as useless. They were thought to be shapeshifters who could turn themselves into young women or animals. An old woman risked execution as a witch if she criticized or insulted men, or torture by "a scold's bridle which locked the victim's head inside an iron cage that drove spikes through her tongue or cheeks" (B. Walker, 137, 139).

Even though the witch-hunts occurred centuries ago, they lasted so long and their fury was so intense that their influence has not been entirely erased. "The real threat posed by older women in a patriarchal society," Walker concludes, "may be the 'evil eye' of sharp judgment honed by disillusioning experience, which pierces male myths and scrutinizes male motives in the hard, unflattering light of critical appraisal. It may be that the witch's evil eye was only an eye from which the scales had fallen" (122). Sharp judgment and critical appraisal may not be necessary to make some old women threatening. Merely withdrawing attention from men may be enough.

It is unnerving to acknowledge that hatred of old women is an important strand in Euro-American culture. In many other cultures, by contrast, post-menopausal women gain power and status. The witch craze is like a toxic waste site covered up for a long time but still emitting poisons. The hatred of old women that is its legacy is fairly well concealed in our society by senti-mentalized images of grandmothers, patronizing deference to "granny," and the invisibility of most women over sixty in politics, the media, and business. Barbed insults and jokes directed at old women give a glimpse of the residual hatred, as does an assumption that illness, silent suffering, and even depriva-tion are natural concomitants of their old age. In many years of attending conferences on women and a few years of attending gerontology conferences, I have never heard a talk or a panel discussion that focused on hatred of old women.

Certain words, phrases, and ways of speaking communicate negative stereo-types. Someone who says grandparenting "keeps me young" offers a pious falsehood. Attributing youthfulness to old women, intended as praise, rein-forces the idea that being old is bad. When a woman over sixty is addressed as "young lady," she can be certain that her age has been seen as a deficit. "Young at heart" suggests fun-loving and active, while the unstated contrast "old at heart" implies boring, passive, and a "wet blanket" (Palmore, 91). Gerontologists perpetuate ageist language by using the term "young-old" to distinguish people under seventy-five from the "old old." These tags imply a sharp separation between groups that does not exist, calling to mind S. I. Hayakawa's line, "the map is not the territory."

In the introduction to Imogen Cunningham's collection *After 90*, a book of portraits she took when she herself was over ninety, the photographer is praised several times for her "youthful qualities," as if energy, whimsy, and intense professional commitment are to be found only among the young. The introduction rises to a crescendo of condescension when the photogra-pher is described as "this ageless, frisky, elfin creature, a crone in a black wool cloak, our heroine of the camera, bright-eyed, quick-witted, and working—even after ninety" (Mitchell, 23). Cunningham's great force of personality is lost in "frisky" and "elfin" and the word "creature" distances her from us. Even the word "our" is revealing, the equivalent of a pat on the head. Cun-ningham's statements quoted in the introduction make clear that she did not see herself as a heroine; this false identity is grafted onto her. The surprise in the last phrase, "even after ninety," patronizes the photographer.

An article in the Sunday Styles section of the *New York Times*, "90 Can-dles and a Second Wind," describes four socially prominent women over ninety whose lives are filled with activity. The phrase "enduring youth" is repeated in the article to characterize the women; the writer cannot otherwise account for their vitality (Hayt, 1–2). "90 Candles" reveals how hard the four must work to maintain a conventionally attractive look, and thus it inadvertently suggests rather constricted lives. The women dare not relax. Ten years ago, the *Times* probably would not have run a series of pictures of women in their nineties outside of a nursing home.

Language is ageist when it expresses surprise that an old person retains his or her competence or assertiveness, as for example in phrases that begin "still creative at. . ." or "still attractive at. . ."(Williams and Giles, 151). "Tired" is sometimes a code word for old, as in the 1996 presidential campaign, when Bob Dole was said to have "tired ideas." The word "older" is sometimes a euphemism for "old." The comparative term takes youth or midlife as the norm. The popularity of "feisty," used especially for old women, reveals surprise that vigor, assertiveness, or strong opinions are expressed by a person over sixty-five. A pamphlet from Old Lesbians Organizing for Change asks, "Would you call Superman 'feisty'?" Another belittling word is "spunky," used on old women but better reserved for spirited pets.

No magazines or products list "anti-black" or "anti-woman" as benefits, but "anti-aging" is a very common label for commercial products, including books. Being against aging is like being against pregnancy or season change. The currently popular phrase "senior moment," used to call attention to forgetfulness, is oppressive. A twenty-year-old who forgets her car keys or leaves a burner on does not say she is having a "twenties moment." Implicit in "senior moment" is an acknowledgement of status loss. "The frail elderly" sounds like an innocuous phrase but suggests an identity that is meaningful only to service providers. In a group of twenty elders given this designation, individual differences are probably far more important than similarities.

Psychologists and communications researchers study elderspeak, a pattern observed in interactions between people of different ages. Elderspeak is characterized by a slow rate of speaking, simple sentence structure and vocabulary, and repetitions. It is not necessarily "cued by older adults' comprehension problems" (Kemper and Harden, 656). Studies of elderspeak provide good empirical evidence of ageism. Other researchers use "patronizing speech" to describe speech directed at old women and men that is marked by careful articulation, a demeaning tone (either overbearing or overly familiar), superficial talk, and in its most extreme form, baby talk (Hummert, 162). Among the stereotypes that evoke patronizing speech are perceptions of the old as severely impaired, curmudgeonly, and depressed

(Hummert, 164). In a study of patronizing speech, subjects denied they were treated differently because of their age but agreed that others were (Williams and Giles, 151).

Patronizing speech damages the self-esteem of elders. Moreover, the unsatisfactory social exchange between the two speakers affects the younger as well, for it reinforces negative stereotypes (Hummert, 165–171). Doctor-patient interaction studies have shown that compared to young patients, the old are addressed with less respect and less patience, given less precise information, and asked fewer open-ended questions (Williams and Giles, 138). Patronizing speech in medical settings occurs in the tone, simplicity, or brevity of the communication.

Ageist language is particularly dismaying when used by writers on aging. The book titled *Coping with your Difficult Older Parent* creates a category out of certain behaviors that may be interpreted quite differently by the parent. Behavior that a parent herself might acknowledge as stubborn or angry is just behavior, not an identity. Even worse is another title, *Working with Toxic Older Adults*, from a leading publisher in gerontology.[5] This insulting label reveals the sinister side to the helping profession's dominance of aging. Once a person in a relatively powerless position has been stigmatized as toxic, he or she can easily be disregarded. Labeling an older person toxic effectively erases the possibility that her needs and desires may not coincide with the services provided by the "helper." In both of these book titles, the older person is seen as marginal, while the point of view expressed is that of an authority. A pronounced "us versus them" mentality is apparent here. No book titles target "difficult adult children" of old women and men.

Ageist stereotypes also play out in the media, the workplace, the law, and the family.

Media

Television has been called a major source of ageism (Palmore, 98). On television, "women can now be forty or fifty but they must look thirty" (Mellan-camp, 316). Lucille Ball was in her forties when *I Love Lucy* began its run in 1951, but she played a twenty-nine year old (316). The age difference between male and female TV anchors is dramatic. The popular Angela Lansbury was whisked off stage, suggesting that one visible old woman on television, Barbara Walters, is considered enough. Representations of blacks and women have evolved since the 1950s, but where aging is concerned we are still in the era when Jack Benny's jokes about his thirty-ninth birthday were a staple of mainstream humor. An analysis of television commercials showed that 12 percent portrayed people over fifty, nearly three-fourths of whom were male. They tended to pitch health and hygiene products or food (Quadagno, 1999, 7). Television programs are written by and for the young. Television commercials would probably not depict old women with any sensitivity, and thus their increased appearance might reinforce rather than weaken negative stereotypes. At the same time, the absence of old women from this mirror of American life suggests a social consensus that they do not matter.

Today the media avoid overtly racist or sexist messages in advertising or programs (with the obvious exception of talk radio). Covert prejudice and misrepresentations still occur. What is unique about ageism is the crude directness with which prejudice is communicated on radio and television, in newspapers, in news magazines, on talk shows, and even in publications geared to an older audience.

In an interview, an acclaimed novelist, sixty, calls herself "an old crock," apparently oblivious to the malignancy of her self-ridicule. A face cream commercial gushes that in an experiment, women "were given a chance to look years younger," as if that were a great benefit any woman would be thrilled to receive. Other ads urge people to cover up or de-emphasize their age, ads for creams that cover up liver spots, for example, or ads for hair dye. The message is that being old is undesirable, something to disguise in order to be acceptable. A telling example of the force of this prejudice appeared when a dermatologist concerned about the increase in skin cancer told San Francisco reporters that young people were still sunbathing and could not be discouraged from the practice by warnings about skin cancer. He found another, scarier warning: tanning will make you look old early.

In the media, old women and men are portrayed as sick, as needing help, and as costing too much. An obstacle to combating ageism is the dearth of realistic, complex images of elders. How different media images would be if aging were seen as a process rather than an affliction. The vigorous old are not featured in the media unless they perform some remarkable feat. The ordinary, healthy old are invisible except to their friends and families. The covers of Modern Maturity, the magazine AARP publishes, used to feature affluent looking heterosexual couples in their early fifties wearing warm-up suits. Now young celebrities appear on the cover, with an occasional middle-aged star such as Susan Sarandon. If you look old enough to join AARP, you can't be on the cover. The failure of the media to present varied images of old women "reinforces an unattainable cultural standard"—that aging must be fought at all cost (Bazzini, 542).

In films, a double standard of aging is upheld by portrayals of men enjoying an active, vigorous old age, whereas women "project images of decline," a pattern that has not changed in sixty-five years (Markson and Taylor, 155–56, 137). Another sign of the double standard is that no equivalent of the irrational fear of old women exists for men (Sceriha, 313), no equivalent to "primal loathing."

Workplace

The Age Discrimination in Employment Act, making it illegal to use age as a criterion in hiring, firing, and layoffs, was passed in 1967 and amended in 1986 to end mandatory retirement from most jobs. In the 1960s, Simone de Beauvoir found studies of European workers showing that their skills did not decline in their sixties and seventies if they were healthy (229–31). Stereotypes about older workers persist, however, despite evidence that they are as efficient as other workers, have a lower rate of absenteeism and a higher rate of job satisfaction, are less likely to be injured on the job and continue to learn. Nevertheless, some managers see older workers as resistant to change, unimaginative, cautious and slow, less physically competent than younger workers, uninterested in technology, and untrainable (Atchley, 234–36).

A worker already perceived as less competent because of racial or sex bias is further disadvantaged if age prejudice figures in decisions to cut her job rather than another's. The 1990s layoffs in many American companies disproportionately affected older workers, some of whom did not realize they were "older workers" until they lost their jobs. Once out of work, they remain unemployed much longer than younger workers and experience a greater earnings loss in their next job, if they find one (Palmore, 120–21). The economic cost of the lost productivity of unemployed workers over fifty has been estimated at sixty billion dollars annually (Palmore, 107).

At work, sexism and ageism may be interconnected. A study of a large geriatric center in England found that female nurses treated male residents better than female residents. Nurses knew far more about the lives of the men and were more likely to describe women residents as difficult. The researcher speculates that caring for old women threatened the nurses because each day they had to face images of their own future lives and thus distanced themselves emotionally from the women (Evers, quoted in Bernard, 636).

The Law

Early in 2000, the Supreme Court ruled 5–4 that state employees cannot go to federal court to sue over age bias (New York Times, January 12, 2000, A1). Sandra Day O'Connor wrote that age discrimination is unlike sex or race discrimination, reasoning that old age "does not define a discrete and insular minority because all persons, if they live out their normal life spans, will experience it." Her logic is flawed because at any given moment, the old *are* a minority group, 12.4 percent of the population. If old workers are discriminated against, it is no comfort to tell them they escaped this treatment when they were young. Furthermore, forcing individuals out of the workplace because of their age has social and economic costs that conservatives on the Supreme Court do not recognize.

In a more favorable recent decision, the Supreme Court ruled that if some evidence of age bias exists and if the employer's reason for dismissal is not persuasive, a jury can decide whether age discrimination was a major factor in the firing. The case involved a Mississippi supervisor who was fired after forty years with a manufacturing company. Not long before the dismissal he was told that he was "too damned old to do the job" and "must have come over on the Mayflower" (*AARP Bulletin* 41, no. 8 [2001]: 21).

High-profile sex discrimination cases and racial discrimination lawsuits like the one against Texaco helped solidify a collective belief that differential treatment based on race or sex is wrong. Older workers, by contrast, have not benefited from a history of comparable litigation, even though discrimination against them is well documented. A southern worker in his early fifties was fired, for example, after a new supervisor repeatedly mocked him for being as old as Methuselah. The state court ruled that he was not a victim of age discrimination. Historically, members of minority groups have gone to federal court because their rights were not fully protected by state courts. State workers prevented from taking age discrimination cases to federal court have fewer legal protections than other citizens.

Families

Two works cited above, Barbara Macdonald's *Look Me in the Eye* and *Over the Hill* by Baba Copper, examine the family's role in fostering ageism. Young women are conditioned to align themselves with powerful fathers rather than mothers and to see older women as servants of both their fathers and themselves (Macdonald, 40). Old women's "labor energy," that is favors or services provided without reciprocity, is available to all family members (Copper, 22). An older woman may unknowingly trigger in a younger woman anger she feels towards her mother. The older woman then finds herself "bearing a burden of projected hostility" that mystifies her (Copper, 24).

The grandmother's place is in the home; her role defines her so strictly that "her right to exist depends on her loving and serving." She is not supposed to believe that her last years are as important as her grandchildren's early years (Macdonald, 105–06). An old woman may feel a sense of help-lessness when her capacity to serve others diminishes (Sceriha, 310). Grand-mothers are expected to represent the past and to provide memories that evoke nostalgia. Thus their present concerns go unnoticed (Copper, 10–11). The traditional family is not set up to nurture late-life development.

Not all women are grandmothers, of course, but the role extends to all, for it envisions the model old woman as passive, cheery, devoted to others, and easily controlled. Barbara Bush, though hardly passive, projects an exag-gerated grandmother image by calling herself "everybody's grandmother." By not dyeing her hair or trying to be thin, she has resisted stereotypic female norms only to become "a disembodied maternal archetype" (Dinnerstein and Weitz, 16). A recent study of film images of old women over many decades found that when they were portrayed as powerful, it was usually within a family setting (Markson and Taylor, 153).

Just as no single Asian Pacific woman or black woman can speak for all, no single old woman can represent everyone over sixty-five. The burden of representation may fall on her, however, if she is the only old woman in a social group, at a public forum, in a college class, or in a family.

In some families and social settings, old women assume the guise of a clown. This is a strategy for age denial: "I'm not old, I'm just eccentric!" (Macdonald, 92). I have observed old women mocking themselves, as if to include themselves in a circle of fun rather than risk being targeted by others' derisive humor. Is this dynamic more likely to occur among white women than women of color? Among women once considered beautiful? Is it more characteristic of women in their eighties or nineties than of younger women? Old women do not have to act like clowns to be treated like mascots.

Appearance

Bodies change. Faces become lined and wrinkled, and loosening flesh takes away their firm definition. The face in the mirror may be grandmother's face. Breasts sag. Knees and ankles thicken. Upper arm flesh hangs down and abdominal fat accumulates. Pubic hair and underarm hair thins. Joints stiffen. Fingers lose some dexterity. Within these common changes are myriad indi-vidual differences.

One of the biggest obstacles to women's complete self-acceptance in late life is the judgment that loss of attractiveness (by conventional norms) is a tragic fact of life rather than a belief that can be examined and repudiated, like the belief that blacks are less intelligent than whites or that women are inferior to men. The judgment that old women's bodies are unattractive is so pervasive as to be almost inescapable. Few women can regard even their mid-life bodily changes with complete equanimity. Disdain for old women's bodies is "very similar to the distaste anti-Semites feel towards Jews, homophobes feel towards lesbians and gays, racists toward Blacks—the drawing back of the oppressor from the physical being of the oppressed" (Rich in Macdonald, 143).

Is this problem as onerous for women of color as for white women? One way to find out would be through extensive interviews with women of different ages that would take into account class differences and differences between women of color born here and those who have come from other countries. Literary images shed light on this question. Poets such as Judith Ortiz Cofer, Lucille Clifton, and Mary TallMountain have described old women's bodies with loving detail, for example in "Paciencia" (Cofer), "Miss Rosie" (Clifton), and "Matmiya" (TallMountain). The poets express unique sensibilities and should not be read simply as cultural representatives. Puerto Rican, black, and Athabaskan cultures differ greatly from each other. Nonetheless, the stark difference between the poets' positive views of old women's bodies and the contempt expressed by M.F.K. Fisher (see below) is striking. For Cofer, Clifton, and TallMountain, power resides in old bodies; they make no distinction between weak/bad/defeated flesh and indomitable spirit.

Women, especially white women, face a double standard according to Susan Sontag: men are judged as "face and body, a physical whole," while women are identified with their faces. The range of acceptability is much wider for men's faces than for women's, and men's well-worn faces are thought to convey maturity, character, and experience. A woman's face, on the other hand, is valued for staying the same. Ideally, it is a mask.[6] Old men often want much younger women for wives and companions. In Western culture the old woman lacks appeal to men because "she is such a long way from their ideal of flattering virginal inexperience" (Rich in Macdonald, 141). Moreover, men's fear of an "all-engulfing mother" is intensified when women are old (Woodward, 1995, 87). In 1873, the radical feminist theorist Matilda Joslyn Gage wrote that a woman who no longer interests men sexually was thought to have "forfeited the right to live" (quoted in Mollenkott, 4). Although much has changed for women since Gage wrote, the perception that old women's bodies are ugly has not changed. "Old women vanish from ads when they lose their sex appeal for men, appearing only to sell food they can cook and medications they can take, or being foolish in a modern female version of Uncle Tom" (Reinharz, 78).

The relentless emphasis on appearance pressures some women to fit into a youth-centered culture by choosing facelifts and other alterations to their bodies. Those who tried to be as thin as possible when young are victimized again. Some women who get facelifts say they want to erase the difference between the way they look and the way they feel inside. This rationale divides us into "our corpus, which drags us inevitably into our dreaded old age, and our spirit, which remains forever young," so that age denial through "artificial dissection" results in a split self (Andrews, 301). Though portrayed as glamorous, facelifts are actually mutilations, a fact powerfully revealed in a series of self-portraits Anne Noggle took immediately after her surgery. Her swollen and bruised face looks like the face of a woman who has been beaten.[7]

If large numbers of baby-boomers—men as well as women—alter their faces to pass as young, we will all be deprived of seeing the whole range and variety of aging faces. Audre Lorde wrote in *The Cancer Journals* that pressure on women like herself to disguise the fact that they had lost a breast deprived her of knowing who shared her experience. So, too, with the banishment of faces that look fifty, sixty, or seventy. In a way, the massive age denial that the boom in cosmetic surgery represents is a superstition as powerful and irrational as any observable in so-called "primitive" societies. Praying to rain gods and cutting out one's wrinkles and sagging face flesh express two kinds of magical thinking. People who have their faces altered try to escape the wrathful gods of inexorable change. Their cosmetic surgeon is Zeus. If they pretend they are not old, they won't really *be* old. No mockery is directed at their delusion; it is too widely shared to be named make-believe. Botox-stiffened faces lose both individuality and a full range of expression.

The NPR program *Marketplace* reported that in a two-year period, 1997 through 1999, cosmetic surgery increased by 50 percent in the U.S. (June 3, 1999). Some women grow ever more desperate to hide the signs of aging, at least women who can afford expensive surgery. The increasing prevalence of cosmetic surgery demonstrates the limited influence of feminism on aging attitudes. More girls play sports in schools today, thanks to Title IX pioneers of the 1970s; more women work in professions previously closed to them; sexual harassment has been identified as a barrier to working women since the 1980s; and in the 1990s, many women of color entered professional schools. Where aging and appearance are concerned, on the other hand, no comparable progress can be claimed.

The shame of aging is perpetuated when old bodies are hidden from view. Young naked female bodies are everywhere, including the magazine section of the Sunday *New York Times*, but where can naked bodies of old women be seen? This is terra incognita. The absence of naked old female bodies deprives women of all ages from knowing what old bodies look like.[8] This deprivation is both aesthetic and psychological. The ways beauty can be expressed through old female forms is yet to be known, although a few artists are breaking the taboo. The cover of Kathleen Woodward's *Figuring Age: Women, Bodies, Generations* is a photograph by Jacqueline Hayden of a nude, one-breasted woman over sixty, sitting on a stool with her arm resting against her raised knee.

Book cover photos of Betty Friedan and Madeline Albright picture women thirty years younger than they are today: two notable woman over sixty with easily recognizable old faces are pushed back into a closet of youth, the better to enhance their market value. A well-known social historian on the campus lecture circuit uses a photo that appears to have been taken forty years ago. The book jacket of a California therapist in her sixties makes her look twenty-five.

As these examples illustrate, a youthful image is so prized that many older people want to freeze early images of themselves and pretend that image is the real one. Newspapers run obituary photos taken forty or fifty years earlier. Granted, people are entitled to choose whatever picture they wish to represent them, but newspapers could encourage families to supply pictures that come close to suggesting a full life span. Obituary pages reinforce age shame when they could instead depict old women and men as they really look.

Looking old can lead to being ignored. Perceiving a woman over sixty as asexual because of her appearance is a way to ignore her. "Sometimes other people don't bring the same level of attention that I bring to them," writes Lucille Clifton,

> and sometimes that makes me sad, or angry, as the case may be. For instance, I've been widowed for ten years, and have noticed that other people, especially men, do not always notice my human characteristics but are quick to pin a label on me: poet, for example, or professor. Sexually and romantically, they are interested in women of my daughter's age. It hurts my feelings. It puts me in a slot, and I go uneasily into slots of any kind (53).

How does an older woman find the courage to accept bodily change? What values or emotional history let her acknowledge what she sees happening in her body without trying to alter it? She may never have been much influenced by conventional beliefs about female beauty, or she may grasp the connection between profit and culturally-induced body loathing. Whatever her ethnicity, she may have aunts and grandmothers whose power or life satisfaction does not come from looking a certain way or denying their age.

Old as a Category

Learning to be old means being conditioned to "lean on the concept of age" (Bodily, 254). It becomes a ready explanation. Children's books typically portray old characters as if age were their defining characteristic (Sorgman and Sorensen, 120). Once designated "old," writes Barbara Myerhoff, we are sharply separated from the members of society deemed useful, full participants, usually "without reference to individual desire or capability. Here nature and culture stand at great remove from each other" (1984, 320). A keen awareness of our individual desire and capability allows us to resist the total category of "old," while at the same time accepting the facts of bodily change and the inevitability of further change.

The well-intentioned Age Page in some newspapers assumes a uniformity among elders that does not exist. Just as the now-defunct Women's Page inadvertently revealed inferiority through segregation, the Age Page signals specialness where it has no bearing. The arbitrary chronological marker of sixty-five creates a class of people who get important benefits, are denied resources and opportunities available to others, and suffer "denigration ranging from well-meaning patronage to unambiguous vilification" (Bytheway, 14). The other meanings of old, including decline, shift like colored pieces in a kaleidoscope. The category looks fixed because it is familiar and provides a convenient way to rank people. The self-confident ease and assertiveness of the well-off white old may insulate them from contemptuous treatment, but if institutionalized, they devolve into the merely "old," and if cared for at home, they enter into the unequal power relationship of caregiver and care recipient. At a time when most people acknowledge that a woman worker's lower pay does not result from her personal shortcomings, we are much less aware that decline among the old is created by social policy as well as by individual bodily processes.

Just as a heightened sense of racial difference interferes with communication, a heightened sense of age can impede straightforward and unselfconscious interaction. If I speak to a seventy-five-year-old woman with a strong awareness of her age and thus her difference from me, a category unnecessarily shapes our communication. If socialized to see this difference as extremely important, I will have trouble letting it fade back into relative insignificance, even after I suspect that seeing "old" limits my perceptions. The woman can probably do most of what she has done in the past; focusing on her losses rather than her continuities gives too much weight to the conventional meaning of "old." If, trying to be helpful, I grab the arm of an old woman as she crosses the street because I think she needs help, I lean on the concept of old. If I assume a friend will enjoy discussing Medicare with me because she is eighty-five, I see her in monochrome. Conditioned by ageist stereotypes, I see helplessness where it does not exist or focus on the medical and economic dimensions of aging as if they were its totality.

I learned what I missed by seeing only "old" while teaching a class called "All About Aging" at the Montefiore Senior Center in San Francisco. The students were amused that a woman under fifty presumed to speak on this topic to an audience made up of people over eighty. One woman who sat near the front of the room paid close attention and made perceptive and lively comments. Not long after the class ended, I was amazed to see her in the hallway of the center, groping her way along slowly and uncertainly. She could barely see. If that had been my only impression of her, age and infirmity would have been the most striking aspects of her identity. But in class I had the opportunity to see her as a competent and fully-functioning individual.

Another woman at the center wore a long coat and a babushka. "Old" was my only impression of her until one day when she joined a group chatting in the hallway and mentioned that she had lived in China and spoke Mandarin. She then became an individual and the category "old" no longer covered her like a blanket.

In *Look Me in the Eye*, Barbara Macdonald claims old as an identity, and in *Over the Hill*, Baba Copper writes, "I take to myself the word everyone seems to fear" (75). The parallel to ethnicity, sex, and sexual orientation is implicit. Writing in the 1980s, Macdonald and Copper tended to see old women as a monolithic group, as acted upon by an ageist culture but not as having influence upon it. At that time it seemed obvious that old women should counter ageist stereotypes by proudly calling themselves old and that their well-known reluctance to do so signified internalized ageism. They needed consciousness raising to adopt Gray Pride. Now their reluctance seems more complex. It may well be that resisters to the designation "old" neither deny their bodily changes nor believe that their interests are the same as those of younger women. Perhaps they sense that "old" erases their individual differences and creates a separation from others that they do not feel, or even an artificial separation from their former selves. Being old may be a less salient identity marker than being black, female or gay because it fits only part of our life span. All stereotyped notions about people of color, women and gay people are demonstrably false, while a key stereotype about late life, the equation with illness, is harder to dismiss because old age and illness are undeniably associated. The stereotype is *equating* the two. A woman who takes on the identity "old" has no mass social movement to back her up.

A larger problem with embracing "old" as an identity is that it facilitates social control. Even the innocuous phrase "the tasks of aging," popular among psychologists who study late life, implies that "old" is a tightly fitting identity with requirements imposed by others. "Task" is a good word for strivers and doers; it seems unsuitably standardized for a group as diverse as people over sixty-five or seventy, some of whom may live for another thirty years. The expectation that the old will be docile illustrates the coercion implicit in the category "old." When Celia Gill vigorously protested the introduction of plastic tablecloths in the nursing home where she lives and was threatened with expulsion, the Associated Press reported the story (Jan. 10, 2002). Her age, 94, was a key factor in her new notoriety.

Bill Bytheway alludes to the social control aspect of the category "old" when he terms ageism "an ideology upon which dominant groups. . . justify and sustain not just the inequalities between age groups but also the belief that these groups exist and are different" (116). Physical differences exist but their meaning does not automatically arise from the aging process itself. The difficulty with full-blown social construction, however, the challenge to the idea that age groups exist, is that it reflects what another British scholar, Molly Andrews, has called "the seductiveness of agelessness" (301–18). Being old means something beyond being exploited and stereotyped. Andrews believes that "development is the project of a lifetime" and thus living to old age is an accomplishment (310). This view of late life as unique is shared by Barbara Macdonald and Baba Copper.

Despite the problems with old as an identity, group consciousness among old women and men is highly desirable, because social change will not occur unless these members of a denigrated group identify with each other (Williams and Giles, 151). Thus the Older Women's League and Old Lesbians Organizing for Change make combating ageism their special agenda, and the Gray Panthers challenge it as well.[9] "Old" can be thought of as an affinity group rather than an identity. Such groups form, grow, dissolve, and spring to life again depending on circumstances. Within affinity groups, "old" can seem fluid and indeterminate, relevant to this situation or issue, irrelevant to that. It may not be necessary to take on "old" as an identity to feel completely at ease with one's physical appearance or the number of years one has lived. Much space exists between denying age and claiming it as an identity.

Internalized Ageism

Just as colonized people may internalize messages about their own inferiority, many old women feel ashamed of their age. This is the most insidious form ageism takes. Consciously working through the negative associations with age that are nearly universal in this society requires effort. If she does not continually examine her ageist notions, writes Shevy Healey, "false expectations and assumptions cloud and diminish my ability to actually experience my life" (1993, 47). Internalized ageism keeps people from accurately assessing their own abilities, and even worse, sets them up to "rationalize unfair assessments from others" (Bodily, 251).

The old appear as likely or more likely than others to perpetuate ageist stereotypes by their jokes and comments, but at the same time they know far better than others that these stereotypes distort and demean them. Studies of attitudes toward the old among people of various ages found less complex views of aging among the young and more complex and more positive attitudes among the old themselves (Hummert, 165), a sign of resistance to internalized ageism. A study of attitudes toward aging in Japan concluded that although Japanese elders held many negative opinions about their own age group, they also had strong self-concepts protecting them from what would otherwise have been "the damaging effects of social environment" (Levy, 1999, 142). The mental gyrations needed to exempt oneself from membership in a group that others assume one belongs to, however, would seem to complicate self-understanding and to require vigilance. A similar process of distancing occurs among old women and men in the U.S. The assumption that being old is shameful is illustrated by the oppressive practice at some senior centers of fining members who use the word "old" (Palmore, 110).

Age passing (i.e., pretending to be younger than you are), is a form of internalized ageism. Copper speculates that it may be easier for small, "cute" older women than for their "more bulky peers" (31). Another self-defeating strategy is to say "nothing has changed but our bodies," a split that erases "the unique insights of our time of life" (11).

Apologies for slow movements also reflect internalized ageism. I recall many times when an old woman boarding a bus apologized for what she perceived as her slowness. The cultural bias favoring speed is so powerful that slow movements mark inferiority. As some colonized people identify with the dominant group rather than their own to deflect stigma, some old women call other old women "little old ladies," thereby evading an undesirable category.[10]

The importance of liberation from socially-constructed inferiority has been demonstrated by psychologist Ellen Langer in an ingenious way, by comparing expectations of age-related memory loss with actual loss in three groups: Chinese elders, American deaf elders, and hearing Americans. She found that the deaf Americans and the Chinese outperformed the hearing Americans. "Negative views correlated with poorer performance" (Power, 97). The hunch that internalized ageism may negatively affect not just self esteem, motivation, risk taking and other hard-to-measure traits, but physical capacity as well is also supported by a recent study of gait speed and swing time (time spent with one foot in the air while walking). To test their hypothesis that activating positive stereotypes could partly reverse age-related changes in walking, researchers had subjects aged sixty-three to eighty-two play a video game that exposed them to either positive or negative stereotypes about the old. Those given positive stereotypes showed significant increases in walking speed and swing time. Researchers concluded that stereotypes of aging "apparently have a powerful impact on the gait of older persons" (Hausdorff, Levy, and Wei, 1346). The mind/body link demonstrated here and in another study in which internalized negative stereotypes of aging were shown to influence cardiovascular function (Levy, 2001, 579) should inspire other researchers to think about measurable effects of ageism.

A study of Canadian women at a senior center who view themselves as "not old" discusses this labeling as a way of "negotiating" aging and concludes that it helps the women contradict negative stereotypes. Most of their statements suggest, however, that the strategy does not work, comments for example on the ugliness of their bodies (Hurd, 431–32). The women feel a sharp separation between themselves and those they designate as old. All are widows, though, a status that definitely coincides with being old. Additionally, the women are well aware that illness could take the "not old" mantle away from them (430). One of the chief ways they lock in "not old" is by being busy (427).

The dilemma faced by these women and others like them is excruciating:

if they take on the despised identity of old, they cannot think well of themselves. If they identify as "not old," on the other hand, they can avoid stigma for a time by dissociating themselves from others but this requires a degree of self-deception. They must deny that aging is a process, one that includes them. Living in a society in which women are ruthlessly judged by physical appearance, they trust that the trivializing self characterization of "young at heart" gives them protective cover. The reprieve is only temporary. The various rationalizations of the "not old" are often regarded as cute by others, a sure sign of their transparent failure.

Instead of rebuking women who exhibit internalized ageism, however, it is fairer to adopt a double consciousness that recognizes both the harm this stance of shame causes and the heavy weight of cultural baggage that makes full self acceptance and honest disclosure of age difficult. An especially poignant example of internalized ageism comes, surprisingly, from M.F.K. Fisher, a writer who has described other people's aging with unusual insight and sensitivity. The afterword to her book *Sister Age* is luminous, but in an interview she reports:

> My [late] husband told me that every self-respecting woman must have a full-length mirror in her house, to see herself from top to bottom cruelly. Mine is facing me at a distance of about ten feet from my bed when I get up in the morning. About a year ago I realized—I sleep without pajamas or a nightie—I suddenly realized I could not face walking toward myself again because here was this strange, uncouth, ugly. . . toad-like woman, long, long thin legs, long, long thin arms, and a sort of shapeless little toad-like torso and this head at the top with great staring eyes. I thought, "Jesus! Why do I have to do this?" So I bought some nightgowns. I felt like an idiot. But I couldn't face it in the mornings. If I'm going to hide myself I want to *hide*. And I have long-sleeved, high-necked, long-to-the-ground granny gowns. They're pretty. I hate them. I'd much rather not have to wear them. But I will not face that strange, that humanoid toad walking toward *me* in the morning.[11]

In this paroxysm of body-loathing, Fisher reduces herself to "it," sharply separating "it" from "me," the true self residing outside of her body. The contortion demanded by the rules of a dead husband is shocking.

To be truly comfortable in old age one must have a keen perception of ageism—its prevalence, its destructive impact on self-esteem, and the particular harm it does to women. An ageist birthday card may seem funny to family and friends, a comic's joke on television or an older person's self-deprecating humor amusing. On these apparently trivial words and commercial products, the scaffolding of ageist stereotypes holds firm. The prejudice implicit in these stereotypes obscures a fundamental truth: at sixty-five, a woman is "still in process" (Macdonald, 41).

Ageism is a form of oppression that harms not only its targets but also those who express it (Laws, 11). An eloquent passage in *Over the Hill* elaborates this point:

> Ageism screens communication between young and old women like a one-way mirror—the old can see the young, aided as they are by memories of their own youth, but the young cannot—or will not—see their future in old women. Sensing that vital information may be hidden on the other side of the mirrored surface, the young press their faces against the barrier, only to scan their own reflections nervously for the imperfections of age. The old, on the other side, watch with sadness, recognizing their own denial of aging in the young women's faces (Copper, 57).

A similar theme is expressed by Evelyn Rosenthal when she writes that younger women "look past us and through us as if by denying our existence they will magically avoid growing old" (6). Anti-aging is not just a marketing slogan but a stance toward life.

A possible defense against the distortions of ageism and the shame it engenders is simultaneously seeing what age means to others and what it means to ourselves. If we experience continuity with our past selves and feel as worthy as before, dismissive judgments based on age may be less wounding. Conscious aging entails mindful resistance to stereotypes, those implicit in the increasingly popular "geezer," for example, a demeaning tag that insults men and erases women in one fell swoop.

Conclusion

In the 1970s, Alex Comfort wrote that ageism is "not only idiotic but anachronistic, and the old to come will not acquiesce in it" (Age Prejudice, 1976, 8). Will baby boomers live up to Comfort's expectation or will they find themselves engulfed in oppressive stereotypes? Ageism is probably too deeply rooted in American culture to be eradicated by mere population aging. The struggle against it is worth pursuing, however, even if it presently concerns only a few. Like advocates for civil rights in the 1940s and defenders of women's equality in the 1950s, critics of ageism today find their voices drowned out. But better health, an analysis of ageism, a stronger drive for self determination than their grandmothers could express, and the support of like-minded friends may inspire many old women to accept their aging without shame or apology.

Notes

1. To call discrimination based on age unconstitutional "boggles my mind," writes Justice Scalia *New York Times* (October 14, 1999): A21. Justice O'Connor's view of ageism is discussed later in this chapter.

2. Originally published in 1983, Barbara Macdonald and Cynthia Rich's *Look Me in the Eye: Old Women, Aging and Ageism* was reissued in an expanded version in 1991. Both editions consist of alternating chapters by Macdonald and Rich, but the title page reads "Barbara Macdonald with Cynthia Rich" rather than listing Rich as a coauthor. To avoid confusion in text references, I cite Macdonald when the quotation is from one of her chapters and Rich in Macdonald when quoting or paraphrasing a statement in one of her chapters. A revised edition of *Look Me in the Eye* was published in 2001.

3. According to the *Compact Oxford English Dictionary*, "geezer" is a derisive term for a man, not necessarily an old man. *Merriam Webster's Collegiate Dictionary* traces geezer to the Scottish term "guiser," one in disguise, an odd or eccentric person, especially an elderly man. D. H. Lawrence used "guiser" to mean a mummer, according to the O.E.D. Thus "guiser" once had a positive meaning, disguised merrymaker. The *Scientific American* article appears in vol. 11, no. 2 (2000): 22–25.

4. The abandonment or killing of elders in some societies may appear to be parallel cases, but typically the reason was extreme food shortage. The well-known example of the Inuit putting their old on ice floes is misleading because the custom was practiced only by some Inuit and because elders themselves determined when their lives were to end. The Japanese folktale "Oyasuteyama" or "The Mountain of the Old" describes the custom of taking aged parents far into the mountains and abandoning them, but first a ritual farewell ceremony takes place and the family grieves.

5. Barbara Lane and Grace Lebow, *Coping with your Difficult Older Parent* (New York: Avon, 1999). Gloria M. Davenport, *Working with Toxic Older Adults* (New York: Springer, 1999).

6. Susan Sontag, "The Double Standard of Aging," in *The Other Within: Feminist Explorations of Women and Aging*, ed. Marilyn Pearsall (Boulder, Colo.: Westview, 1997). Originally published in 1972, Sontag's essay presents outdated views of women and aging. Sontag calls old age an "ordeal," for example, and a "shipwreck." She was far ahead of her time, however, in recognizing that "aging is much more a social judgment than a biological eventuality" (21).

7. Anne Noggle, *Silver Lining* (Albuquerque: University of New Mexico Press, 1983). One facelift photograph from this collection is reprinted in *Women and Aging*, eds. Jo Alexander et al. (Corvallis, Ore.: Calyx Books, 1986).

8. A San Francisco institution for fifty years before it was torn down and replaced by

a parking lot, Finnila's sauna on the corner of Market and Noe streets was a place where naked bodies of many diverse old women could be seen.

9. Maggie Kuhn (1905–1995) founded the Gray Panthers in 1970 after being forced to retire from a job with the Presbyterian church. A dynamic speaker and leader, she inspired many Americans to recognize ageism. Kuhn is profiled by Jeanne E. Bader in *Contemporary Gerontology* 6, no. 4 (2000): 104–108. Among the concerns of the 40,000 members of Gray Panthers are jobs, housing, the environment, health care, and military spending.

10. A conversation with San Francisco writer Judy MacLean clarified this point for me.

11. Excerpt from "I'm Too Busy to Talk Now: Conversations with American Artists over 70." Connie Goldman Talks with M.F.K. Fisher. University of Wisconsin Extension Educational Radio, 1985.

CHAPTER NINE

~

Prescribed Busyness and Spirituality

The inequalities outlined in chapters 6 and 7 tell a story of women's aging often obscured in discussions of late life. What else is missing? Conscious aging additionally requires an awareness that busyness has the force of a prescription for elders in this society. Just as they receive social approval for being sick and accepting sickness as their natural condition, they are expected (when not sick) to stay as busy as possible. Resistance to the path of illness and prescription drug dependency is easily justified because health is valued. With busyness, however, the defense is less obvious because lack of busyness can be equated with laziness, withdrawal from others, or lack of imagination. Women typically are busy for most of their lives. Late-life busyness may be a trap for them, however, encouraging age denial, numbing feelings, and keeping them in familiar grooves. This chapter examines prescribed busyness and offers one antidote, spirituality.

Prescribed Busyness

Learning to be old in the conventional sense means following the direction Be Busy, for busyness is equated with worth and mental competence. When workers approach retirement, colleagues ask what they will do with their time and later, the new retirees commonly report that they are as busy as ever. This accomplishment meets with social approval. Sitting around, doing nothing, having no plans, looking out the window for hours at a time are all frowned upon. To admit to not being busy invites suggestions for remedying this unfortunate condition. "We are busy people," boast Sun City, Arizona, residents. There people "race with time" and "fill time so that they will not be swallowed by emptiness. And they avert their eyes when the ragged tooth marks of time begin to appear around the edges of a neighbor's mind or body" (Kastenbaum, 178).

Old women and men who keep busy resemble the young and the middle-aged, at least in one respect. Busyness has nothing to do with frailty, disability, slowing down, dependence. It encourages emotional distance from those no longer able to boast of a crowded schedule. Perhaps the emphasis on busyness is a way of keeping the terror of aging at bay, as Kastenbaum's gloss on Sun City suggests. Busyness blocks recognition of one's future self as (possibly or probably) unable to be busy. It is a shield, even an amulet.

When Connie Goldman titled her series of radio interviews with artists over seventy "I'm Too Busy to Talk Now,"[1] she offered a positive image of late-life vigor and creativity, but behind the title lurks a shadow of a prescription: for a good old age, stay busy. Former film star Alice Faye travels across the country promoting a giant pharmaceutical company as its good health ambassador. Her message to older Americans is "Keep on Moving" (Wheeler, 147). That may be hard if her audience uses too many of the company's products. "Keep on moving" is a variation of the busy theme.

A belief that the old are intrinsically worthy or that life beyond wage earning is intrinsically good runs counter to a belief that busyness is redemptive for them. Busyness is a utilitarian value. It is an unimaginative expectation to hold for people in late life. Accepting busyness allows one to overlook the possibility that old age has meanings not shared with mid-life. In addition, by uncritically applauding busyness, gerontologists have reinforced a pragmatic view of aging and, until recently, have de-emphasized the possibilities of late-life spiritual development.

In Tennyson's famous dramatic monologue "Ulysses," the speaker values his former life of adventure at sea and chafes against his present idleness. Telling his companions that old age is a time for honor but also for toil, Ulysses urges them to set out with him once more. The lure is fresh experience and action itself:

> How dull it is to pause, to make an end,
> To rust unburnished, not to shine in use!

From the poetry of Victorian England to the pages of *Modern Maturity*, pausing is linked to rusting.

Activity and engagement differ from busyness in being more mindful and allowing space for inactivity and reflection. These broad descriptions are hard to apply to an individual's choices and schedule, of course; one person's level of activity would be far too busy for another. But a distinction can be made between busyness and the more purposeful and thoughtful engagement with life suggested by *Vital Involvements in Old Age*, the title of a book by Erik Erikson, Joan Erikson, and Helen Q. Kivnick (1986).

Prescribed busyness functions as social control. It is a hidden rule. Old women and men who hurry from one task or appointment to the next have no time to notice that their age group is disfavored or to ask what they have in common with other old people. What if no social approval accompanied a crowded schedule? Would older women and men stay busy then? Some would have to decrease their activity in response to health problems, loss of energy, or declining incomes. For others, leisure is not an option; many more black women than white women remain in the labor force when they are aged sixty to sixty-five, for example.

A common justification for busyness is that it is healthy. For some, it may be true that staying in harness is healthy, but the health benefits of retirement are well documented. Robert Atchley found that walking for exercise was far more common among retirees than among people the same age who still worked, and he concluded that the false link between retirement and physical and mental harm serves to emphasize the value of work (260).

The strong social message to keep busy in late life is analyzed by David J. Ekerdt, who notes that workers and nonworkers alike share the expectation that the old will keep busy. Why is this idea so firmly rooted in our ideology of old age? It protects a person from suspicions that she or he may no longer be capable of busyness and it "tames the potentially unfettered pleasures of retirement to prevailing values of engagement that apply to adulthood" (138–39). What are these unfettered pleasures and why must they be tamed?

We could have an "ethic of repose, with retirees resolutely unembarrassed about slowing down to enjoy leisure in very individual ways," says Ekerdt, or we could espouse an ethic of "hedonism, nonconformity, and carefree self-indulgence" as appropriate for late life (138–39). To choose either repose or happy hedonism in old age, Americans would have to throw off the Puritanism that underlies prescribed busyness and find value in being as well as in doing. Since this is unlikely to happen, options less extreme than either repose or hedonism would have to be encouraged.

As a supposedly desirable mark of aging well, busyness is related to gerontologists' prescriptions for productive aging and by implication to the successful aging discussed in the introduction. At first glance, this worthy goal seems unassailable. Who would defend its opposite? Martha Holstein offers several reasons for questioning this norm, however. Productive aging may come to be defined as paid work; it may reinforce traditional patterns of work inequality that have harmed women; and by setting a narrow standard for a meaningful life, productivity obscures the complexities of old age. In Holstein's view, emphasizing productivity can devalue the relationships women create as primary caregivers of the old and as recipients of care and "hide the creativity and moral integrity that are developed and realized in these relationships" (1992, 26). Another danger is that the productivity model may discount those who are not vigorous and independent, thus intensifying negative attitudes toward frail or impaired elderly citizens (27). Moreover, older women are least likely to be the "gatekeepers" who define productive aging and thus they risk living by others' norms. At the same time, it is they who would "benefit most profoundly from a re-imagining of old age" (Holstein, 1999, 364).[2] A woman who resists busyness, who moves to her own inner rhythms, need not find her self-worth through accomplishment. She may find pleasure in relaxing the ego drive that busyness often requires. But as Ram Dass observes, we Americans are uneasy in "retirement from achieving" (83).

Productivity interprets aging through values of growth, energy, activity, and accumulation when a broader vision is needed, one that stresses "altruism, citizenship, stewardship [and] creativity" (Moody, Age, 1993, 36, 38). The latter do not require physical stamina to be enacted. As Theodore Roszak observes, productivity as an old age ideal makes the loss of physical stamina "all the more frightening" (108). Keeping busy creates an illusion of invulnerability and control that cannot be sustained. "A human culture is only possible," writes Thomas Rentsch, if humans understand their lives not only in production, consumption, and domination of the natural world but also in "their materiality, corporeality, fragility, and vulnerability" (271). Busyness draws attention away from our vulnerability.

It is useful nevertheless to relate productivity narrowly to aging because older workers are often pushed out of the labor market, and widespread layoffs in the last decade and unemployment caused by jobs moving overseas have limited outlets for many workers over fifty to be productive. Paradoxically, older people are urged to stay busy while opportunities to be busy at paid work are decreasing. To maintain a good self-concept in late life is difficult because social worth in our society depends on productivity, and elders find themselves "stripped of the power to freely produce" (Stannard, 13). The absence of a wide range of well-paid flexible jobs for people over sixty is a structural problem that is disguised as a personal problem when workers are told to retrain, adapt, accept lower wages, or take early retirement. Lack of opportunity to be productive in paid work is made worse by the inadequacy of lifelong learning programs, either academic or technical.

Volunteer work may preserve a self-image of usefulness. It is urged on older Americans as a way to keep busy, but as Baba Copper points out, projects needing the work of elders, especially of old women, are typically designed by others (86). In *Prime Time*, Marc Freedman predicts that volunteers of the future will expect to be in charge of activities rather than simply providing extra hands.

Models of productive aging or "good aging" are inherently coercive. Nearly always they are proposed by the non-old. Rather than illuminating aging they reveal the anxieties and needs of the non-old. In much gerontological writing, notes Margaret Urban Walker, late-life meaning comes "either through 'productive aging' in which we keep 'busy' . . . or through a final project of life review," in which we "prove to ourselves and to others that at least we *were* socially acceptable persons before our adulthood expired" (Getting, 1999, 104), i.e., that we *used* to be busy.

If being old in America were seen as a natural process, models for doing it properly would not exist. A few guidelines and recommendations would suffice. In *The Coming of Age*, Simone de Beauvoir explains the relativity of old age by saying that in France she needn't think about her French identity, but in another country, she is required to adopt some attitude toward being French (291). If being old in America were as nonproblematic as being French in France, norms for successful or productive aging, or exhortations to keep busy, would not be necessary. Some have proposed that the definition of productivity be expanded to include not just paid work but a wide range of socially beneficial activities. Caregiving would be an example. But as long as caregiving is uncompensated labor for which women are expected to make large sacrifices, calling it productive will not gain for it the respect given to paid work.

In her book *Be An Outrageous Older Woman*, Ruth Jacobs tells of a woman who expresses frustration at having scheduled events every night for two weeks. "Yet this same woman becomes anxious if her calendar is not filled" (98). Learning to be old means noticing whether a busy life is truly satisfying or simply conforms to social expectation. The old, knowing they are expected to be busy, will say they are (Ekerdt, 140–41).

Not surprisingly, some dissent from this orthodoxy. It may be hard to redirect one's focus in late life if hard work has been central to one's identity, but outgrowing busyness can be liberating and exhilarating. This discovery shapes "Just Desserts," a personal essay by Hila Colman published in the *New*

York Times Magazine. At eighty, she felt pressured by thinking of all the things she felt she had to do, or that others believed she should do, find a hobby, take classes, work out at a gym, devote money and time to looking younger than her age. Then she decides that her old age will be different from her youth because old age is a new experience. Not having commitments or demands on her time is a luxury, and she resists inducements to become busy. "I am tired of being useful," she concludes. "This is my time to enjoy the quietness of just being, of stopping to look and feel and think, of indulging myself. Time for myself at last" (84).

This is hardly hedonism, simply healthy nonconformity. The expression of one woman's values, "Just Desserts" reflects the experience of many women who have worked hard all their lives taking care of families, responding to others' expectations, and overtaxing themselves meeting multiple responsibilities. At some point, they want to stop. Another writer in her eighties who enjoyed "the quietness of just being" was Florida Scott-Maxwell. Written in the 1960s, her book *The Measure of My Days* has become a classic. "Goals and efforts of a lifetime can be abandoned," she writes. "What a comfort. One's conscience? Toss the fussy thing aside. Rest, rest" (119).

Slowing down is seen negatively when it means only bodily change, but this dimension of aging is more complicated. Late life is the time when "our being slows on all levels in order to experience situations and persons with more attentiveness and care than is possible when a youthful, fast-paced metabolism and an energetic, vigorous body inspire us to cover great distances at high speed, to finish quickly with one experience in order to hasten on to the next" (Berg and Gadow, 227). Maybe a purpose of late life, then, is to recover physically and psychologically from the busyness binge of the previous decades.

Recently children, or at least middle-class children, have become overscheduled and subject to busyness pressures previously felt only by adults. They no longer roam about unsupervised or go long distances on their bicycles. Whatever these trends suggest about childhood, one meaning for the life course is clear: late life is now the only period characterized by ample free time. The growth-inducing possibilities of contented idleness, disappearing from childhood and unattainable by most workers, will increasingly be found only among the old. Creative play will be a long-deferred gratification. Creativity itself, among those whose primary work is not artistic or intellectual, may in time be associated with the old.

Spirituality

A good antidote to the busy ethic is an awareness of spiritual values. By spirituality I mean attitudes, beliefs, and practices expressed privately or in small groups, independent of formal religious institutions, or an inner awareness of meaning that transcends the ordinary. In *Still Here*, a book full of insights about aging and spirituality, Ram Dass asks, "What has all this been about?" and, "Where am I in the flow of all this?" The old in America think they are supposed to keep busy, he notes, but "slowing down, drawing in, can open us to some of the most fruitful experiences of life" (52).

Gerontologists have linked church participation to psychologically healthy aging, but more recently they have become less sure of the correlation. The social networks often provided by churches are perhaps as beneficial as religious belief itself.[3] Unitarians, Quakers, and black churchgoers seem especially supportive of the old. Ruth Jacobs reports in *Be An Outrageous Older Woman* that after her divorce she found that all of the activities at her church were organized for couples. In her new Quaker group, by contrast, she feels like a "full-status person, not a second-class person" (98). Even though churchgoing is far from universal in America, gerontologists tend not to study old agnostics, atheists, pagans, witches, or people who have left congregations and synagogues to find their own spiritual paths.

The confluence of aging and spirituality has several sources. Since the 1970s, humanities scholars have published work speculating on the meanings of age.[4] Secondly, within mainstream religions awareness of the aging of congregations has led to programs and publications linking spirituality to aging. Examples are the Institute of Spirituality and Aging, founded in 1992 and affiliated since 1994 with the Graduate Theological Union in Berkeley, and the Center for Aging, Religion, and Spirituality at Luther Seminary in St. Paul. A third influence has been the proliferation of groups growing out of the Spiritual Eldering Institute founded in Philadelphia in 1986 by Rabbi Zalman Schachter-Shalomi, and "Conscious Aging" programs sponsored by the Omega Institute for Holistic Studies.[5] The popularity of "conscious aging" has been related to the aging of participants in alternative movements of the 1960s (Atchley, 294). The Forum on Religion, Spirituality, and Aging of the American Society on Aging, a national, multidisciplinary group, holds an annual conference and links participants through ASA's Web site. In addition to these groups are others hard to document for they consist of spontaneously forming friendship groups among old women and men interested in the spiritual dimension of aging.

Contributing less directly to interest in aging and spirituality are New Age beliefs, feminist spirituality, American Buddhism, and the various mind-body techniques associated with Esalen such as humanistic psychology, massage, and altered states of consciousness. An experimental program in Berkeley called SAGE (Senior Actualization and Growth Explorations) created by Gay Luce and others in 1974 introduced a group of elders to body movement, breathing exercises, visualization, dream work, massage, and various holistic healing practices. The main rule of SAGE was "pay attention."[6]

Although the term "New Age" has become so elastic as to be nearly meaningless except as a marketing tag, the phenomenon has profoundly altered many Americans, especially in the middle class, and will undoubtedly shape the ways they age. Whatever techniques or practices they espouse, those influenced by New Age beliefs look for meaning that busyness cannot provide. Those who have adopted spiritual practices identified as Native American have been rebuked for cultural appropriation, however. Indian writers such as Beth Brant, a Mohawk, who link nineteenth-century theft of their land with theft of their religion today, make a powerful moral claim. Whites drawn to the cosmology and ceremonies of American Indians understandably seek something meaningful, but they can never recreate the context in which the beliefs, rituals, and practices are rooted. Certainly, respect for elders is one feature of American Indian culture that others wish were part of their own. In an unusual instance of bridging cultures, some elderly Navajo in Arizona spend summers with their families on reservations and winters in nursing homes.

In feminist spirituality, the central place of old women is recognized, for it was they who lost influence in the rise of patriarchal religion. Writers such as Charlene Spretnak and Starhawk explore pre-Christian spiritual traditions in which women are honored. Feminist spirituality has strong links to the environmental movement. Some feminists revere Hildegard of Bingen, the medieval German mystic, healer, abbess, composer, artist, writer, and visionary ecologist who clashed with the pope over the fine points of Christian burial on the grounds of her convent. Feminists value Hildegard's concept of "greening power," a translation of *viriditas* by Matthew Fox.[7]

A counter to prescribed busyness is the idea that aging is a time for personal growth. An "often invisible gift of age," writes Martha Holstein, is the freedom "to discover ways to flourish that are personally satisfying" (1999, 372). Growth may be construed as a spiritual or moral task as it is for May Sarton's Caro Spencer in *As We Are Now* who says, after being put in a nursing home, "I intend to make myself whole here in this hell" (4). She wants to avoid the "corroding impurity" of the rage she associates with suicide (13). Personal growth may seem suitable to late life when a person has fewer responsibilities; has less ego need to be competitive; is less constrained by the opinion of others; and is motivated by the knowledge that time is short (Kalish, 126). Some old women are still caregivers, however, and when those they care for have dementia, the responsibility is heavy.

Personal growth is an aspect of aging comfortably. For some it may mean that racist, sexist, homophobic, or fat-phobic messages lose some of their power to wound. The death of a critical or authoritarian parent or spouse may allow an older person to grow into greater self acceptance. Or a caregiver may feel compassion for the first time for a parent whom she now experiences as vulnerable. Whatever form growth takes, many artists and writers see aging as "becoming oneself" (Rentsch, 263). Extremely busy lives leave scant room for that quest. At the end of an engrossing story of escape from calcified systems of belief and practice, from a "universal viewpoint," Don Hanlon Johnson writes, "Now I could relax into particularity" (219). That phrase sums up what aging might be.

Both *The Miracle of Mindfulness* by Thich Nhat Hahn and *Mindfulness* by Ellen Langer describe the value of paying attention and living in the present moment. This practice allows one to face the slow physical decline usual to aging. Not necessarily to *accept* it, although for some, acceptance of this change is part of a spiritual practice. In her essay "Aging as a Russian Doll," Leonore Friedman writes, "If we don't spin stories of failure and humiliation, what's happening is not a private, personal tragedy, but just what's happening in the great scheme of things" (77). One can practice mindfulness at any age, of course, but busyness is a huge obstacle for paid workers, parents, caregivers, and others. Retirement or a change to part-time work may be the occasion for adopting a spiritual practice such as meditation, unless non-work life becomes as busy as working life used to be. The sense of having enough time is a luxury in our society. Practices that change our relationship to time help us become aware that busyness is often self-inflicted. Undeveloped parts of the self may send out faint signals when we make time for quieting down and reflecting.

Silence is part of spirituality. People now over seventy must remember well a time when noise was less polluting, no boom boxes or Blue Angels roaring overhead, no blaring television commercials, no beepers going off in concerts or movies, no jet skis, ATVs, or leafblowers, no Muzak accompanying "please hold." Retreating from the assault of noise is challenging at a time when farmland falls to developers and hillsides are flattened by construction. Few Americans can easily get to totally quiet places. For an old woman or man who has lost a partner, silence must be desolating. And between spouses who have been unhappily together for decades, silence is neither calming nor comforting. But for the old who choose to turn inward to reflect on the meanings of their experience, silence is welcome. Silence restores the psychic energy that busyness depletes. It brings surprising (and sometimes unwelcome) insights. Healing touch offered in silence is a rare gift. In old age, if we have no family or friends nearby to turn to, silence can be a protector.

Late-life spirituality has been viewed as a compensation for loss of physical strength and mobility, but that is a limited notion, separating mind from body. Spirituality is rooted in the body, especially in breathing. Any breath work is useful to the old because our respiratory systems tend to weaken as we age. Focusing on the breath allows us to become more aware of our natural body rhythms and the relationship of parts of the body to each other. Asian practices now popular in the U.S. such as Tai Chi and Qi Gong encourage mind-body unity, as do yoga, meditation, and the various bodywork methods described in chapter 5.

Spirituality grounded in the body requires frankness about decline and loss of capacity. To speak of this honestly, writes Barbara Hillyer, an old woman "must defy the cultural prescription of false cheerfulness." Details such as fear of falling and fear of sight or hearing loss will counter our expectation "that an old feminist continues to be superwoman or is always optimistic about her aging" (55). After Doris Grumbach published her memoir *Coming Into the End Zone*, some readers complained that she had been too negative when she reported signs of physical decline (1993, 126–27). They wanted a favorite author to filter out the bad news.

A tendency among some old women and men to pare down to essentials may reflect spirituality, whether it is manifested in an ordinary way such as giving away possessions or moving to a smaller home or apartment, or more interiorly by shedding old prejudices, grievances, antipathies, or competitive feelings with siblings. If one likes slowing down and being quiet, worldly goods matter little. The local mall may appear a surreal circus. Lightening our load of accumulated possessions goes along with turning inward, not to tune out the external world but rather to lessen its intrusiveness. When this happens, one develops a heightened sense of integrity, in the old meaning of completeness. This impression is conveyed by writers over eighty such as Doris Grumbach, Florida Scott-Maxwell, and M.F.K. Fisher.

Learning to be old means noticing that where materialism sets the tone, determines priorities, and assesses meaning, the old lose value. Moving quickly is so valued in our culture, for example, that old women and men typically apologize when they are aware of moving more slowly than others. How could old women using canes or walkers believe their pace is not inferior, only different? What subtle harm does the speeded-up quality of much of American life cause the old? Appropriate to late life is "a consciousness of the value of slowness, of pausing, of calmly looking backward" (Rentsch, 271). Whether or not such values are associated with spirituality, their psychological benefit seems obvious.

Without an awareness of spiritual values, it is hard to connect the youth-worshipping materialism of American culture with the corresponding denigration of the old. Nineteenth-century American writers worried about the production/consumption model overtaking the ideals of the founders. The Transcendentalists, for example, linked conformity to materialism. Walt Whitman proposed that emotional bonds between men might create spiritual values as a counterweight to dehumanizing industrialism, and Margaret Fuller believed that democracy could flourish only through women's cooperative energy, "self-dependence," regard for old women, and respect for citizens of diverse backgrounds (Avallone, 140).

More recently, in the past decade, big business has pushed itself into spheres that were formerly somewhat independent of it, education, the arts, national parks. If you admire the view at Mirror Lake in Yosemite today, for example, you stand near a sign announcing that a major oil company gave money to the park. Baseball fields are now littered by advertising banners and college athletic events saturated by commercial posters and billboards. The old Metropolitan Opera is now the Texaco Exxon Metropolitan Opera. Many colleges have a contract with Coca-Cola agreeing to keep competitors off campus, and student and faculty ID cards have an ad for AT&T—stamped on the back. Credit card vendors peddle their wares on campuses, offering free gifts to lure students into the adult world of overconsumption and debt. "Corporations are remaking our public institutions and space" (Schor, 9). What all of this means for old women and men is that the values of commerce are now even more pervasive in American society than they were in the time of Whitman, Emerson, Thoreau, and Fuller, and that the materialism that tends to devalue the old is even more rampant than it was in the nineteenth century or even a decade ago.

On the other hand, the sheer number of older people now alive emphasizes a spiritual dimension to life or at least a non-material dimension. A significant part of the population is no longer caught up in the production of goods and services, in the cycle of "getting and spending," as Wordsworth succinctly described life in the Industrial Age. Therefore the meaning of their lives must be more than material. Otherwise, they are simply drags on everyone who does produce. Many believe this, of course, including proponents of rationing health care for the old. They see neither the economic value of the informal, unpaid work performed by many of the old, especially old women, nor the more abstract value of their friendships, knowledge, and life experience. Individuals who are old naturally see value in their own lives and regard their continued existence as desirable, but they are aging in a society that undervalues anyone deemed unproductive. By conspicuously not working, elders implicitly challenge the very great value placed on work in our society.

Conclusion

An increasing number of Americans will live twenty-five or thirty years in retirement, an opportunity for meaningful leisure and enjoyment that their parents and grandparents could not have imagined. Instead of responding to this demographic change with a set of values appropriate to late life, however, we are stuck with mid-life's emphasis on work and productivity. Unwisely, by "celebrating efficiency, productivity or power, we subordinate any moral claim for the last stage of life in favor of values that ultimately depreciate the meaning of old age" (Moody, Age, 1993, 34). This is not only shortsighted but manifestly sexist if productive aging becomes a rationale for weakening public support of the oldest old, the poorest of whom are usually women (Holstein, 1999, 366).

What would constitute a moral claim for the last stage of life? One component could be a belief that the survival of many to old age is intrinsically good, like the infinite variety and abundance of the natural world (at least before species began to disappear at an accelerated rate). The long-lived whose talents have fully flowered show the rest of us something about human potential. At any age, we benefit from contact with those in whom the life force is very strong. As recently as twenty years ago, the full spectrum of life was not as apparent as it is today. Long-term emancipation from work offers possibilities for growth, pleasure, enjoyment, and awareness that were once barely imaginable. Without that hope, old age is still inherently good, even allowing for all of the misery and degradation that often accompany it. To accept the proposition that old age is intrinsically good, it is not necessary to hold a religious view that suffering has meaning. A moral claim for the last stage of life must clearly separate aging from disease. The despair of some old women and men who are chronically ill or cut off from others seems a natural response to their hopeless situation, but that has been misread as a reason to devalue old age itself.

Robert Butler alludes to a spiritual view of aging when he describes lengthening lives as "the triumph of survivorship." His word suggests a good, like friend*ship* or fellow*ship*, and it connotes luck. Survivorship also suggests some action on our part. Each human who reaches eighty is a model of regeneration and adaptation. Centenarians tend to be resilient, mellow, and positive, often surprised by lasting as long as they have and amused by their singularity. So much threatens human life at every turn that mere survival surely deserves to be celebrated. Whatever survivorship means in the future as more people attain it, busyness is too limited a value to have a central place in its definition. It fits only the hearty survivors, and ultimately even they will fail to live up to it. Behind the busy ethic is the secret wish that midlife will extend indefinitely. Fear of the unknown and uncontrollable is natural, and attempts to ward it off through busyness understandable. But the inexorable process of change sweeps away our protective cover of busyness and deposits us, ready or not, at the border of old age.

Notes

1. Connie Goldman Productions, 1985. This excellent series broadcast on Wisconsin Public Radio includes interviews with M.F.K. Fisher, Josephine Miles, John Huston, Louise Nevelson, Burl Ives, John Cage, Hume Cronyn, and Jessica Tandy.

2. In "Productive Aging: A Feminist Critique," *Journal of Aging and Social Policy* 4, nos. 3–4 (1992): 17–34, Martha Holstein's policy recommendations include taking into account elder care in Social Security calculations and providing respite and income for grandmothers who parent.

3. For summaries of research on religion and aging, see Robert Atchley, *Social Forces and Aging*, 9th ed. (Belmont, Calif.: Wadsworth, 2000), chapter 11, and Jill Quadagno, *Aging and the Life Course* (Boston: McGraw-Hill, 1999), chapter 9. Several essays in Robert Atchley and Susan H. McFadden, eds., *Aging and the Meaning of Time* (New York: Springer, 2001) consider aging and spirituality. For an excellent brief discussion of the subject, see the last section of Margaret Urban Walker's essay "Getting Out of Line: Alternatives to Life as a Career," in *Mother Time*, ed. Margaret Urban Walker (Lanham, Md.: Rowman & Littlefield, 1999). See also Robert Atchley, "Spirituality," in *The Handbook of the Humanities and Aging*, 2nd ed. (New York: Springer, 2000).

4. An example is Stuart Spicker, Kathleen Woodward, and David Van Tassel, eds., *Aging and the Elderly: Humanistic Perspectives in Gerontology* (Atlantic Heights, N.J.:

Humanities Press, 1979). Van Tassel also edited *Aging and the Completion of Being* (Philadelphia: University of Pennsylvania Press, 1989). *Aging Today*, published by the American Society on Aging and edited by Paul Kleyman, features articles on the humanities and aging.

5. See Zalman Schachter-Shalomi and R. S. Miller, *From Age-ing to Sage-ing* (New York: Warner Books, 1997).

6. Gay Gaer Luce, *Your Second Life. Vitality and Growth in Middle and Later Years.* (New York: Delacorte Seymour Lawrence, 1979). Though out of print, this book is relevant today.

7. See his *Illuminations of Hildegard of Bingen* (Sante Fe: Bear Books, 1985). For a comprehensive and illuminating account of Hildegard's medical knowledge, see Victoria Sweet, "Hildegard of Bingen and the Greening of Medieval Medicine," *Bulletin of the History of Medicine* 73, no. 3 (1999): 381–403.

~

CHAPTER TEN

Gerastology: A Feminist's View of Gerontology and Women's Aging

I enter Payson Hall at the University of Southern Maine with a few students. They walk up the stairs to our classroom; I take the elevator. Women and Aging is our subject. For them, it is far off, like a trip to Mars. For me, it feels as imminent as the next baseball season. Noticing our different placements along the life course, I wonder why age gets so much attention in our society. How bizarre it would seem if one of the students didn't know her age. Though favored with only the faintest dusting of postmodern thought, I decide that power must be central here. "Old" is a category determining who has more and less power. Apparently we do not take on the identity "old"; it befalls us. It requires others to give it meaning. Like gender, aging can be performed.

The identity "old" can fade in and out of significance. If two seventy-five-year-old neighbors are talking, "old" need not be central to who they are, unless they happen to refer to bodily changes commonly attributed to the aging process. Even then, a conversation about arthritis remedies, for example, can occur outside of the web of meanings "old" has for the people around them. It need not focus on decline. When one of these women talks to a thirty-year-old, on the other hand, her old identity comes into play. She performs being old in relation to the younger woman not by any words or gestures, necessarily, but by having projected onto her the younger woman's culturally shaped notions of what old is. The older woman's statements or movements may be evaluated by the younger woman as being like those of an old woman, or unlike. She is progressive "for her age"; she walks vigorously "for her age."

Bodily differences between the women are undeniable. The older could wish for the metabolism, the vision, the taut skin, and the thick foot padding of the younger. Compared to her, the older woman has a greater risk of developing heart disease or of losing her autonomy. Otherwise, their similarities may be strong, but when hyperawareness of age blurs these similarities and creates expectations of difference, old women become the Other.

I perform "old" when I take the elevator to class instead of walking up the stairs. Clothes don't seem to mark me as different; we all wear pants and vests. No Doc Martens boots for me, though, or body piercings. When a student reports sighting a woman over sixty with a nose ring, other students applaud, and their surprise reflects a culturally-determined idea that "old" limits certain behavior or style choices. As I expound the social construction of aging, I wonder if I should not instead be talking of leaky bladders, morning stiffness, and impaired night vision. I shrink from such personal revelation. Students describe rehearsals for *The Vagina Monologues* and I can't even say the word "bladder." My generation brought the speculum into women's studies classrooms and planned nude solstice rituals, but the *aging* body is harder to present in an upbeat spirit. My reticence embarrasses me. It's as if the cogs in my feminist brain are running off track.

At least I can point out to students that "geron" is the Greek word for old man, and gerontology is literally the study of old men. I propose "gerastology" instead, the study of old women from a feminist perspective. Until my coinage catches on, feminist gerontology will have to do. The latter term is deficient, though, in that it presupposes a body of knowledge given a particular slant sometime after its creation. Gerastology begins in feminism.

But another embarrassment: old women have been missing persons in women's studies. And even though gerontologists have discovered gender, its multiple meanings have yet to be explored. "Like diners at separate tables, aging theorists and feminist sociologists [and other feminists] have been exchanging some meaningful glances but without pooling their conceptual resources" (Arber and Ginn, 1995, 2). To change the metaphor, the territory at the intersection of women's studies and gerontology has drawn only a few settlers.

This chapter first considers women's studies' neglect of aging, then turns to critiques of gerontology from within the discipline and critiques from a feminist perspective, and finally examines other issues for gerastology.

Women's Studies

The women's movement and women's studies have been very slow to name aging a women's issue and some would argue that the acknowledgement has not yet come. Why not? Many of us were young at the beginning of the second wave of feminism. Reproductive issues, workplace inequality, and violence against women have claimed our attention during the past thirty years. In addition, as Shulamit Reinharz points out, for some white, middle-class women adopting feminism seemed to require rejecting mothers, for they represented volunteering, housework, and living for husbands and children (81). To confront aging would have been not only to acknowledge our mothers but to stress likeness to them rather than the radical difference we exulted in. We suffered from "mother flu."[1]

In "Indian Summer," an autobiographical essay that is partly a reminiscence about her grandmother, Paula Gunn Allen writes that maturation in white America involves separation of generations and a struggle "to defuse the power mothers have over daughters." Among Indians, by contrast, the young are not inclined "to overthrow or trivialize elders" (189–90).

Another reason why women's studies has not taken on aging issues is that academic gerontology is a small field compared to sociology, history, literature, psychology and anthropology, where feminists have long been influential. A large number of the gerontologists who work outside of the academy are women, but that majority in itself has not ensured a feminist viewpoint, and thus the benefits of collaboration between women gerontologists and women's studies' faculty so far have not been realized.

Moreover, aging indisputably changes bodies, and we in women's studies have not wanted to locate too much meaning in bodies. If anatomy is not destiny, neither should biology be destiny. From Mary Wollstonecraft onward, feminists have argued that women's inferior status comes not from our bodily differences from men but from custom. Many falsehoods have originated in misunderstandings about women's bodies, the late nineteenth century fear that higher education would destroy ovaries and cause madness in women, for example. Given the need to find explanations outside of bodies, we in women's studies have averted our gaze from women over sixty, even if we are over sixty ourselves. But biology does play a role in aging. Accepting this requires a shift in our thinking. Yes, aging like gender is socially constructed, and culture determines the meanings we ascribe to physical change. But bodies matter.

Even so, women's studies professors and students, like others, are influenced by academic fashions, and aging is emphatically not a trendy subject. More approval greets an essay on the hegemonic discourse of valorized vapors than an essay on old women. The old are a stigmatized group that feminist students and teachers may unconsciously avoid. Like others, feminists fear changes in our appearance and our social power and thus aging has not seemed to be a promising subject for study (Arber and Ginn, 1991, 30).

Internalized ageism may be the most important reason most women's studies practitioners have paid little heed to old women. "Self-directed ageism," Mary Carpenter calls it in an essay on academic feminists. "The irrational loathing and terror of female aging casts a long shadow," writes Baba Copper. It divides generations and "robs women of the continuity of identity necessary for successful feminist resistance" (55). Irrational terror and loathing are much harder to examine in the classroom than wage discrimination or abortion.

The sorry record of the women's movement and women's studies on aging must be acknowledged before we can recognize our internalized ageism and from that analysis come to understand the strengths of old women. Without our contributions, public discussion of old women's issues where it exists at all will continue to be insubstantial, fragmented, or confined to economics. We in women's studies have yet to acknowledge three major demographic trends: the shift to an aging population; the increasing longevity of women; and the particularly rapid increase in the number of minority elders. All of these changes will profoundly shape the lives of American women in the twenty-first century.

Betty Friedan laid out many of the issues for white, middle-class women in *The Fountain of Age*, but her book seems to have had little impact. *Look Me in the Eye: Old Women, Aging, and Ageism* by Barbara Macdonald and Cynthia Rich (1983, 1991, 2001) is occasionally mentioned but Baba Copper's *Over the Hill: Reflections on Ageism Between Women* (1988) is rarely cited. These books were original and provocative enough to have inspired a body of work on ageism or the development of many courses on women's aging. That did not happen. Perhaps only after retirement or after caregiving responsibilities are thrust upon large numbers of us will feminists begin to focus on aging with the same awareness of social injustice that we brought to studies of reproduction, work, and violence against women.

In the following complaints about women's studies, I write as a loyalist, one whose life has benefited immeasurably from participation in the field.

From women's studies texts, course listings, conferences, videos and periodicals, one would never guess that population aging is one of the most important facts of contemporary American life or that aging is a major women's issue. The silence is remarkable. Old women are missing from *Feminism: The Biological Body* (Lynda Birke), from *Feminist Theory and the Body* (edited by Janet Price and Margrit Shildrick), and from many other women's studies books having the word "body" in the title. Among hundreds of books on display at the National Women's Studies conference in 2000, the only book on women's aging I found was *Mother Time: Women, Aging, and Ethics*, a collection of essays by feminist philosophers edited by Margaret Urban Walker. At the 2001 conference, a few books featuring old women's lives were displayed, but analytical work remains rare. The essays in *The Other Within: Feminist Explorations of Women and Aging*, edited by Marilyn Pearsall (1997), are an exception.

In *Women's Studies Essential Readings*, edited by Stevi Jackson, information about old women is not deemed essential. Old women get a brief mention under economic need in *Open Boundaries: A Canadian Women's Studies Reader*, edited by Barbara A. Crow and Lise Gotell, but are left out of the Annual Editions *Women's Studies 99/00*, edited by Patricia Ojea and Barbara Quigley. Old women and aging are two subjects missing from the index of the 561-page *Radically Speaking: Feminism Reclaimed*.[2] Articles on old women rarely appear in feminist periodicals aimed at a women's studies audience.

Ageist stereotypes appear in an introductory women's studies text.[3] The aging section begins by stating that "aging is a painful process for many mid-life and older women whose lives are marked by vulnerability to poverty, crime, poor health, and inadequate housing," and then attributes "physical fragility" to old women. The first problem here is that when middle-aged and old women are lumped together, their differences are overlooked, and attention is deflected from women over sixty-five. A forty-five-year-old may have little in common with a ninety-year-old. Second, the vulnerability mentioned in the text certainly exists, but it results not from age *per se* but from racism, sexism, heterosexism, and class bias. The privilege of upper-middle-class white old women is invisible here. In addition, nothing in the editors' introduction suggests that late life might be a time of growth and fulfillment for a woman. Finally, "fragility" characterizes some old women but not all. Of herself, an old woman might say that she moves slowly, uses a walker, or can't climb stairs. These specifics are more telling than the blanket term "fragility."

In a speech at the 1985 National Women's Studies Association conference, Barbara Macdonald denounced her audience for neglect of aging issues and exploitation of old women. You come to us when you need something, she charged, oral histories, material for grants or theses, histories of social movements. "You come to old women who have been serving young women for a lifetime and ask to be served one more time, and then you cover up your embarrassment as you depart by saying you felt as though we were your grandmother or your mother or your aunt" (124). Macdonald expressed anger at being either ignored or guiltily honored. "I don't know which is worse" (127). Her blunt assessment of women's studies—"we planned curriculum with an entire piece omitted, that of old age and the oppression of ageism"—remains accurate (127). Feminists have been more willing to reify a few extraordinary old women than to notice the many whose lives may resemble their own. The quality of May Sarton's work won her an audience, for example, but scarcity made her an icon.

Critiques of Gerontology from within the Discipline

Gerontology covers a wide territory "stretching from the microscopy of cells to the macrosociality of populations" (S. Katz, 119). Gerontologists work in the natural sciences, the social sciences, and the humanities, but little collaboration occurs across disciplines. In spirit, if not in practice, the field is interdisciplinary because gerontologists grapple with many of "life's big questions—its purpose, value, meaning, potential, and mystery" (Manheimer, 1992, 427). Social gerontology has produced a great quantity of data that are difficult to integrate (Birren, 463), and it lacks a unifying core of knowledge and models of interdisciplinary research (Estes, Binney, and Culbertson, 50).

In popular usage, gerontology and geriatrics, the medical study of late-life diseases, are often synonymous, so that the distinction between old-age illness and old age itself is blurred. Gerontology has uncritically accepted a medical model of aging not because of its intrinsic worth but because of medicine's great power. The ideology of biomedicine exerts a powerful influence on gerontology, not only in conceiving of human conditions as requiring medical intervention but also in making the individual the unit of analysis (Estes, Binney, and Culbertson, 51). The important problems in aging, rooted in issues of class, ethnicity, gender, politics, economics, and demographics, do not lend themselves to biomedical solutions (60).

Within a biomedical framework, aging problems result from bodily decline or the failure of individual adjustment, not from state policy, the economy, or social inequality (Townsend, 19). Recent studies of minority aging is an exception but the assumption that aging is a problem of adjustment informs much work in gerontology. Concepts of adaptation or adjustment are applied not only to elders but also to children, the sick, the disabled, prisoners, rehabilitated criminals, and immigrants (Hazan, 21).

Studies of individuals can be illuminating, however, if they tell how elders "resist rather than succumb to the pressures associated with growing old" (Phillipson, 139).

Life satisfaction studies, an example of a focus on individuals, were critiqued by Jaber Gubrium and Robert Lynott, who pointed out that the measurements convey a linear sense of time and assume that subject and questioner share the same understanding of life satisfaction. The measurements cannot reveal the "multiplicity of life," they overlook social ties, and they view subjects' lives as completed (31–37). In other societies, time is round or cyclic (Vincent, 80), or it may be a universal present (Langer, 1989, 32). Aging can be thought of as "nonlinear, simultaneous loss-gain" (Manheimer, 1992, 435). Such perceptions of time would make conventional tests and measurements difficult, and these have been important to gerontology because the discipline has presented itself as "hard" like science, not "soft" like the humanities.

In a review of a work on the psychology of women's aging, Mildred Seltzer notes that the authors' samples were white and middle-class and asks, "How generalizable are the findings?" (103). This is a large question for gerontology as a whole, not just for women's aging. Lars Tornstam coined the phrase "gerotranscendence" to describe the last stage in a "natural process moving toward maturation and wisdom" in which people exhibit less fear of death, less materialism, less self-centeredness and less focus on their bodies, more selectivity in friendships, a new self-knowledge, an ability to see patterns in their lives, and a heightened spiritual awareness (11–12). Working with Swedes and Danes, Tornstam used both quantitative and qualitative methods to develop his theory. Did his subjects demonstrate these qualities because they are old or because they are old Swedes and Danes? Material ease very likely underlies gerotranscendence.[4] It is an appealing theory that invites speculation about late-life growth, but the notion that a non-biological process is natural for older people seems questionable.

In surveys assessing elders' attitudes, making future plans is sometimes equated with good morale and mental health, but the capacity for planning implies sufficient resources and control over one's life, characteristic of middle-class people rather than those who are just getting by. Similarly, a researcher may design a questionnaire that assumes age is a primary status when that is not the case for many blacks, Chicanos, Asian Pacific Islanders and American Indians for whom survival is the main concern (Dressel, Minkler, and Yen, 280).

The impact of multiculturalism on gerontology is weak compared to other fields such as women's studies. The word "diversity" is used but often just as a banner (Calasanti, 1996, 147). Diversity is confused with heterogeneity, the former marking group difference and the latter referring to individual difference (148). A more serious problem is that diversity is seen as relating to a special group or problem rather than involving a power relationship between oppressed and privileged groups (155). Research on difference makes the dominant group the unacknowledged norm, whereas research that asks "why groups diverge relates the dominant group to racial/ethnic groups and all groups to each other" (148). Other aspects of cultural diversity within gerontology are discussed in chapters 6 and 7.

Traditionally, gerontology has been grounded in positivism, the philosophy of knowledge based on observable phenomena that can be measured. Under its influence, gerontology has focused on aging as a disease or deficiency (Manheimer, 1992, 427). More recently, knowledge has been regarded as variable, relative, and subject to different interpretations, and facts seen as "inseparable from our 'perceptual filters'" (Hendricks, 1992, 32), which include our ideas, research methods, and politics (Hendricks and Achenbaum, 33).

Critical Gerontology Overview

The term critical gerontology broadly describes perspectives developed in the 1980s and 1990s that challenge the positivism of earlier work. Seeing aging as socially constructed, it raises questions not considered by mainstream gerontology (Phillipson, 14).[5] A central issue in critical gerontology, for example, is the "emancipation of older people from all forms of domination" (Moody, Overview, 1993, xv). Thus critical gerontology parallels feminist theory. It fits in with a postmodern spirit of "play and relativity," shifting boundaries, and uncertainty about fixed categories such as youth, adulthood, and old age (xx). Contributors to *Critical Gerontology*, edited by Meredith Minkler and Carroll L. Estes, explore the consequences of declining state support for older Americans and the nature of interdependence between generations. Among their concerns are the political power of the old; aging economics; health care; and race, class, and gender differences that influence late life.

Another issue in critical gerontology is the export of U.S. aging models to countries in which they are inappropriate. Models from Western gerontology are falsely assumed to be universally applicable (137). In his article, "No Aging in India," Lawrence Cohen describes how programs such as senior day care and Meals on Wheels end up benefiting only relatively well-off Indian elders, not the vast numbers of the elderly poor. Questions about this issue or about the colonialist implications of overseas sales of prescription drugs aimed at the old are more likely to be raised by critical gerontology than by mainstream gerontology.

In *Old Age: Constructions and Deconstructions,* Haim Hazan expresses skepticism about gerontology, believing that "only a smattering of research is dedicated to deciphering the world of old people as subjects" (3). Thus it cannot do justice to the contradictions and ambiguities of aging (14). Moreover, the pursuit of knowledge about aging "endows the phenomenon with the illusion of intelligibility, but that very quest renders it unique and inexplicable" (93). Hazan is right about the limits of gerontology as an explanatory system, but feminists do not have the luxury of his degree of postmodern doubt because we have barely begun our investigation of women's aging.

In *Disciplining Old Age,* Stephen Katz applies Foucault's analysis of power, knowledge, and disciplinarity to tell how the elderly became *the elderly,* a separate and distinct group. Old bodies became a problem for science and medicine to define and control. The search for "normal" aging concealed class and gender bias as well as its own role in "relegating the aged to the margins of corporate industrial society" (Cole, 1992, 210). Gerontology has used nonscientific language and metaphors to "shore up its conceptual limitations" (Katz, 91).

Under the umbrella of critical gerontology fall political economy, moral economy, and the humanities.[6]

Political Economy

According to Carroll L. Estes, political economy relates treatment of the old to the national and global economy, the state, labor market conditions, and the social divisions of class, race, sex, and age (1991, 29). Implicit in this approach is a concern for social justice (Overbo and Minkler, 290). Estes coined the phrase "the aging enterprise" to denote all the service providers, agency workers, policymakers, and other professionals who foster dependency in the old and exert social control over them (1991, 25). "Enterprise" indicates that older Americans are often "processed and treated as a commodity" and that age policies that segregate the old stigmatize and isolate them (1979, 2). Aging bureaucracies serve their own interests, an Estes theme expressed in Isabelle Maynard's story "The House on Fell Street," in which a social worker pressured by her supervisor to take an elderly Russian refugee from his cramped room gradually realizes that his needs are more important than the needs of the system she serves.[7]

Blaming the old for the structural flaws of capitalism masks the shift of responsibility for elders from the state to individuals (Estes, 1991, 123). Thus the scapegoating of older Americans, described in chapter 2, has an economic dimension; ageism insufficiently explains it. A premise of political economy is that social structures influence both the way the old are viewed and the way they view themselves, thereby affecting "their sense of worth and power" (Estes, Critical, 1999, 29). Here political economy is aligned with the humanities. It is also aligned with feminist theory, although the emphasis on women's oppression distinguishes feminist theory from political economy (Hooyman and Gonyea, Feminist Perspectives, 18).

Moral Economy

Moral economy is defined by Meredith Minkler and Thomas Cole as "collectively shared assumptions defining norms of reciprocity" (38). Aspects of aging such as subjectivity, spirituality, and morality are lost sight of in gerontological theory; they are not just "dependent variables" to be explained in material terms (37–38). The mutually beneficial relationships of the old with others were noted in chapter 2. And, as Theodore Roszak notes, an accurate picture of the transfer of wealth between generations might show "aging parents keeping an underemployed son or jobless daughter afloat in the swirling waters of the global economy" (38). A moral economy perspective challenges the view that the individual is an "autonomous moral agent" (Robertson, 85), considers obligations as well as rights, and takes questions of need out of the marketplace where they are "commodified" (86). What is due the old, as members of a community? Without a framework of reciprocity, they are typecast as economic burdens.

The Humanities

The humanities include literature, philosophy, history, cultural studies, religion and art, both visual and performance art. Since the 1980s and especially since the 1990s, humanistic gerontology has been both corrective and illuminating, corrective in balancing ideas about aging set forth in the natural sciences and social sciences, illuminating in its new perspectives on aging. Humanists seek to restore a spiritual and moral dimension to aging and to resist management of old age, believing that many aging policies foster dependency and "fail to nurture basic strengths" (Moody, 1988, 11). This perception is reinforced by anthropological studies, for without romanticizing preliterate, preindustrial societies, anthropologists show that Western societies have "dealt with aging far less directly and less satisfactorily than many simpler societies" and that in America, the old are "a dislocated group—societal refugees—structurally alienated and unabsorbed" (Myerhoff, 1992, 107, 126). This summary helps to explain why the old in America are feared, why sickness is such an important role for many of them, and why busyness is culturally prescribed.

The humanities implicitly challenge prescriptions for aging based on materialism, for as Haim Hazan has remarked, "the accumulated capital of a lifetime of human experience has no direct equivalent in the economic marketplace" (19). The "productive aging" model comes from this market-place but paradoxically, it is not material enough, for it retreats from the material conditions of advanced old age. Someone with Alzheimer's, for example, can hardly be "productive" in a marketplace sense. Meaning for that person and her friends must therefore be found in more capacious views of aging.

The "facts" about aging from science and social science do not provide a neutral, objective understanding of late life but a value-laden interpretation. A deep tension between the humanities and mainstream gerontology arises from the difference between "prediction and control versus interpretation and self-actualization" (Moody, 2001, 413). The role of the humanities is to "open a door to new possibilities" (Berg and Gadow, 225). Slowing down, for example, can only be seen as a problem in traditional, science-based ger-ontology, but suppose that slowing down is not primarily a symptom but an opportunity to experience life more attentively (227). The idea is not com-pensation for loss (although that may be a part of healthy aging) but opening to something not available before. Humanities scholars do not simply counter negative views of aging with positive ones—the pains, deprivations, and shriveling of the self that may accompany aging are starkly revealed in modern literature—but seek to move beyond the either/or thinking shown by the division of aging into negative and positive aspects (Achenbaum, 426).

This split appears when writers, including feminist writers, contrast an old woman's diminished body with her spirit, always called "indomitable," as if the latter resides somewhere outside of her body. Another common example is the supposed incompatibility of erotic power and old age, sometimes juxta-posed to highlight dissonance. In a New Yorker review of James Merrill's Col-lected Poems, for example, Helen Vendler states that the poet wrote of "the incongruity of erotic feeling in an aging body" as if this were a truth universally acknowledged rather than a remnant of ancient prejudice (March 12, 2001, 102).

Metaphors transcend these limiting dualisms. Aging is a journey (Cole, 1992), an "abundance of life," (Moody, 1988), or a time of ripening. Aging is a kaleidoscope, its shifting images neither good nor bad. It is a mask that both hides and reveals an identity (Hepworth, 28). In popular culture, roughened and wrinkled old skin is abhorrent. Metaphorically, such changes express "the greater intricacies, the finer articulations that are possible in the person for whom reality has become many-layered, folded upon itself, woven and richly textured, a reality no longer ordered in the more familiar linear fashion, but now a world filled with leaps, windings, countless crossings, immeasurably more intricate and perhaps also more true than the world of one-dimensional thought" (Berg and Gadow, 227–28). Not all artists and writers understand aging in such complex terms, of course.

The contrast between a one-dimensional view of aging and a many-layered one is evident in the difference between two depictions of eccentric and "difficult" old women, Hattie in Saul Bellow's story "Leaving the Yellow House" and Flo in "Spelling" by Alice Munro. Both Hattie and Flo are surly and acrimonious but Hattie is also repulsive and drunken.[8] In her, old age itself appears loathsome. Munro, on the other hand, elicits affection for Flo through a complex blend of humor and irony. Dementia is disruptive but does not make Flo grotesque.

One of the most engaging nineteenth-century depictions of an old woman is Sarah Orne Jewett's protagonist in "The Flight of Betsey Lane" from *The Country of the Pointed Firs* (1896). In this story old age is regarded as normal. The ailments and complaints of Betsey and her friends, who live at a poor farm, are carefully detailed but illness and aging are not equated. A spirited, independent woman, Betsey leaves the farm to make her first long trip from the Maine village where she has spent her whole life. The story shows age gradations: at sixty-nine, Betsey is old, but her friends at the farm consider her "young to settle down 'long of old folks like us." "The Flight of Betsey Lane" is relevant today because Jewett imagines a woman having the most meaningful experience of her life in old age. Few writers have glimpsed that possibility.

The subtleties in Jewett's story foreshadow a promising development in the humanities, close attention to narratives of aging. Ronald Blythe interviewed elderly residents of an English village and presented their stories interspersed with his own observations in *The View in Winter*. *In the Ever After* is a collection of elder tales (fairy tales having an elderly protagonist) that Allan Chinen gathered from many cultures. Barbara Myerhoff found her elder tales among retired Jewish residents of Venice, California; *Number Our Days* is the title of both her book about them and a documentary film. A posthumously published collection of her essays is titled *Remembered Lives: The Work of Ritual, Storytelling, and Growing Older*. Another anthropologist, Sharon Kaufman, has explored narratives of dying to learn how it is understood by patients, families, and hospital workers. Kristin Langellier studies the role of *mémère* (grandmother) stories among Franco-Americans, stories often highlighting large families, hard work, poverty, discrimination, and religion as a force for cultural preservation. The emphasis on narrative marks a shift from the "human values" perspective of early work in the humanities and aging to issues of "personal, textual, historical, and cultural meaning" (Cole, 1993, viii).

In *Beyond Nostalgia: Aging and Life-Story Writing*, Ruth Ray describes narrative themes of people she works with, age, gender and ethnic differences, and the impact of groups on the writing process. In *The Journey of Life: A Cultural History of Aging in America*, Thomas R. Cole traces changing ideas about aging from the communal and religious ideas of early America to the secular, individualistic meanings dominated by science and medicine (xxx). The term "age studies" was coined by Margaret Morganroth Gullette to propose that "whatever happens in the body, human beings are aged by culture first of all" (1997, 3), an argument that works better for midlife than for old age but rightly challenges the view that old age is something we must adapt to. Age theory encourages resistance to "fragmentation of the life course" (1999, 228). A parallel to ethnic studies and women's studies is suggested by "age studies," in that all arise from differences based on bodies, but being old differs from being female or being black because bodily change is central to the process.

Another important theorist, Kathleen Woodward, edited *Figuring Age: Women, Bodies, Generations*, which includes analyses of painting, photography, and television and movie depictions of old women, accompanied by striking reproductions. *Aging and Gender in Literature*, edited by Anne Wyatt-Brown and Janice Rossen, examines late-life creativity. Ann Basting's work in performance and aging crosses several disciplines, including anthropology and theater. In an essay on the 1995 revival of *Hello Dolly* with Carol Channing, Basting concludes that Channing has changed and that "staying the same is really quite frightening" (260).[9]

Taken together, the humanistic scholarship cited here and work in social science influenced by the humanities is perhaps the most vital theoretical force in gerontology today. With feminist gerontology, it has the potential to transform the way Americans think about aging. But two large obstacles exist: the humanities so far have had little influence on gerontology as a whole and their practitioners have not found a large, public audience. The 1999 *Handbook of Theories of Aging*, edited by James E. Birren, overlooked theory from the humanities (McFadden, 133), and the ten-year MacArthur Foundation study of aging excluded humanities specialists (Achenbaum, 425–426). Moreover, when journalists or television interviewers need comment on some aging issue, they turn to doctors, scientists, government officials or demographers, not to philosophers, critics or artists (Achenbaum, 430). Thus one-dimensional views of aging are perpetuated. Learning to be old requires at least as much familiarity with the humanities as with social science.

A Feminist's Critique of Gerontology

A few feminist essays on women's aging were published in the 1970s and 1980s, but it was not until the mid-1990s that a small body of work could be identified as feminist gerontology.[10] "The aging woman" has been replaced by aging *women*. Whether the latter phrase can embrace those as diverse as black women in Alabama, working-class or middle-class, and the New England widows ensconced in twelve-room coastal "cottages" remains to be seen.

As objects of study, old women have been seen as a discrete group with knowable characteristics that remain fairly constant. Researchers almost always have higher status than their subjects. They study the most easily accessible subjects, typically those most like themselves. Conclusions or questions from studies frame future studies, and within this closed circle, the artifice is well concealed.

Attitudes toward women in mainstream gerontology are characterized by "androcentrism, biological determinism, and dualism" (Gannon, 8). A good example of the first is the Baltimore Longitudinal Study of Aging, begun in 1958 and carried on for twenty years without women. Biological determinism makes reproduction women's primary purpose and thus views menopause as a "deficiency disease," not as a life transition (Gannon, 9). Dualism is evident in the sharp division of women into premenopausal and postmenopausal, a way of overemphasizing reproduction (9).

In addition to being excluded from research, women have been included in distorting ways, for example when the conceptual models are taken from men's lives and women then measured against men (Quadagno, 1999, 39). Past research was limited to menopause, depression, widowhood, the empty nest, and poverty (Sapiro, 132), excluding equally relevant topics such as work, retirement, sexuality, diversity of women's aging experiences, stereotypes, and the social meanings of limited income (McDaniel, 1989, 60–61). Furthermore, when gender appears as a variable in quantitative research, it "flattens women into a single dimension, ignoring their heterogeneity" (Lopata, 116). Gender's impact is complex and pervasive, for the lives of old women tend to be marked by lower incomes, more chronic illness, stronger support networks, more social activity, loss of spouse, and longer lives (D. Gibson, 443). Early work used population samples that were flawed because they excluded people in institutions (mostly women) and excluded the oldest of the old (Herzog, 138, 140).

Research on older women has been limited by the assumption that they develop only through family roles and thus future studies should emphasize their individuality (Sinnott, 150–51). Alternatives to family focus and family dependency need to be explored, and future work should broaden the meaning of "families" to include those created by gay, lesbian, bisexual, and transgendered elders. Studies should no longer use the blanket category "unmarried" to cover divorced women, those separated from male partners, widows, never-married lesbians, and never-married heterosexual women.

Gerontology students are often assigned readings in the lifestage theories of Erik Erikson and Daniel Levinson, male models in which values such as separation, achievement, and autonomy are valued, "to the neglect of attachment, connection, and relationship." Thus, when these models are used to explain women's adult development, women may appear "inferior, incomplete, or deviant" (LeVande, 168). Moreover, the Erikson and Levinson models miss differences among women as they age (168). Feminists have studied attachment, connection, and relationship among children and adolescent girls, but not among old women (171). Late in his own life, Erikson modified his belief that wisdom is the particular province of old age by acknowledging that wisdom does not characterize this life stage if it has not been present long before (Hoare, 192).

The limitation of a male-centered perspective is vividly illustrated by Richard Posner's remark that women "might actually prefer a slightly shorter life expectancy if the consequences were to increase the utility of their lives when old by making it more likely that they would have male companionship" (280). Sometimes when conservative theorists leap into the Sea of Abstractions, they drown. Women's subordination to men is taken for granted here, and Posner assumes not only that all women are heterosexual but that all heterosexual women want male companionship late in life. "Utility" is the wrong measure for old women's lives.

Mainstream gerontology has tended to marginalize or neglect altogether lesbians and women of color. Lesbians are missing from Jean M. Coyle's *Handbook on Women and Aging* (1997), even from the essay on unmarried women, but the *Handbook* includes more women of color than Coyle's earlier work *Women and Aging: A Selected Annotated Bibliography* (1989). Gerontology on the whole has not made the progress reflected in the *Handbook*. One issue is the need to train culturally competent gerontologists. A study of predominantly white female college students who planned to enter the helping professions found they held stereotyped views of black elders based on television and movies: the elders were seen as stubborn, resentful, resistant to change, unintelligent, weak, and passive (Conway-Turner, 581). Simply adding information about black aging to the gerontology curriculum will not be sufficient to change attitudes, however; black studies courses are needed as well (586). Compared to gerontology, women's studies has been far more receptive to anti-racism work and more likely to require students to read works by public intellectuals such as bell hooks, Patricia Williams, and Gloria Anzaldúa. Although they do not treat aging directly, their analyses of racism, popular culture, the law, difference, and interlocking systems of oppression could influence social gerontology.

Feminists value reflexivity, by which they mean an awareness of the ways their identities—shaped by particular circumstances of time, place, gender, ethnicity, class—influence their work, and conversely, of the ways their work shapes their identities (Crawford and Kimmel, 3). Gerontologists, on the other hand, have been "singularly unreflective about their craft." They have not asked themselves about the consequences of their research or stepped back from explanations to ask why their theories are plausible (Estes, Binney, and Culbertson, 63). Critical gerontology and feminist inquiry acknowledge the hidden ways who we are determines what we see; neither this issue nor the related issue of power differences between researcher and subject is likely to be raised in mainstream gerontology.

Power in other forms is sometimes an unnamed but important aspect of gerontological studies, for example those focusing on prescription drugs, hip fractures, elder abuse, and reminiscence. Feminists must vigorously question the so far unchallenged central place of prescription drugs in women's aging. Although it contains much useful information, the Winter 2001 issue of *Generations* on medication and aging omits any discussion of gender, even though a woman is pictured on the cover.[11] By contrast, *Psychopharmacology from a Feminist Perspective* (Hamilton and Jensvold) covers many drug research and medical practices affecting women. The difference between these two publications reveals a chasm between mainstream gerontology and feminist gerontology. The prospect of increasing numbers of old women becoming increasingly drug dependent should prompt feminists to act. A good place to start would be demanding that the F.D.A. reinstate its ban on television drug advertising. Much more work needs to be done on the connection between prescription drugs and falls. Drug-induced lethargy, confusion or dizziness erodes the power of old women.

Feminists may also ask why reminiscence, a popular theme in gerontology, is now referred to in some publications as an "intervention," a word that shifts its focus from a creative process to managerial skill. A person's life story may be all that remains under her control. Social workers, health care providers, senior center directors, and others attribute benevolent intentions to themselves and speak of "empowering" the elderly, but the exercise of professional power over them remains largely unexplored. In an essay on nursing ethics, Sally Gadow notes that in clinical settings, "the discrepancy between the hidden body of the professional and the exposed, emphasized body of the patient is not just an expression of power: it is one of its sources" (1988, 9). Reminiscence is another kind of exposure, in the presence of one who need make no personal revelation herself, one whose power derives in part from not being known. (Other aspects of reminiscence are discussed in chapter 3.)

On a more practical level, women who suffer hip fractures deserve longer and better rehabilitation than is now available to them; restoration of full function should be the goal. When current practice emphasizes accommodating problems, it indirectly encourages dependency (Estes, Aging Enterprise Revisited, 1999, 140). The voices of women who have experienced falls must be incorporated into research and into recovery programs. Old women who have not fallen realistically fear that they will. How does this fear limit them physically and psychologically?

In mainstream gerontology, elder abuse is usually thought to result from caregiver stress or, more recently, from dysfunctional family patterns. Gender is missing from the analysis. A *Generations* issue on elder abuse published in 2000, for example, considers many different aspects of the problem but not gender. Current approaches obscure the role of men as perpetrators (Whittaker, 147). A feminist alternative to the caregiver stress or dysfunctional family models is to locate elder abuse in the patriarchal family (156). While noting that women may also be abusers, this perspective asks how power operates in different contexts (152). Since few voices of elder abuse survivors have been heard, little is known about the social context of abuse or the strategies women use to cope (153). When elder abuse is seen through conventional models, a person or family is identified as the problem, not the large structures that create and maintain power differences.

The inadequacy of individualism as a model for aging, suggested by this point, was noted in the preceding section and in earlier chapters. For women in small, rural communities, lack of public transportation may be the single largest impediment to healthy aging, but they must cope with this systemic failure as if it were their individual problem. Have they aged "unsuccessfully"? In this case, a social and economic problem having nothing to do with bodily change may decrease women's mobility and thus lessen their strength and energy.

Feminist theorists have questioned the emphasis on competition that often accompanies individualism and the belief that each person's interest is sharply separated from that of others (Grimshaw, 175), a belief underlying exaggerated fear of an aging population for example. Since the lives of many women involve service to others, feminists grapple with the difficult problem of staking out a claim for their own interests while attending to those of others (184).

Some feminists have turned away from quantitative analysis, while others believe it can be useful either by itself or in combination with qualitative methods. They value the latter because it recognizes that the data reflect not only the social and cultural worlds of subjects but also their inner lives (Herzog, 150). Quantitative work *on* elders must be balanced by research *with* them so that the work is shaped by their perceptions and concerns (Arber and Ginn, 1995, 13). It is useful and sobering to know, as *JAMA* reported, that one in five elders has taken prescription drugs such as tranquilizers and anti-depressants that leave them susceptible to falls (December 12, 2001), but what is the subjective experience of this statistic for individual old women?

The terms "old age" and "elder abuse" disguise gender differences, just as "teen violence" masks the fact that boys are nearly always the culprits, and "family violence" diverts attention from the sex of the perpetrators. Gerontology, even to some degree its revisionist branch, critical gerontology, has unwittingly helped perpetuate the relative powerlessness of old women by regarding them as marginal figures, even though their numbers clearly place them at the center of aging. Thus feminists must challenge the authority of mainstream gerontology to draw the maps of our third age and thoroughly rethink aging itself. Women's aging must now be seen in light of the cumulative impact of discrimination over a lifetime (Ollenburger and Moore, 213). A feminist model for aging, according to Nancy Hooyman, would examine not only inequities across the life span but also consider women's strengths and potential for change (Research, 1999, 116). This is a more ambitious and complex model than one that envisions feminist thought on aging as primarily a response to ageism.

Gerastology

Besides identifying the flaws and shortcomings of mainstream gerontology's understanding of old women, feminists must propose other approaches. This is the harder task. A few feminist essays have been published in the *Gerontologist* and in the *Journal of Women and Aging*, suggesting receptivity to alternative viewpoints, but gerastology will require multiple voices because of the breadth of women's aging issues. In the following pages, I consider several topics that lend themselves to a feminist analysis: the strengths evident among many old women; longevity; life changes; housing; aging research; standpoint theory and crones.

Strengths

These have been noted in previous chapters in amongst the dangers and problems of women's aging. Feminists stress "agency," the concept that women are not completely controlled by their circumstances. Even though women are "variously molded" by social location and by cohort, they "resist denigration and domination by whatever means available" (Markson, 1999, 501). Literary examples bear this out. In Alice Walker's story "The Welcome Table," for example, an old black woman who is expelled from a segregated church finds her own path to Jesus. In "Trifles," a play by Susan Glaspell (1916), farm women conceal evidence that would convict their neighbor, a woman who has killed her abusive husband, of murder. Forms of resistance to domination differ in a group as heterogeneous as old women. Those sustained by an ethic of sturdy individualism will make different choices than those who live collectively, for example. Class privilege will insulate some older women but at the same time it may also pressure them to alter their bodies to disguise signs of physical aging.

Cross-cultural research demonstrates that in many societies, women's power and status increase with age. Old women are not only energetic and capable, they are leaders (Cool and McCabe, 108). Thus obstacles to old women functioning as powerful figures in mainstream American society are cultural, not biological. Certainly many were and are powerful among American Indians, Onondaga women of the Iroquois nation, for example. In *Women: An Intimate Geography*, Natalie Angier summarizes anthropological research suggesting that "selection favors robustness after menopause" because the food gathering skill of a grandmother helps increase the survival chances of her grandchild (248). The inference is that robustness after menopause could be seen as usual, not anomalous.

Some old women give each other informal help, an important aspect of women's aging that may be invisible to social science researchers. A drawback to documenting this help might be appearing to show that old women's needs can be met privately, for example that the gaps created by cutbacks in home health care can be filled by individual effort. The informal help older women give each other has been called "peer care," an alternative to institutional care or care by families. Reciprocal help characterizes a relationship between two individuals, but peer care envisions networks of old women developing ways of care that "they both construct and manage" (Fiore, 247).[12] If women's longevity increases, such networks will be invaluable.

Longevity

The dramatic twentieth-century extension of longevity was caused by changes such as better diet and health care, notes Alice Rossi, but these "environmental changes" (as opposed to genetic) could be reversed by other environmental changes, so that

> all future generations in developed societies may not necessarily live as well or as long as have recent generations. It is therefore only an optimistic faith in the persistence of improved diet and health that underlies the prediction that future generations in Western societies will be healthy, large, long-lived creatures, and that the age composition of society will be increasingly tipped to an older population (112).

A pessimist might note that AIDS has already lowered longevity rates in Africa. Neither the government nor scientists can predict the impact on longevity of global warming, bio-chemical terrorism, air and water pollution, genetically modified food, or the increasing use of antibiotics and hormones on farm animals. In thinking about women's greater longevity, feminists must ask not only what benefits it confers but also how it is suppressed by social policies that deprive many old women of adequate incomes and health care. If indeed selection favors robustness after menopause, how does cultural aging get in the way?

Change

Old women's potential for change, a theme touched on in earlier chapters, is expressed metaphorically by Gloria Wade-Gayles:

> I was always interruptible, always accessible and available. . . . I was like a plant from which one takes cuttings. A piece for this one. A piece for that one. . . . Although there were times when I could feel the blade, I did not regret the cuttings. They strengthened my roots. . . .
>
> But there is a time when a plant should be left still, when the number of cuttings should be reduced, when it should be left undisturbed in the light of its own nourishing sun. Now is that time for me (20).

A survey of work on women's aging concluded that processes are more important than events; women go through "transitions and transformations" (Seltzer, 1994, 163), such as the one Wade-Gayles describes. We need primary sources to illuminate these changes: hundreds of diaries, oral histories, reminiscences, letters, novels, poems, plays, interviews, speeches, essays, and dialogues between women of different ethnic and class backgrounds. Other useful sources include labor archives, legislative testimony, and court records (Herzog, 151–52). The Canadian Film Board's outstanding documentary *Strangers in Good Company* offers a glimpse of the past and present lives of diverse old women, one of whom, Mary Meigs, described the process of making the film in her book titled *In the Company of Strangers*.

The importance of primary sources is emphasized by Gloria Wade-Gayles when she points out that she cannot find books in which black women describe *their* aging. "The way that racism exacerbates ageism, which is further exacerbated by class, is our project and nobody else's" (14). Unfortunately, many black writers have died before they could become old, including Audre Lorde, Pat Parker, Barbara Christian, Toni Cade Bambara, Rhonda Williams, and June Jordan. In "Indian Summer," Paula Gunn Allen reports seeing "virtually nothing written by elder women for elder women that is connected to my own experience of this part of my life journey" (186).

How can we teach ourselves and each other to heed our aging bodies? What constitutes close and loving attention to them? The study of old bodies could encourage us to perform ordinary actions like sitting, walking, standing, and driving more comfortably. How can we breathe more easily and deeply? Imagine a massage club for old women. No body shame here, no apologies for wrinkles, sagging skin, or thickened middles. No self-denigrating humor. To understand aging bodies, we need more work like Mary Felsteiner's essay "Casing My Joints: A Private and Public Story of Arthritis," in which she explores the meanings of rheumatoid arthritis as a woman's disease.

In another important essay, "The Embodiment of Old Women: Silences," Barbara Hillyer asks why so little has been written about the physical changes women experience. To notice them and not comment makes the aging female body "an unspeakable subject or at least beneath notice" (53). Discussing physical changes should be a normal part of self care for women as they age. Instead, menopause is considered the most important physical event for older women, accounts of "successful" aging focus on activity or accomplishments as if old bodies don't matter, and gerontologists do not inquire about physical changes unless they point to diseases or social problems. If an old woman talks of stiff joints or an unsteady gait, she may be discounted as a whiner. An old woman who honestly describes her bodily experience rebels against the expectation that she be cheerful (48–55).

Housing

To refute the stereotype that the old are lonely or isolated, gerontologists cite statistics about frequency of contact with families, but quality of contact eludes measurement. Suppose that living alone, the pattern for more than half of women over seventy-five, is not conducive to optimal physical and psychological health. It is true that many old women report a preference for living alone. They like the freedom from obligation. Would daily contact with a circle of friends better satisfy companionship needs? Old women alone in their houses, apartments, or rooms may pay a high price for the extreme individualism of our culture. Living alone, considered a personal choice, is perhaps more significantly a conditioned response to social circumstance.

Communal or group living for older women is imagined only as confinement in board and care houses or nursing homes. But if a group of middle-class women pool their resources, they could have individual dwellings and common areas—dining room, laundry room, recreation room, reading room—an arrangement that might better suit them than living with families or living alone, the only choices now available. Many women could not envision such an arrangement because their lives center on family rather than friends. But families are not organized to meet the needs of old women, while alternative living could be so arranged. Intergenerational housing of non-relatives could be one form. Why does housing designed for older people assume that they will be a married couple or a single woman? Why not have units for two or more women living together? (Burwell, 202).

Aging Research

What would aging research look like if old women themselves conducted in-depth interviews with thousands of diverse old women? Research on this scale would be hard to fund and carry out, and if a large quantity of data could be gathered, it might reveal the limits of generalization. Aging research was simpler when samples were 17,000 male doctors who went to Harvard. They are easy to find. Locating participants in barrios, on reservations, in hospitals and nursing homes, in community college classes, in rural churches, would be harder. Frieda Kerner Furman found her subjects in a beauty parlor. A large body of data would give feminists a clearer sense of the implications for social policy and for individual lives of women's greater longevity, chronic illness, and likelihood of living alone and being poor.

Feminists must ask questions that others do not ask. How does lesbians' aging differ from that of heterosexual women, for example? When minority women elders age in a new homeland away from their extended family, will their experience be more isolating than that of men (Arber and Ginn, 1995, 12). What about gender difference in treatment of terminally ill patients?[13] What is unique about the concerns of the oldest old women? How much of the late-life physical and psychological illness of women is caused by or exacerbated by long-repressed memories of childhood sexual abuse? That question is unasked in mainstream gerontology and in critical gerontology. The loss of driving ability signals social, religious, recreational, and aesthetic losses for old women in this culture; it marks official obsolescence (Carp, 256). How does a woman withstand this private shame? How will globalization and the loss of union jobs affect older women? (McDaniel, 2001, 43). What do we lose individually and collectively by attempting to reduce old age "to the wide and widening expanse of middle age," asks Martha Holstein. Does aging still have a special place in human life? (2000, 329).

Obstacles to the development of feminist gerontology noted by Ruth Ray are the small number of women doing the work, the lack of places to publish, and the suspicion of colleagues that feminist gerontology is not scholarly. It's time to "step out of bounds," she concludes (1999, 182). Out there we will need to find ways to bring health care, social science, and the humanities into closer alignment when the subject is old women. That ambitious agenda will require resistance to academic specialization as it is currently practiced.

A method for studying sexual harassment has applications for research on old women. Canadian scholars asked teenaged girls to keep journals recording their feelings about harassment they experienced. Groups met monthly to discuss relevant issues. Only after these had been identified and discussed by students did researchers formulate their questionnaires on sexual harassment (Larkin, 17–18). In a similar collaborative spirit, Sharon Jacobson designed her dissertation on lesbians and leisure with the help of an advisory panel who gave her feedback at every stage of her work. Members of Old Lesbians Organizing for Change created a slogan expressing their attitude toward research: "Nothing About Us Without Us."

In both women's studies and gerontology, advocacy has an awkward relationship with academic specialization. When careers are built on the study of disadvantaged people, what are the ethical obligations to advocate for those whom one studies? If the group known as "the old" dissolves, who will lose power? The facile use of the term "empowerment" by some feminist gerontologists (in the way "diversity" and "multiculturalism" are invoked as feel-good words) suggests a benevolent regard for those seen as less able than themselves. Who has asked old women what power means to them?

Postmodernism complicates the relationship between advocacy and academic specialization by questioning traditional categories such as "woman" and "old" and by challenging the validity of authoritative statements. But feminists cannot easily reject authoritative theoretical or political statements because women are oppressed and feminism aims to improve women's lives (Gagnier, 24). While it is probably inevitable that academic feminists reject a belief in "one single unseamed reality 'out there' composed of facts which researchers can establish as the 'truth' about social life" (Stanley, 263), there is a danger in seeing all as relative and contingent, for from this perspective, suffering and the political action that aims to alleviate it seem remote or futile.

Standpoint Theory

A lively debate among feminists centers on standpoint theory, the idea that women have access to a special knowledge, leading to a "truer (or less false) image of social reality" than the image available to white men (Harding, 185). Standpoint theory presupposes that people will develop different knowledge frameworks depending on their experiences and their circumstances (Hirschmann, 167) and that knowledge is particular rather than universal (Hekman, 25). A black woman's standpoint has a "legacy of struggle" at its core (Collins, 1997, 581), for example. The relevance of this debate for women's aging is that some have claimed for old women a special knowledge of the aging process. Shevy Healey believes for example that gerontology credentials do not create aging experts; the old themselves are "the *only* experts available" (1994, 109). But aging is not only an individual process; it is also a social construction whose workings are often hidden from view. Healey gives too much weight to personal experience. Being old does not by itself produce an understanding of the biology of aging, the ways that other cultures conceive of old age, or the intricacies of the federal aging bureaucracy. Gerontological knowledge is admittedly limited, partial, and contested, but some familiarity with it can inoculate against social control. The idea that old women have a special knowledge of aging is too attractive to cast aside, however. But which old women? Feminist theory posits that "women" is not a universal category. If the same is true of "old women," who are the privileged knowers of aging? Those who have paid the closest attention might be one answer.

Crones

In response to ageism, some feminists have created crone ceremonies to celebrate empowerment and creative aging when a woman turns fifty.[14] Perhaps we remember our mothers' dread of reaching this age and reluctance to acknowledge it. The received meaning of crone, an ugly, withered old woman, is rejected in favor of wise and powerful. Crones defy social messages to conceal their age in shame. They are "free to be who we are and to speak out as we must" (Onyx, Leonard, and Reed, 176). The Biblical figure Naomi is viewed as a crone by Shoni Labowitz, who notes that "crone" is related to "crown" and that in many societies, the crone was the "crown citizen." Naomi gave advice wisely and self-confidently. "A crone, like Naomi, doesn't ask, 'Am I doing it right? What are they thinking of me?' Instead she asks, 'Do I want to do this? How can I do it most consciously and effectively?'" (228–29, 239).

Although these notions of crones are attractive, crones and croning exemplify the social construction of aging by replacing negative stereotypes with positive ones; they still assume that chronology confers fixed meanings. Declaring women over fifty wise and powerful simply by virtue of their age obscures their individuality. It is a way of not seeing them. When young and middle-aged feminists attribute wisdom to women older than themselves, their effort to be positive about aging perhaps masks their anxieties. At the end of her illuminating essay on menopause, Jacqueline Zita writes, "To deconstruct the meaning of menopause in a male gerontocracy is to construct a social and cultural space for the empowerment of crones," whom she praises as "unruly. . . old, wise, and furiously heretical" (110). This statement essentializes old women. It sees them as monolithic. The notion that they should be unruly or heretical says more about the needs of younger women than about old women themselves. When we project onto an old woman our wish that she be rebellious, we romanticize her.

Furthermore, when old women are positively stereotyped as crones, white women mistake their experience for universal experience. The crone is a European figure taken over by white Americans to compensate for the hatred of old women in mainstream culture. Blacks, Latinas/os, Indians, and Asian Americans are not burdened by this tradition, although they may be influenced by it because of its cultural dominance. Figures analogous to the crone may be familiar to them, *curanderas* in Latina culture, for example, and many grew up with grandmothers and other female relatives who were powerful and revered.[15]

Whisper the Waves, the Wind, a beautiful film about a diverse group of old women, takes place on a beach in La Jolla.[16] All wearing white, the women sit at round tables discussing their lives. A few stroll on the beach. They obviously love being together; later they gather for a reunion. They speak profoundly about their aging. As the film opens, the women are on a bus listening to one of the filmmakers thank them for participating. "You are our goddesses," she tells them, "you are our oracles, voices of experience that we can turn to." In the conversations that follow, however, neither the goddess nor the oracle appears, and the women do not present themselves as guides for others. The roles imposed on them by the filmmaker apparently have no meaning for them. Calling an old woman an oracle treats her as if her life were over. She is seen as a finished product.[17]

If, on the other hand, we think that an old woman continues to develop, we may be less likely to put her on a pedestal. Invoking positive stereotypes shows an understandable wish to take the sting out of aging, but instead makes signs and emblems of old women. Assigning attributes such as wisdom and power to a class of people was perhaps justified when only a few reached old age and those who did stood out. The situation is very different now. The crone holds an honored place, but she is not a template.

Conclusion

Whatever students take away from Women and Aging, I hope that their fears will be eased. Specific concerns are realistic—poverty, loss of mobility, age discrimination—but the generalized fear of getting old is an insidious and debilitating fear that feminists must bring into the light. If my students' aging will mirror others' attitudes about how it should unfold and if these attitudes are socially constructed, how much freedom will they have to age in their own ways, and how can they determine what their ways are? Years from now, hyperawareness of their age by others may construct images that they will have to notice in order to resist. They will then share with women of color, poor women, and disabled women the need to expend psychic energy deflecting distorted images of themselves.

Aging has been called the "ultimate challenge in a woman's life, testing the limits of her resources and capabilities" (Gaylord, 64–65). Because her resources and to a lesser extent her capabilities will largely be determined by the politics of aging, gerastology must be skeptical of "successful" aging, "productive" aging, or other prescriptions that disguise inequity and power difference. "One size fits all" aging models will not do for women. Pressures to keep busy, for example, can coerce old women into prolonging the service role that gerontologists, including feminist gerontologists, have uncritically accepted as appropriate for them. If feminist gerontology develops theory connecting individual aging with the structures that shape it (McDaniel, 2001, 44), a bridge between women's studies and critical gerontology can be created.

The most pressing question in gerastology is how can we—we old women, we service providers inside and outside the home, we researchers, students and teachers—improve the health, well-being, and social standing of women in late life? This question does not deny the value of knowledge for its own sake or require that every study have practical application. But it assumes a double focus: the lives of old women and the professional work made possible by those lives. Twenty years ago, Nancy Datan wrote that old women are doubly disadvantaged by the "narrowing horizons of old age" compounded by traditional discriminations they face, but at the same time, their late-life potential is greater than that of men (124). This paradox still defines women's aging.

The influence of postmodernism on feminism has shifted the focus from things to words, "from concern with 'real' things—the everyday realities of women's oppression—to critiquing representations" of them (Rendell, 20). This insight helps to explain women's studies' neglect of aging, but whatever our reservations about postmodernism, we feminists cannot return to an essentialized, sentimentalized and ultimately patronizing view of old women as either uniformly wise or universally oppressed. By virtue of their experience and their placement in the social hierarchy, some old women may have a special knowledge of aging, and previous neglect of them gives this knowledge great importance. But the category of wise old woman can be relinquished. At this unique, historical moment of a burgeoning population of old women, meaning lies in particulars. Having no models, we improvise. Later, perhaps, we organize.

Notes

1. Natalie Angier, *Women: An Intimate Geography* (New York: Anchor Books, 1999), 254. She adds, "We daughters, like pit vipers, have nonretractable fangs."

2. I picked these examples at random, but other women's studies books could as easily have been used. It is somewhat unfair to look at only one aspect of a work, but without being specific, I could not emphasize the point that old women's issues are usually absent from texts.

3. Amy Kesselman, Lily D. McNair, and Nancy Schniedewind, eds., *Women, Images and Realities: A Multicultural Anthology,* 2nd ed. (Mountain View, Calif.: Mayfield, 1999). Their selections on aging are excellent.

4. I base this inference on Tornstam's statement that some subjects in his study volunteered after hearing a lecture on gerotranscendence.

5. In discussing critical gerontology, Chris Phillipson overlooks the important contributions of women scholars, including Kathleen Woodward, Anne Wyatt-Brown, Ruth Ray, Toni Calasanti, Nancy Hooyman, Judith Gonyea, Jill Quadagno, Martha Holstein, Sally Gadow, Kathleen Slevin, and Margaret Morganroth Gullette. Chris Phillipson does cite the work of Meredith Minkler and Carroll L. Estes. See *Reconstructing Old Age: New Agendas in Social Theory and Practice* (London: Sage, 1998), chapter 2.

6. Others have a different schema. Phillipson divides critical gerontology into political economy, the humanities, and biographical and narrative perspectives. In her essay "A Postmodern Perspective on Feminist Gerontology," Ruth E. Ray considers feminist gerontology to be a part of critical gerontology. Harry R. Moody's "Overview: What is Critical Gerontology and Why is it Important" omits feminism. In *Disciplining Gerontology,* Stephen Katz identifies cultural studies as part of critical gerontology, and Margaret Morgenroth Gullette's essay in the *Handbook of the Humanities and Aging,* 2nd ed., is titled "Age Studies as Cultural Studies." The *Handbook* is edited by Thomas R. Cole, Robert Kastenbaum, and Ruth E. Ray (New York: Springer, 2000).

7. For political economy, see Carroll L. Estes and Associates, eds., *Social Policy and Aging. A Critical Perspective* (Thousand Oaks, Calif.: Sage, 2001); and Carroll L. Estes and Jane L. Mahakian, "The Political Economy of Productive Aging," in *Productive Aging,* ed. Nancy Morrow-Howell, James Hinterlong, and Michael Sherraden (Baltimore: Johns Hopkins, 2001)

8. The depiction of old characters as alcoholics reverts to a stereotype in Greek and Roman drama. Why contemporary writers rely on it is a question worth investigating.

Perhaps writers see old age as depressing and drinking as a means of escape. Drunken characters are also supposed to be funny and they have an identifying tag.

9. See also Lois Banner, *In Full Flower: Aging Women, Power, and Sexuality* (New York: Knopf, 1992); Barbara Frey Waxman, *To Live in the Center of the Moment: Literary Autobiographies of Aging* (Charlottesville, Va.: University Press of Virginia, 1997); *What Does it Mean to Grow Old*, ed. Thomas R. Cole and Sally Gadow (Durham: Duke, 1986); *Images of Aging: Cultural Representations of Later Life*, ed. Mike Featherstone and Andrew Wernick (London: Routledge, 1995); *Aging and Identity, A Humanities Perspective*, eds. Sara Munson Deets and Lagretta Tallent Lenker (Westport, Conn.: Praeger, 1999); and Ruth Ray, "The Search for Meaning in Old Age: Narrative, Narrative Process, Narrativity, and Narrative Movement in Gerontology." *Gerontologist* 42, no. 1 (2002): 131–136.

10. Work on women from a mainstream gerontological perspective was published in these decades. Marilyn Pearsall's anthology *The Other Within* (Boulder, Colo.: Westview, 1997) reprints some of the notable early feminist work including Pauline Bart's essay on older Jewish women, Jacquelyn Johnson Jackson's essay on older black women, Emily Abel's study of caregivers, and an essay on older women in the city by Elizabeth W. Markson and Beth B. Hess.

11. Janice L. Feinberg edited the *Generations* issue on medication. Women have been well-represented in *Generations* as authors and guest editors.

12. See also the other essays in the "Living Arrangements" section of *Mother Time*: Anita Silvers on reciprocity and interdependence, Martha Holstein on home care, and Joan C. Tronto on age-segregated housing.

13. See, for example, N. Jane McCandless and Francis P. Conner, "Working with Terminally Ill Older Women: Can a Feminist Perspective Add New Insight and Direction?" *Journal of Women and Aging* 11, nos. 2–3 (1999): 101–114; and S. Miles and A. August, "Courts, Gender, and the 'Right to Die'" *Law, Medicine, and Health* 18 (1990): 85–95.

14. For interpretations of crones, see Edna Ward, *Celebrating Ourselves: A Crone Ritual Book* (Portland: Astarte Shell Press, 1992); Barbara Walker, *The Crone* (San Francisco: Harper and Row, 1985); and Ursula LeGuin, "The Space Crone" in *The Other Within*, ed. Marilyn Pearsall.

15. I thank Mirtha Quintanales for this connection.

16. *Whisper the Waves, the Wind*, directed by Suzanne Lacy and Kathleen Laughlin, produced by Suzanne Lacy, Terra Nova Films, 1986.

17. Stephanie Ross pointed this out to me.

Conclusion: The Paradoxes of Aging

Aging is full of contradictions, ironies, and paradoxes. Our chronological age is both meaningful and meaningless. Nothing special, the aging process is made special by fear, denial, and the belief that it is a problem or a disease, all attitudes that are culturally determined. Our aging bodies carry these meanings because we age here, now. Old women and men are resented for their costly illnesses, but the health promotion programs that would keep them well are denied them. In this society, we have low expectations of elders, many of whom have untapped potential for social good. The loss of what they could offer is hard to calculate, but the incidence of late-life depression, alcoholism, and sickness would probably decline if meaningful social roles were available for them. The role of wise elder cannot be translated to industrial societies, but neither can the discarding of the old characteristic of American society continue. As their already large numbers grow, the gap between capacity and opportunity must be addressed.

In late life our bodies demand more attention, but giving them too much is a trap because it leads to the sick role and overdrugging. Decline is thought to be the main theme of aging, and yet for many old age is a time of ripening, of becoming most ourselves. For women it may be both freeing and limiting—freeing if latent power and creativity can be expressed; limiting if chronic illness or lack of money narrow life possibilities. Aging is increasingly a female phenomenon; yet health care, public policy, and gerontology have not adapted to the rise in the numbers of women over eighty, and women's studies continues to focus on the young and middle-aged. Our aging population is multicultural, but the institutions that deal with aging tend to be monocultural.

Paradoxically, aging is both within our control and beyond our control.

How much of each depends on class, ethnicity, and gender. Grasping this paradox is liberating for it says our responsibility is only partial. Norms such as "successful aging" and "productive aging" put the whole burden of aging well upon us. Instead, we might grade Social Security or Medicare as unsuccessful or unproductive. Comfortable aging or conscious aging, possibilities rather than models, recognize the social forces of aging. The preceding chapters have attempted to shed light on these forces and to suggest the limits of individualism as an aging philosophy. At the same time, individualism in the sense of nonconformity may be stressed too little in aging. The old who ignore ageist messages march to their own drummer. Women who outgrow subordination to men, who know their own minds and speak for themselves, are nonconformists.

Another paradox is that the many agencies and organizations for the old, run by caring professionals, have an uncaring dimension. They not only assume need (and sometimes create dependency) based on the arbitrary classification of "senior citizen," but also assume a match between elders' needs and existing programs. Many of these organizations could be run by elders themselves, or elders could decide that other services would better suit them. Or they could decide that whatever their needs, they do not fit neatly into an age-segregation model. Pieties about the wisdom of the old notwithstanding, they are often treated like people who require management. Aggregation of "the old" is convenient for service providers, but may not be in the best interest of elders themselves. Even the term "elder," which conveys more dignity than "senior citizen," may be an unwelcome, superimposed designation.

Learning to Be Old is about resistance, not only to the all-encompassing category of "old" that places such strong emphasis on *difference* from others. The notion that aging is mainly biological must also be resisted because it obscures cultural aging. Even as a biological process, aging can be misunderstood if our capacity for repair, regeneration, and healing is underestimated. I have urged resistance to white, middle-class male bias in gerontology, to ageist stereotypes, to prescribed busyness, and to scapegoating the old for population aging. I have tried to depict women over sixty-five as very diverse.

Examples from other cultures demonstrate that the way we age now in America is only one way. Some castes in Nepal, for example, have the custom of carrying a person through the village in a palanquin once he or she has attained the age of 60, a celebratory event quite different in spirit from our own age markings.[1]

Resistance to medicalized aging is now extremely difficult, but we can at least be aware of its dangers and limitations, especially for women. Above all,

Learning to Be Old urges resistance to overdrugging, to the unacknowledged power the drug industry now exerts over our aging and would like to exert over the aging of people in other countries. Beyond resistance, we need to imagine new ways of understanding and experiencing late life, ways that emphasize development in the face of some decline. The body/mind split will have to be overcome. The stigma attached to frailty and dependence will have to be lifted. A change in consciousness similar to that brought about by the civil rights movement and the women's movement will be necessary to achieve these transformations.

From stories, poems, plays, memoirs, oral histories, and interviews with elders have come complex and illuminating interpretations of aging, and as more old women write and tell about their experiences, the many dimensions of their aging will be better understood. If the humanities play a larger role in shaping our common awareness of late life, and if they can balance bio-medicine and social science, new ways of knowing aging may be possible. Power, resilience, and rediscovery of skills and knowledge are the themes for example of *Two Old Women*, an Athabaskan legend retold by Velma Wallis. Abandoned in a time of famine, the women survive against great odds and eventually save the lives of their tribe.

In the Nevelson gallery of the Farnsworth Museum in Maine is an abstract etching of a woman titled "The Ancient One" (1953–1955). Neither fear nor revulsion are projected onto the figure, and she is not romanticized. In this striking work, Louise Nevelson transcends the social construction of aging. Will others be able to do the same?

Note

1. Satyam Barakoti told me about the palanquin rides in Nepal.

References

Abel, Emily K. "Family Care of the Frail Elderly: Framing an Agenda for Change." *Womens Studies Quarterly* 17, nos. 1–2 (1989): 75–85.

———. *Who Cares for the Elderly? Public Policy and the Experiences of Adult Daughters.* Philadelphia: Temple, 1991.

Achenbaum, W. Andrew. "Afterward." In *Handbook of the Humanities and Aging*, 2nd ed. Edited by Thomas R. Cole, Robert Kastenbaum, and Ruth E. Ray. New York: Springer, 2000.

Adams, Chris. "FDA Scrambles to Police Drug Ads' Truthfulness." *Wall Street Journal* (Jan. 2, 2000): A4.

Aging News Alert. "Program Improves Frail Seniors' Lives." (April 20, 1999): 7.

———. "Vitamin D Deficiency is a Major Factor in Half of Women's Falls." (May 4, 1999): l0.

Agronin, Marc E. "The New Frontier in Geriatric Psychiatry: Nursing Homes and Other Long-term Care Settings." *Gerontologist* 38, no. 3 (1998): 388–91.

Alcon, Arnaa and Judith Apt Bernstein. *Women of Labor Speak Out on Retirement, Finances, Health Care and Caregiving.* Waltham, Mass.: National Policy and Resource Center on Women and Aging, Brandeis, n.d.

Allen, Jessie. "Caring Work and Gender Equity in an Aging Society." In *Women on the Front Lines.* Edited by Jessie Allen and Alan Pifer. Washington, D.C.: Urban Institute, 1993.

Allen, Paula Gunn. "Indian Summer." In *Long Time Passing: Lives of Older Lesbians.* Edited by Marcy Adelman. Boston: Alyson, 1986.

———. *Off the Reservation.* Boston: Beacon Press, 1998.

Andrews, Molly. "The Seductiveness of Agelessness." *Ageing and Society* 19 (1999): 301–18.

Angel, Jacqueline L. "Coming of Age: Minority Elders in the United States." *Gerontologist* 40, no. 4 (2000): 502–07.

Annan, Kofi. "Address at Ceremony Launching the International Year of Older Persons (1999)." *Journal of Gerontology: Psychological Sciences* 54B, no. 1 (1999): P5–P6.

Anzaldúa, Gloria. Introduction to *Making Face, Making Soul: Haciendo Caras*. Edited by Gloria Anzaldúa. San Francisco: Aunt Lute Books, 1990.

Anzick, Michael A. and David A. Weaver. "Reducing Poverty Among Elderly Women." ORES Working Paper Series, no. 87. Washington, D.C.: Office of Research, Evaluation, and Statistics, Social Security Administration (2001): 1–25.

Applebome, Peter. "Second Acts and Beyond." *New York Times* (November 22, 1998): 4:1.

Arber, Sara and Jay Ginn, eds. *Connecting Gender and Ageing: A Sociological Approach*. Buckingham: Open University Press, 1995.

———. *Gender and Later Life*. London: Sage, 1991.

Archbold, Patricia A. "The Impact of Parent Caring on Women." *Family Relations* 32, no. 1 (1983): 39–45.

Arluke, Arnold and John Peterson. "Accidental Medicalization of Old Age and its Social Control Implications." In *Dimensions: Aging, Culture and Health*. Edited by Christine L. Fry. New York: Praeger, 1981.

Ashliman, D. L. "Aging and Death in Folklore." 1997. www.pitt.edu/aging.html (accessed 10–7–2000).

Atchley, Robert. *Social Forces and Aging*, 9th ed. Belmont, Calif.: Wadsworth, 2000.

Avallone, Charlene. "The Red Roots of White Feminism." In *Teaching and Research In the Academy*. Edited by Mary Anderson et al. East Lansing: Michigan State University Women's Studies Program, 1997.

Baltes, Margret M. *The Many Faces of Dependency in Old Age*. Cambridge: Cambridge University Press, 1996.

Barker, Pat. "Alice Bell." *Union Street*. New York: Putnam, 1983.

Barusch, Amanda S. *Older Women in Poverty*. New York: Springer, 1994.

Basting, Anne Davis. "Dolly Descending a Staircase: Stardom, Age, and Gender in Times Square." In *Figuring Age*. Edited by Kathleen Woodward. Bloomington: Indiana, 1999.

Bayne-Smith, M. "Health and Women of Color: A Contextual Overview," in *Race, Gender and Health*. Edited by M. Bayne-Smith. Thousand Oaks, Calif.: Sage, 1996.

Bazzini, Doris G. "The Aging Woman in Popular Films: Underrepresented, Unattractive, Unfriendly, and Unintelligent." *Sex Roles* 36, nos. 7–8 (1997): 531–44.

Beizer, Judith. "Medications and the Aging Body: Alteration as a Function of Age." *Generations* 8, no. 2 (1994): 13–17.

Bell, Diane and Renate Klein, eds. *Radically Speaking: Feminism Reclaimed*. North Melbourne: Spinifex, 1996.

Bellow, Saul. "Leaving the Yellow House." In *Literature and Aging: An Anthology*. Edited by Martin Kohn, Carol Donley, and Delese Wear. Kent, Ohio: Kent State University Press, 1992.

Bennett, James. "Hidden Malnutrition Worsens Health of Elderly." *New York Times* (October 10, 1992): 1: 10.

Berdes, Celia and Mary Erdmans. "Aging in Polonia: Polish and Polish American Elderly." In *Age Through Ethnic Lenses: Caring for the Elderly in a Multicultural Society*. Edited by Laura Katz Olson. Lanham, Md.: Rowman & Littlefield, 2001.

Berg, Geri and Sally Gadow. "Toward More Human Meanings of Aging." In *Fierce with Reality: An Anthology of Literature about Aging*. Edited by Margaret Cruikshank. St. Cloud, Minn.: North Star Press, 1995.

Bergman, Barbara R. and Jim Bush. *Is Social Security Broke? A Cartoon Guide to the Issues*. Ann Arbor, Mich.: University of Michigan, 2000.

Bernard, Miriam. "Backs to the Future? Reflections on Women, Ageing, and Nursing." *Journal of Advanced Nursing* 27 (1998): 633–40.

Binstock, Robert H. "Public Policy and Minority Elders." In *Serving Minority Elders in the 21st Century*. Edited by May L. Wykle and Amasa B. Ford. New York: Springer, 1999.

Birke, Lynda I. *Feminism and the Biological Body*. New Brunswick: Rutgers, 2000.

Birren, James. "Theories of Aging: Personal Perspective." In *Handbook of Theories of Aging*. Edited by Vern Bengtson and K. Warner Schaie. New York: Springer, 1999.

Black, Helen K. and Robert L. Rubinstein. *Old Souls: Aged Women, Poverty, and the Experience of God*. New York: Aldine De Gruyter, 2000.

Blakeslee, Sandra. "A Decade of Discovery Yields a Shock About the Brain." *New York Times* (January 4, 2000): D1.

Blythe, Ronald. *The View in Winter*. New York: Harcourt Brace, 1979.

Bodily, Christopher. "'I Have No Opinions. I'm 73 Years Old!' Rethinking Ageism," *Journal of Aging Studies* 5, no. 3 (1991): 245–64.

Bonner, Joseph and William Harris. *Healthy Aging*. Claremont, Calif.: Hunter House, 1988.

Bortz, Walter. "Aging and Activity," in *The Practical Guide to Aging*. Edited by Christine Cassel. New York: New York University Press, 1999.

———. *We Live Too Short and Die Too Long*. New York: Bantam, 1991.

Brandler, Sondra M. "Aged Mothers, Aging Daughters." *NWSA Journal* 10, no. 1 (1998): 43–56.

Brant, Beth. "Anodynes and Amulets." In *Writing as Witness*. Toronto: The Women's Press, 1994.

Brody, Jacob A. "Postponement as Prevention in Aging." In *Delaying the Onset of Late Life Dysfunction*. Edited by Robert N. Butler and Jacob A. Brody. New York: Springer, 1995.

Brody, Jane. "Americans Gamble on Herbs as Medicine." *New York Times* (February 9, 1999): D1.

———. "Changing Nutritional Needs Put the Elderly at Risk Because of Inadequate Diets." *New York Times* (February 8, 1990): B7.

———. "Drunk on Liquid Candy: U.S. Overdoses on Sugar." *New York Times* (November 24, 1998): D7.

Bruner, Jerome. "Narratives of Aging." *Journal of Aging Studies* 13, no. 1 (1999): 7–9.

Buell, John. "Drug Prices that Fuel Monopolies." *Bangor Daily News* (October 12, 2000): A11.

Burkhauser, Richard V. and Timothy M. Smeeding. "Social Security Reform: A Budget Neutral Approach to Reducing Older Women's Disproportionate Risk of Poverty." Syracuse, N.Y.: Maxwell School of Citizenship and Public Affairs/Center for Public Policy Research, 1994.

Burton, Linda M., Peggye Dilworth-Anderson and Vern L. Bengtson. "Creating Culturally Relevant Ways of Thinking about Diversity and Aging: Theoretical Challenges for the Twenty-First Century." In *Diversity: New Approaches to Ethnic Minority Aging*. Edited by E. Percil Stanford and Fernando Torres-Gil. Amityville, N.Y.: Baywood, 1992.

Burwell, Elinor J. "Sexism in Social Science Research on Aging." In *Taking Sex into Account: The Policy Consequences of Sexist Research*. Edited by Jill McCalla Vickers. Ottawa: Carleton University, 1984.

Butler, Robert. "Ageism: Another Form of Bigotry." *Gerontologist* 9 (1969): 243–46.

———. "Butler Reviews Life Review." *Aging Today* (July-August 2000): 9.

———. Letter to the Editor. *New York Times* (January 8, 2001): A20.

———. "New World of Longevity: 12 Ideas for Vital Aging." www.ncoa.org/news (accessed September 1999).

———. "Revolution in Longevity." In *Delaying the Onset of Late-Life Dysfunction*. Edited by Robert Butler and Jacob A. Brody. New York: Springer, 1995.

———. "The Life Review: an Interpretation of Reminiscence in the Aged." *Psychiatry* 26 (1963): 65–76.

———. *Why Survive? Being Old in America*. New York: Harper and Row, 1975.

Butler, Sandra S. and Barbara Hope. "Relying on Themselves and Their Communities: Healthcare Experiences of Older Rural Lesbians." *Outward: Newsletter of the Lesbian and Gay Aging Network of the American Society on Aging* 5, no. 1 (1998): 2, 8.

Bytheway, Bill. *Ageism*. Bristol, Pa.: Open University Press, 1995.

Calasanti, Toni M. "Bringing in Diversity: Toward an Inclusive Theory of Retirement." *Journal of Aging Studies* 7, no. 2 (1993): 133–50.

———. "Incorporating Diversity: Meaning, Levels of Research, and Implications for Theory," *Gerontologist* 36, no. 2 (1996): 147–156.

Calasanti, Toni M. and Anna M. Zajicek. "A Socialist-Feminist Approach to Aging: Embracing Diversity." *Journal of Aging Studies* 7, no. 2 (1993): 117–131.

Calbom, Cherie and Maureen Keene. *Juicing for Life*. Garden City, N.Y.: Avery, 1992.

Callahan, Daniel. "Age, Sex, and Resource Allocation." In *Mother Time: Women, Aging, and Ethics*. Edited by Margaret Urban Walker. Lanham, Md.: Rowman & Littlefield, 1999.

Callahan, James J. "Imagination: a Resource Policy." *Gerontologist* 38, no. 3 (1999): 388.

Cameron, Kathleen A. "Drug Risk Should Not Be Ignored." *Aging Today* (Nov.-Dec. 1999): 10.

Campbell, Steve. "Allen Stirs Up Drug Industry with Senior Discount Bill." *Maine Sunday Telegram* (June 30, 1999): 1A.

Carp, Frances M. "Living Arrangements for Midlife and Older Women." In *Handbook on Women and Aging*. Edited by Jean M. Coyle. Westport, Conn.: Greenwood, 1997.

Carpenter, Mary Wilson. "Female Grotesques in Academia: Ageism, Antifeminism, and Feminists on the Faculty." In *Antifeminism in the Academy*. Edited by Veve Clark et al. New York: Routledge, 1996.

Caselli, Graziella. "Future Longevity Among the Elderly." In *Health and Mortality Among Elderly Populations*. Edited by Graziella Caselli and Alan D. Lopez. Oxford: Clarendon Press, 1996.

Cassel, Christine. "Ethics and the Future of Aging Research." *Generations* 16, no. 4 (1992): 61–65.

———, ed. *The Practical Guide to Aging*. New York: New York University Press, 1999.

Cather, Willa. "Paul's Case." In *The Troll Garden* (1905).

Chinen, Allan B. *In the Ever After: Fairy Tales and the Second Half of Life*. Wilmette, Ill.: Chiron, 1989.

Christian, Barbara. "The Race for Theory." In *Making Face, Making Soul: Haciendo Caras*. Edited by Gloria Anzaldúa. San Francisco: Aunt Lute Books, 1990.

Claire, Thomas. *Bodywork*. New York: William Morrow, 1995.

Clark, Margaret. "Contributions of Cultural Anthropology to the Study of the Aged." In *Cultural Illness and Health*. Edited by Laura Nader and Thomas Maretzki. Washington, D.C.: American Anthropological Society, 1973.

Clifton, Lucille. "The Things Themselves." In *What We Know So Far: Wisdom Among Women*. Edited by Beth Benatovich. New York: St. Martin's, 1995.

Cohen, Lawrence. *No Aging in India: Alzheimer's, The Bad Family, and Other Modern Things*. Berkeley: University of California, 1998.

———. "No Aging in India: The Uses of Gerontology." *Culture, Medicine, and Psychiatry* 16 (1992): 123–61.

Cole, Thomas R. *The Journey of Life: A Cultural History of Aging in America*. Cambridge: Cambridge University Press, 1992.

———, ed. *Voices and Visions of Aging: Toward a Critical Gerontology*. New York: Springer, 1993.

Collins, Patricia Hill. "Defining Black Feminist Thought." In *The Woman That I Am*. Edited by D. Soyini Madison. New York: St. Martin's, 1997.

———. "Toward a New Vision: Race, Class, and Gender as Categories of Analysis and Connection." In *Women's Voices, Feminist Visions*. Edited by Susan M. Shaw and Janet Lee. Mountain View, Calif.: Mayfield, 2001.

Colman, Hila. "Just Desserts." *New York Times Magazine* (May 3, 1998): 84.

Comfort, Alexander. "Age Prejudice in America." *Social Policy* 7, no. 3 (1976): 3–8.

———. *A Good Age*. New York: Crown, 1976.

Conway-Turner, Katherine. "Inclusion of Black Studies in Gerontology Courses." *Journal of Black Studies* 25, no. 5 (1995): 577–88.

Cool, Linda E. "The Effects of Social Class and Ethnicity on the Aging Process." In *The Elderly as Modern Pioneers*. Edited by Philip Silverman. Bloomington: Indiana, 1987.

———. "Ethnicity: Its Significance and Measurement." In *New Methods for Old-Age Research*. Edited by Jennie Keith and Christine L. Fry. South Hadley, Mass.: Bergin and Garvey, 1986.

Cool, Linda E. and Justine McCabe. "The 'Scheming Hag' and the 'Dear Old Thing': The Anthropology of Aging Women." In *Growing Old in America*, 3rd ed. Edited by Beth B. Hess and Elizabeth W. Markson. New Brunswick, N.J.: Transaction, 1986.

Cool, Lisa Collier. "Forgotten Women: How Minorities are Underserved by Our Healthcare System." In *Women's Health Annual Editions 98/99*. Edited by Maureen Edwards and Nora L. Howley. Guilford, Conn.: Dushkin-McGraw-Hill, 1998.

Coontz, Stephanie. *The Way We Never Were: American Families and the Nostalgia Trap*. New York: Basic Books, 1992.

Copper, Baba. *Over the Hill: Reflections on Ageism Between Women*. Freedom, Calif.: Crossing Press, 1988.

Coyle, Jean M., ed. *Handbook on Women and Aging*. Westport, Conn.: Greenwood, 2001.

———. *Women and Aging: A Selected Annotated Bibliography*. Westport, Conn.: Greenwood, 1989.

Crawford, Mary and Ellen Kimmel. "Promoting Methodological Diversity in Feminist Research." *Psychology of Women Quarterly* 23 (1999): 1–6.

Crimmins, Eileen M. "Defining Disability and Examining Trends." *Critical Issues in Aging*, no. 2 (1998): 10–11.

Crow, Barbara A. and Lise Gotell, eds. *Open Boundaries: A Canadian Women's Studies Reader*. Toronto: Prentice-Hall Canada, 2000.

Cruikshank, Margaret, ed. *Fierce with Reality: An Anthology of Literature about Aging*. St. Cloud, Minn.: North Star Press, 1995.

Dailey, Nancy. *When Baby Boom Women Retire*. Westport, Conn.: Praeger, 1998.

Datan, Nancy. "The Lost Cause: Aging Women in American Feminism." In *Toward the Second Decade*. Edited by Betty Justice and Renate Pore. Westport, Conn.: Greenwood, 1981.

Davidson, Warren. "Metaphors of Health and Aging: Geriatrics as Metaphor." In *Metaphors of Aging in Science and the Humanities*. Edited by Gary Kenyon, James E. Birren, and Johannes J.F. Schroot. New York: Springer, 1991.

Davis, Karen, Paula Grant, and Diane Rowland. "Alone and Poor: the Plight of Elderly Women." In *Gender and Aging*. Edited by Lou Glasse and Jon Hendricks. Amityville, N.Y.: Baywood, 1992.

Deaton, Gail, et al. "The Eden Alternative: an Evolving Paradigm for Long Term Care." In *Annual Editions Aging, 02/03*. Edited by Harold Cox. Guilford, Conn.: Dushkin-McGraw-Hill, 2002.

de Beauvoir, Simone. *The Coming of Age*. Translated by Patrick O'Brian. New York: Norton, 1996. Paris: Editions Gallimard, 1970.

Delaney, Sarah Louise and Annie Elizabeth Delaney. *Having Our Say: The Delaney Sisters' First 100 Years*. New York: Kodansha International, 1993.

Dembner, Alice. "Research Integrity Declines." *Boston Globe* (August 22, 2000): E1.

DeParle, Jason. "Early Sex Abuse Hinders Many Women on Welfare." *New York Times* (November 28, 1999): 1.

Dinnerstein, Myra and Rose Weitz. "Jane Fonda, Barbara Bush and Other Aging Bodies: Femininity and the Limits of Resistance." *Feminist Issues* 14, no. 2 (1994): 3–24.

Donovan, Josephine and Carol J. Adams, eds. *Beyond Animal Rights: A Feminist Caring Ethic for the Treatment of Animals.* New York: Continuum, 1996.

Doress-Worters, Paula B. and Diana Lasker Siegal, eds. *The New Ourselves Growing Older.* New York: Simon and Schuster, 1994.

Downes, Peggy, ed. *The New Older Woman.* Berkeley: Celestial Arts, 1996.

Dressel, Paula. "Gender, Race, and Class: Beyond the Feminization of Poverty in Later Life." In *The Other Within: Feminist Explorations of Women and Aging.* Edited by Marilyn Pearsall. Boulder, Colo.: Westview, 1997.

Dressel, Paula, Meredith Minkler, and Irene Yen. "Gender, Race, Class, and Aging: Advances and Opportunities." In *Critical Gerontology. Perspectives from Political and Moral Economy.* Edited by Meredith Minkler and Carroll L. Estes. Amityville, N.Y.: Baywood, 1999.

"Drugs Fuel Health Costs." *AARP Bulletin* 41, no. 1 (2000): 8.

"Drugs and Older Women: How to Protect Yourself." *Women's Health Advocate* (September 1997): 4–6.

Eastman, Peggy. "Drugs that Fight Can Hurt You." *Modern Maturity* 40, no. 3 (1999): 14–16.

Ebersole, Priscilla and Patricia Hess. *Toward Healthy Aging,* 5th ed. St. Louis: Mosby, 1998.

Edmonds, Mary McKinney. "The Health of the Black Aged Female." In *Black Aged.* Edited by Zev Harel, Edward A. McKinney, and Michael Williams. Newbury Park, Calif.: Sage, 1990.

Eichenwald, Kurt and Gina Kolata. "A Doctor's Drug Studies Turn into Fraud." *New York Times* (May 17, 2000): A1.

Ekerdt, David. "The Busy Ethic: Moral Continuity between Work and Retirement." *Annual Editions Aging.* 13th ed. Edited by Harold Cox. Guilford, Conn.: Dushkin-McGraw-Hill, 2000.

Emerman, Jim. "Futurecare: The Web, Virtual Services and even 'Carebots.'" *Aging Today* 22, no. 1 (2001): 11–12.

Emerson, Ralph Waldo. "Self Reliance." 1841; 1847. *The Heath Anthology of American Literature,* 3rd ed., vol 1. Edited by Paul Lauter. Boston: Houghton Mifflin, 1998.

Estes, Carroll L. *The Aging Enterprise.* San Francisco: Jossey-Bass, 1979.

———. "The Aging Enterprise Revisited" In *Critical Gerontology: Perspectives from Political and Moral Economy.* Edited by Meredith Minkler and Carroll L. Estes. Amityville, N.Y.: Baywood, 1999.

———. "Critical Gerontology and the New Political Economy of Aging." In *Critical Gerontology.* Edited by Meredith Minkler and Carroll L. Estes. Amityville, N.Y.: Baywood, 1999.

———. "A Feminist Perspective on the Privatization of Social Security." Paper presented at the annual meeting of the Gerontological Society of America, Chicago, November 17, 2001.

———. "The New Political Economy of Aging," In *Critical Perspectives on Aging.* Edited by Meredith Minkler and Carroll L. Estes. Amityville, N.Y.: Baywood, 1991.

Estes, Carroll L., Elizabeth Binney, and Richard Culbertson. "The Gerontological Imagination: Social Influences on the Development of Gerontology, 1945-Present." *International Journal of Aging and Human Development* 35, no. 1 (1992): 49–65.

Estes, Carroll L. and Liz Close. "Public Policy and Long-Term Care." In *Aging and Quality of Life*. Edited by Ronald P. Abeles et al. New York: Springer, 1994.

Estes, Carroll L. and Karen W. Linkins. "Decentralization, Devolution, and the Deficit: The Changing Role of the State and the Community." In *Resecuring Social Security and Medicare: Understanding Privatization and Risk*. Edited by Judith Gonyea. Washington, D.C.: The Gerontological Society of America, 1998.

Evans, W. and D. Cyr-Campbell. "Nutrition, Exercise, and Healthy Aging." *Journal of the American Dietetic Association* 97, no. 6 (1997): 632–38.

Facio, Elisa. "Chicanas and Aging: Toward Definitions of Womanhood." In *Handbook on Women and Aging*. Edited by Jean M. Coyle. Westport, Conn.: Greenwood, 1997.

Fahs, Marianne C. "Preventative Medical Care: Targeting Elderly Women in an Aging Society." In *Women on the Front Lines*. Edited by Jessie Allen and Alan Pifer. Washington, D.C.: The Urban Institute, 1993.

Family Caregiving in the U.S. Findings from a National Survey. Washington, D.C.: National Alliance for Caregiving and AARP, 1997.

Farris, Martha and John W. Gibson. "The Older Woman Sexually Abused as a Child: Untold Stories and Unanswered Questions." *Journal of Women and Aging* 4, no. 3 (1992): 31–44.

Featherstone, Mike and Andrew Wernick, eds. *Images of Aging: Cultural Representations of Later Life*. New York: Routledge, 1995.

Feinson, Margorie Chary. "Where are the Women in the History of Aging?" *Social Science History* 9, no. 4 (1985): 429–52.

Felsteiner, Mary Lowenthal. "Casing My Joints: A Private and Public Story of Arthritis." *Feminist Studies* 26, no. 2 (2000): 273–85.

Fiore, Robin N. "Caring for Ourselves: Peer Care in Autonomous Aging," In *Mother Time*. Edited by Margaret Urban Walker. Lanham, Md.: Rowman & Littlefield, 1999.

Flaherty, Julie. "Preaching the Merits of a Multistep Program." *New York Times* (June 13, 1999) 15: 3.

Fleming, Juanita. "Ensuring Racial and Ethnic Diversity in the Health Professions." *Healthcare Trends and Transitions* 6, no. 4 (1995): 24–32.

Foner, Nancy. "Caring for the Elderly: a Cross-Cultural View." In *Growing Old in America*, 3rd ed. Edited by Beth B. Hess and Elizabeth W. Markson. New Brunswick, N.J.: Transaction Books, 1986.

Foster, Susan E. and Jack A. Brizius. "Caring Too Much? American Women and the Nation's Caregiving Crisis." In *Women on the Front Lines*. Edited by Jessie Allen and Alan Pifer. Washington, D.C.: Urban Institute, 1993.

Fraser, Joy and Janet Ross Kerr. "Psychophysiological Effects of Back Massage on Elderly Institutionalized Patients." *Journal of Advanced Nursing* 18 (1993): 238–45.

Freedman, Marc. *Prime Time*. New York: Public Affairs, 1999.

———. "Senior Citizens: A New Force in Community Service." In *Annual Editions Aging*. Edited by Harold Cox. Guilford, Conn.: Dushkin-McGraw-Hill, 2000.

Freeman, Mary E. Wilkins. "A Mistaken Charity." In *A Humble Romance and Other Stories*. New York: Harper and Brothers, 1887.

———. "A Village Singer." In *A New England Nun and Other Stories*. New York: Harper and Brothers, 1891.

Freund, Katherine. "Surviving without Driving: Creating Sustainable Transportation for Seniors." Speech to the Muskie Forum, Muskie School of Public Service. Speaking in Maine, Maine Public Radio, January 11, 2002.

Friedan, Betty. *The Fountain of Age*. New York: Simon and Schuster, 1993.

Friedman, Leonore. "Aging as a Russian Doll." In *Being Bodies: Buddhist Women on the Paradox of Embodiment*. Boston: Shambhala, 1997.

Fulmer, Terry et al. "The Complexity of Medication Compliance in the Elderly: What the Literature Tells Us." *Generations* 24, no. 4 (2000–2001): 43–48.

Fullmer, Elise M., Dena Shenk and Lynette J. Eastland. "Negative Identity: a Feminist Analysis of the Social Invisibility of Older Lesbians." *Journal of Women and Aging* 11, nos. 2–3 (1999): 131–48.

Furman, Frieda Kerner. *Facing the Mirror: Older Women and Beauty Shop Culture*. New York: Routledge, 1997.

Gadow, Sally. "Covenant without Care: Letting Go and Holding On to Chronic Illness." In *The Ethics of Care and the Ethics of Cure*. Edited by Jean Watson and Marilyn Ann Ray. New York: National League for Nursing, 1988.

———. "Frailty and Strength: The Dialectic in Aging." *Gerontologist* 23, no. 2 (1983): 144–47.

———. "Whose Body, Whose Story? The Question about Narratives in Women's Health Care." *Soundings* 77, nos. 3–4 (1994): 295–307.

Gagnier, Regenia. "Feminist Postmodernism: the End of Feminism or the End of Theory?" In *Theoretical Perspectives on Sexual Difference*. Edited by Deborah L. Rhode. New Haven, Conn.: Yale, 1990.

Gannon, Linda R. *Women and Aging: Transcending the Myths*. New York: Routledge, 1999.

Gaylord, Susan. "Women and Aging: A Psychological Perspective." In *Women as They Age*, 2nd ed. Edited by J. Dianne Garner and Susan O. Mercer. New York: Haworth, 2001.

Gerth, Jeff and Sheryl Gay Stolberg. "Drug Firms Reap Profits on Tax-Backed Research." *New York Times* (April 23, 2000): 1.

Gibson, Diane. "Broken Down by Age and Gender: The 'Problem of Older Women' Redefined." *Gender and Society* 10, no. 4 (1996): 433–448.

Gibson, Rose Campbell. "Reconceptualizing Retirement for Black Americans." In *Worlds of Difference: Inequality in the Aging Experience*. Edited by Eleanor Palo Stoller and Rose Campbell Gibson. Thousand Oaks, Calif.: Pine Forge Press, 1994.

Gomberg, Edith S. "Alcohol and Drugs." *Encyclopedia of Gerontology*, vol. 1. Edited by James E. Birren. New York: Academic Press, 1996.

Goodman, Catherine Chase. "The Caregiving Roles of Asian American Women." *Journal of Women and Aging* 2, no. 1 (1990): 109–120.

Gould, Jean, ed. *Dutiful Daughters: Caring for Our Parents as They Grow Old.* Seattle: Seal Press, 1999.

Gould, Ketayun. "A Minority-Feminist Perspective on Women and Aging." *Journal of Women and Aging* 1 (1989): 195–216.

Gould, Mary-Louise. "Overcoming Blindness: Facing the Effects of Trauma and Interpersonal Violence: What One Holotropic Breathwork Practitioner Has Learned." *The Inner Door: Association for Holotropic Breathwork International* 11, no. 4 (1999): 1, 6.

Grady, Denise. "Not a Simple Case of Health Racism." *New York Times* (October 17, 1999) 4: 1.

———. "Scientists Say Herbs Need More Regulation." *New York Times* (March 7, 2000): D1.

Graubarth-Szyller, Bobbie, Julianna D. Padgett, and Julia Weiss. *Discovering Wellness in a Nursing Home.* New Orleans: Longevity Press, 1987.

Grimshaw, Jean. *Philosophy and Feminist Thinking.* Minneapolis: University of Minnesota, 1986.

Grumbach, Doris. *Coming into the End Zone: A Memoir.* New York: Norton, 1991.

———. *Extra Innings: A Memoir.* New York: Norton, 1993.

Gubrium, Jaber F. and James Holstein. "Constuctionist Perspectives on Aging." In *Handbook of Theories of Aging.* Edited by Vern L. Bengtson and K. Warner Schaie. New York: Springer, 1999.

Gubrium, Jaber F. and Robert J. Lynott. "Rethinking Life Satisfaction," *Human Organization* 42, no. 1 (1983): 30–38.

Gullette, Margaret Morganroth. "Age Studies as Cultural Studies." In *Handbook of the Humanities and Aging,* 2nd ed. Edited by Thomas R. Cole, Robert Kastenbaum, and Ruth Ray. New York: Springer, 1999.

———. *Declining to Decline: Cultural Combat and the Politics of Midlife.* Charlottesville, Va.: University Press of Virginia, 1997.

Haber, David. *Health Promotion and Aging,* 2nd ed. New York: Springer, 1999.

Hall, Stephen S. "Prescription for Profit." *New York Times Magazine* (March 11, 2001): 40–45.

Hamilton, Jean. A and Margaret F. Jensvold. "Psychopharmacology from a Feminist Perspective." *Women and Therapy* 16, no. 1 (1995).

Harding, Sandra. "Conclusion: Epistemological Questions." In *Feminist Methodologies.* Edited by Sandra Harding. Bloomington: Indiana, 1987.

Harper, Mary S. "Aging Minorities." *Healthcare Trends and Transitions* 6, no. 4 (1995): 9–20.

Hatch, Laurie Russell. "Women's and Men's Retirement: Plural Pathways, Diverse Destinations." In *Social Gerontology.* Edited by David E. Redburn and Robert P. McNamara. Westport, Conn.: Auburn House, 1998.

Hausdorff, Jeffrey, Becca R. Levy, and Jeanne Y. Wei. "The Power of Ageism on Physical

Function in Older Persons: Reversibility of Age-Related Gait Changes." *Journal of the American Geriatric Society* 47 (1999): 1346–1349.

Hayt, Elizabeth. "90 Candles and a Second Wind." *New York Times* Sunday Styles (October 8, 2000): Sec. 9, 1–2.

Hazan, Haim. *Old Age. Constructions and Deconstructions*. Cambridge: Cambridge University Press, 1994.

Healey, Shevy. "Calling the Question: Confronting Ageism." Conference paper, National Women's Studies Association, Akron, Ohio, June 1990.

———. "Confronting Ageism: a MUST for Mental Health." In *Faces of Women and Aging*. Edited by Nancy D. Davis, Ellen Cole, and Esther Rothblum. New York: Haworth, 1993.

———. "Diversity with a Difference: On Being Old and Lesbian." *Journal of Gay and Lesbian Social Services* 1, no. 1 (1994): 109–17.

———. "Growing to be an Old Woman." In *Women and Aging*. Edited by Jo Alexander et al. Corvallis, Ore.: Calyx Books, 1986.

Healy, Tara. "Women's Ethic of Care in its Social and Economic Context: Implications for Practice." Paper presented at the Women and Aging conference of Mabel Wadsworth Women's Health Center, Husson College, Bangor, Maine, November 20, 1999.

Heilbrun, Carolyn. Letter to the Editor. *Women's Review of Books* 17, no. 5 (February 2000).

Hekman, Susan. "Truth and Method: Feminist Standpoint Theory Revisited." In *Provoking Feminisms*. Edited by Carolyn Allen and Judith A. Howard. Chicago: University of Chicago, 2000.

Hendricks, Jon. "Creativity over the Life Course—a Call for a Relational Perspective." *International Journal of Aging and Human Development* 48, no. 2 (1999): 85–111.

———. "Generations and The Generation of Theory in Social Gerontology." *International Journal of Aging and Human Development* 35, no. 1 (1992): 31–47.

———. "Practical Consciousness, Social Class, and Self-Concept: a View from Sociology." In *The Self and Society in Aging Processes*. Edited by Carol D. Ryff and Victor W. Marshall. New York: Springer, 1999.

Hendricks, Jon and W. Andrew Achenbaum. "Historical Development of Theories of Aging." In *Handbook of Theories of Aging*. Edited by Vern Bengtson and K. Warner Schaie. New York: Springer, 1999.

Hepworth, Mike. "Images of Old Age." In *Handbook of Communication and Aging Research*. Edited by Jon F. Nussbaum and Justine Coupland. Mahway, N.J.: Lawrence Erlbaum, 1995.

Herzog, A. Regula. "Methodological Issues in Research on Older Women." In *Health and Economic Status of Older Women*. Edited by Herzog, Karen C. Holden and Mildred M. Seltzer. Amityville, N.Y.: Baywood, 1989.

Hillyer, Barbara. "The Embodiment of Old Women: Silences." *Frontiers* 19, no. 1 (1998): 48–60.

Hirschmann, Nancy J. *Rethinking Obligation. A Feminist Method for Political Theory*. Ithaca, N.Y.: Cornell, 1992.

Hoare, Carol Wren. *Erikson on Development in Adulthood. New Insights from Unpublished Papers*. Oxford: Oxford University Press, 2002.

Holstein, Martha. "Home Care, Women, and Aging: A Case Study of Injustice." In *Mother Time*. Edited by Margaret Urban Walker. Lanham, Md.: Rowman & Littlefield, 1999.

———. "The 'New Aging': Imagining Alternative Futures." In *Evolution of the Aging Self*. Edited by K. Warner Schaie and Jon Hendricks. New York: Springer, 2000.

———. "Productive Aging: A Feminist Critique." *Journal of Aging and Social Policy* 4, nos. 3–4 (1992): 17–33.

———. "What is Home Care?" *Park Ridge Center Bulletin* (Sept.-Oct. 1999): 3–4.

———. "Women and Productive Aging: Troubling Implications." In *Critical Gerontology: Perspectives from Political and Moral Economy*. Edited by Meredith Minkler and Carroll L. Estes. Amityville, N.Y.: Baywood, 1999.

hooks, bell. *Where We Stand: Class Matters*. New York: Routledge, 2000.

Hooyman, Nancy. "Research on Older Women: Where is Feminism?" *Gerontologist* 39, no. 1 (1999): 115–18.

———. "Women as Caregivers of the Elderly: Implications for Social Welfare Policy and Practice." In *Aging and Caregiving: Theory, Research, and Policy*. Edited by David C. Biegel and Arthur Blum. Newbury Park, Calif.: Sage, 1990.

Hooyman, Nancy and Judith Gonyea. "A Feminist Model of Family Care: Practice and Policy Directions." In *Fundamentals of Feminist Gerontology*. Edited by J. Dianne Garner. New York: Haworth, 1999.

Hooyman, Nancy and Judith Gonyea. *Feminist Perspectives on Family Care*. Thousand Oaks, Calif.: Sage, 1995.

Hudson, Robert B. "Privatizing Old-Age Benefits: Re-emergent Ideology Encounters Organized Interests." In *Resecuring Social Security and Medicare: Understanding Privatization and Risk*. Edited by Judith Gonyea. Washington, D.C.: The Gerontological Society of America, 1998.

Hummert, Mary Lee. "Stereotypes of the Elderly and Patronizing Speech." In *Interpersonal Communication in Older Adulthood*. Edited by Mary Lee Hummert et al. Thousand Oaks, Calif.: Sage, 1994.

Hurd, Laura C. "'We're Not Old!': Older Women's Negotiations of Aging and Oldness." *Journal of Aging Studies* 13, no. 4 (1999): 419–39.

Hurtado, Aida. "Strategic Suspensions: Feminists of Color Theorize the Production of Knowledge" In *Knowledge, Difference, and Power*. Edited by Nancy Goldberger et al. New York: Basic Books, 1996.

Hynes, Denise M. "The Quality of Breast Cancer Care in Local Communities: Implications for Health Care Reform." *Medical Care* 32 (1994): 328–40.

Illich, Ivan. *Medical Nemesis: The Expropriation of Health*. New York: Random House, 1976.

Innes, J. Bruce et al. "Beyond the Myths of Aging." *Critical Issues in Aging*, no. 1 (1997): 42–45.

"In Search of the Secrets of Aging." National Institutes of Health, National Institute on Aging, 1996. NIH Publication no. 93–2756.

Jackson, Jacquelyne Johnson. "Aging Black Women and Public Policies." *The Black Scholar* (May-June 1988): 31–43.

———. "Race, National Origin, Ethnicity, and Aging." In *Handbook of Aging and the Social Sciences.* Edited by R. Binstock and E. Shanas. New York: Van Rostrand Reinhold, 1985.

Jackson, Jacquelyne Johnson and Charlotte Perry. "Physical Health Conditions of Middle-Aged and Aged Blacks." In *Aging and Health. Perspectives on Gender, Race, Ethnicity, and Class.* Edited by Kyriakos S. Markides. Newbury Park, Calif.: Sage, 1989.

Jackson, Stevi, ed. *Women's Studies: Essential Readings.* New York: New York University, 1993.

Jacobs, Ruth Harriet. *Be an Outrageous Older Woman.* New York: Harper Collins, 1997.

———. "Friendships Among Old Women." In *Women, Aging, and Ageism.* Edited by Evelyn R. Rosenthal. New York: Harrington Park Press, 1990.

Jacobson, Sharon. "An Examination of Leisure in the Lives of Old Lesbians from an Ecological Perspective." Doctoral Dissertation, University of Georgia, 1996.

Jewett, Sarah Orne. "The Flight of Betsey Lane." In *The Country of the Pointed Firs.* Boston: Houghton Mifflin, 1896.

John, Robert, Patrice Blanchard and Catherine Hagan Hennessy. "Hidden Lives: Aging and Contemporary American Indian Women." In *Handbook on Women and Aging.* Edited by Jean M. Coyle. Westport, Conn.: Greenwood, 1997.

John, Robert, Catherine Hagan Hennessy and Clark H. Denny. "Preventing Chronic Illness and Disability Among Native American Elders." In *Serving Minority Elders In the 21st Century.* Edited by May L. Wykle and Amasa B. Ford. New York: Springer, 1999.

Johns, Elizabeth. "Redefining Retirement: Women Who Continue to Work After Age 65." M.A. thesis, Human Development, University of Maine, 2002.

Johnson, Colleen L. "Cultural Diversity in the Late-Life Family." In *Handbook of Aging and the Family.* Edited by Rosemary Blieszner and Victoria Hilkevitch Bedford. Westport, Conn.: Greenwood, 1995.

Johnson, Colleen L. and Barbara Barer. *Life Beyond 85 Years: The Aura of Survivorship.* New York: Springer, 1997.

Johnson, Don Hanlon. *Body, Spirit and Democracy.* Berkeley: North Atlantic Books Somatic Resources, 1994.

Kalish, Richard. "The New Ageism and the Failure Models." In *Aging and the Human Spirit.* Edited by Carol LeFevre and Perry LeFevre. Chicago: Exploration Press, 1985.

Kaplan, George A. "Behavioral, Social, and Socioenvironmental Factors Adding Years to Life and Life to Years." In *Public Health and Aging.* Edited by Tom Hickey, Marjorie A. Speers, and Thomas R. Prohaska. Baltimore: Johns Hopkins, 1998.

Kaplan, George A. and William J. Strawbridge. "Behavioral and Social Factors in Healthy Aging." In *Aging and Quality of Life.* Edited by Ronald Abeles et al. New York: Springer, 1994.

Kaplan, Sheila. "The New Generation Gap: The Politics of Generational Justice." *Common Cause* 13, no. 2 (1987): 13–15.

Kastenbaum, Robert. "Encrusted Elders: Arizona and the Political Spirit of Postmodern Aging." In *Voices and Visions of Aging: Toward a Critical Gerontology*. Edited by Thomas R. Cole et al. New York: Springer, 1993.

Katz, Ira R. "Late-Life Suicide and the Euthanasia Debate: What Should We Do About Suffering in Terminal Illness and Chronic Disease?" *Gerontologist* 34, no. 5 (1997): 269–271.

Katz, Stephen. *Disciplining Old Age: The Formation of Gerontological Knowledge*. Charlottesville, Va.: University of Virginia Press, 1996.

Kaufman, Sharon. "Narrative, Death, and the Uses of Anthropology." In *Handbook of the Humanities and Aging*, 2nd ed. Edited by Thomas R. Cole, Robert Kastenbaum, and Ruth E. Ray. New York: Springer, 2000.

Kelchner, Elizabeth. "Ageism's Impact and Effect on Society: Not Just a Concern for the Old." *Journal of Gerontological Social Work* 32, no. 4 (1999): 85–100.

Kelley, Barbara Bailey. "Running on Empty: Thyroid Problems in Women." In *Women's Health Annual Editions 98/99*. Edited by Maureen Edwards and Nora Howley. Guilford, Conn.: Dushkin-McGraw-Hill, 1998.

Kemper, Susan and Tamara Harden. "Experimentally Disentangling What's Beneficial about Elderspeak from What's Not." *Psychology and Aging* 14, no. 4 (1999): 656–70.

Kennedy, Jae and Meredith Minkler. "Disability Theory and Public Policy: Implications for Critical Gerontology." In *Critical Gerontology: Perspectives from Political and Moral Economy*. Edited by Meredith Minkler and Carroll L. Estes. Amityville, N.Y.: Baywood, 1999.

Kingson, Eric and Jill Quadagno. "Social Security: Marketing Radical Reform." In *Critical Gerontology: Perspectives from Political and Moral Economy*, eds. Meredith Minkler and Carroll L. Estes. Amityville, N.Y.: Baywood, 1999.

Kiyak, H. Asuman and Nancy R. Hooyman. "Minority and Socioeconomic Status: Impact on Quality of Life in Aging." In *Aging and Quality of Life*. Edited by Ronald Abeles et al. New York: Springer, 1994.

Knox, Richard. "Living Longer is the Best Revenge." *Boston Globe Magazine* (May 23, 1999): 40.

Koenig, Harold, et al. "Mental Health Care for Older Adults in the Year 2020: A Dangerous and Avoided Topic." *Gerontologist* 34, no. 5 (1994): 674–79.

Kolata, Gina. "Estrogen Use Tied to Slight Increase in Risks to Heart." *New York Times* (April 5, 2000): A1.

Knight, Eric L. and Jerry Avorn. "Use and Abuse of Drugs in Older Persons." *Gerontologist* 39, no. 1 (1999): 109–11.

LaBouvie-Vief, Gisela. "Women's Creativity and Images of Gender." In *Women Growing Older: Psychological Perspectives*. Edited by Barbara F. Turner and Lillian E. Troll. Thousand Oaks, Calif.: Sage, 1994.

Labowitz, Shoni. *God, Sex, and Women of the Bible*. New York: Simon and Schuster, 1998.

Lamphere-Thorpe, Jo-Ann and Robert J. Blendon. "Years Gained and Opportunities Lost: Women and Healthcare in an Aging America." In *Women on the Front Lines*. Edited by Jessie Allen and Alan Pifer. Washington, D.C.: The Urban Institute, 1993.

Lamy, Peter. "Actions of Alcohol and Drugs in Older People." *Generations* 12, no. 4 (1988): 9–13.

———. "Geriatric Drug Therapy." *AFP* 34, no. 6 (1986): 118–24.

Langellier, Kristen. "Mémère Stories: Reproducing the Franco-American Family." Presentation to Women in the Curriculum lunch series, University of Maine, September 12, 2000.

Langer, Ellen J. *Mindfulness*. Reading, Mass.: Addison-Wesley, 1989.

———. *The Power of Mindful Learning*. Reading, Mass.: Addison-Wesley, 1997.

Larkin, June. *Sexual Harassment: High School Girls Speak Out*. Toronto: Second Story Press, 1997.

Laws, Glenda. "Understanding Ageism: Lessons from Feminism and Postmodernism." *Gerontologist* 35, no. 1 (1995): 112–18.

le Carré, John. "In Place of Nations." *The Nation* (April 9, 2001): 11–13.

LeVande, Diane I. "Growth and Development in Older Women: A Critique and Proposal." In *Doing Feminism. Teaching and Research in the Academy*. Edited by Mary Anderson et al. Lansing, Mich.: Michigan State Women's Studies Program, 1997.

Levin, Jack and William Levin. *Ageism*. Belmont, Calif.: Wadsworth, 1980.

Levy, Becca R. "Eradication of Ageism Requires Addressing the Enemy Within." *Gerontologist* 41, no. 5 (2001): 578–79.

———. "The Inner Self of Japanese Elderly: A Defense Against Negative Stereotypes of Aging." *International Journal of Aging and Human Development* 48, no. 2 (1999): 131–44.

Long, H. Lewis. *Health Care for the Elderly: A Hermeneutic Study of the Role of Culture and Tradition*. Doctoral Dissertation, University of San Francisco, 1998.

Longino, Charles F. "The Gray Peril Mentality and the Impact of Retirement Migration." *Journal of Applied Gerontology* 7, no. 4 (1988): 448–55.

Longman, Philip J. "The World Turns Gray." *U.S. News and World Report* (March 1, 1999): 30–39.

Lopata, Helen Znaniecka. "Feminist Perspectives on Social Gerontology." In *Handbook of Aging and the Family*. Edited by Rosemary Blieszner and Victoria Hilkevitch Bedford. Westport, Conn.: Greenwood, 1995.

Louie, Kem B. "Status of Mental Health Needs of Asian Elderly." In *Serving Minority Elders in the 21st Century*. Edited by May L. Wykle and Amasa B. Ford. New York: Springer, 1999.

Lugones, Maria. "Playfulness, 'World Travelling,' and Loving." In *The Woman That I Am. The Literature and Culture of Contemporary Women of Color*. Edited by D. Soyini Madison. New York: St. Martin's, 1994.

Lyder, Courtney H. et al. "Appropriate Prescribing for Elders: Disease Management Alone is not Enough." *Generations* 24, no. 4 (2000–2001): 55–59.

Macdonald, Barbara with Cynthia Rich. *Look Me in the Eye, Old Women, Aging and Age-ism*, 2nd ed. Minneapolis, Minn.: Spinsters Ink, 1991.

McDaniel, Susan. "A Sociological Perspective on Women and Aging as the Millenium Turns." In *Women as They Age*, 2nd ed. Edited by J. Dianne Garner and Susan O. Mercer. New York: Haworth, 2001.

———. "Women and Aging: A Sociological Perspective." In *Women as They Age*. Edited by J. Dianne Garner and Susan O. Mercer. New York: Haworth, 1989.

McDonald, Kim. "Sport Scientists Gain New Respect as They Shift Focus to the Elderly." *Chronicle of Higher Education*. (September 25, 1998), A15–A16.

McFadden, Susan. "Feminist Scholarship as a Meeting Ground for Age and Disability Studies." *Gerontologist* 41, no.1 (2001): 133–37.

McLeod, Beth Witrogen and Theodore Roszak. "Tomorrow's Caregivers: New Opportunities, New Challenges." *Aging Today* 22, no.1 (2001): 9–10.

McQueen, Anjetta. "Prescriptions Reportedly Claim Growing Share of Health Costs." *Boston Globe*. (March 12, 2001): A3.

Malveaux, Julianne. "Gender Differences and Beyond: An Economic Perspective on Diversity and Commonality Among Women." In *Theoretical Perspectives on Sexual Difference*. Edited by Deborah L. Rhode. New Haven, Conn.: Yale, 1990.

———. "Race, Poverty, and Women's Aging." In *Women on the Front Lines*. Edited by Jessie Allen and Alan Pifer. Washington D.C.: The Urban Institute, 1993.

Manahan, William. *Eat for Health*. Tiburon, Calif.: H.J. Kramer, 1988.

Manheimer, Ronald J. Review of *Handbook of Emotion, Adult Development and Aging*. *Gerontologist* 38, no. 2 (1998): 262–67.

———. "Wisdom and Method: Philosophical Contributions to Gerontology." In *Handbook of the Humanities and Aging*. Edited by Thomas R. Cole, David D. Van Tassel, and Robert Kastenbaum. New York: Springer, 1992.

Mann, Charles C. "Swallowing Hard." Review of *Bitter Pills: Inside the Hazardous World of Legal Drugs* by Stephen Fried. *New York Times Book Review* (June 13, 1998).

Markides, Kyriakos S. "Aging, Gender, Race, Ethnicity, Class and Health: A Conceptual Overview." In *Aging and Health*. Edited by Kyriakos S. Markides. Newbury Park, Calif.: Sage, 1989.

Markides, Kyriakos S., Jeannine Coreil and Linda Perkowski Rogers. "Aging and Health Among Southwestern Hispanics." In *Aging and Health*. Edited by Kyriakos S. Markides. Newbury Park, Calif.: Sage, 1989.

Markson, Elizabeth. "Communities of Resistance: Older Women in a Gendered World." *Gerontologist* 39, no. 4 (1999): 495–502.

———. "Gender Roles and Memory Loss in Old Age: An Exploration of Linkages." In *Growing Old in America*, 3rd ed. Edited by Beth B. Hess and Elizabeth Markson. New Brunswick, N.J.: Transaction Books, 1986.

Markson, Elizabeth and Carol A. Taylor. "The Mirror Has Two Faces." *Ageing and Society* 20 (2000): 137–60.

Matthews, Anne Martin and Lori D. Campbell. "Gender Roles, Employment and Informal Care." In *Connecting Gender and Age*. Edited by Sara Arber and Jay Ginn. Buckingham: Open University Press, 1995.

Maynard, Isabelle. "The House on Fell Street." In *Fierce with Reality*. Edited by Margaret Cruikshank. St. Cloud, Minn.: North Star Press, 1995.

Meigs, Mary. *In the Company of Strangers*. Vancouver, Talon Books, 1991.

Mellancamp, Patricia. "From Anxiety to Equanimity: Crisis and Generational Continuity on TV, at the Movies, in Life, in Death." In *Figuring Age: Women, Bodies, Generations*. Edited by Kathleen Woodward. Bloomington: Indiana University Press, 1999.

Meyer, Madonna Harrington. "Declining Marital Rates and Changing Eligibility for Social Security." Paper presented at annual meeting of the Gerontological Society of America, Chicago, November 17, 2001.

———. "Family Status and Poverty Among Older Women: The Gendered Distribution of Retirement Income in the United States." In *Aging for the 21ˢᵗ Century*. Edited by Jill Quadagno and Debra Street. New York: St. Martin's, 1996.

Meyers, Diana Tietjens. "Miroir, Mémoire, Mirage: Appearance, Aging and Women." In *Mother Time*. Edited by Margaret Urban Walker. Lanham, Md.: Rowman & Littlefield, 1999.

Michocki, K.J. et al. "Drug Prescribing for the Elderly." *Archives of Family Medicine* 2, no. 4 (1993): 441–44.

Miles, Toni P. "Aging and the New Multicultural Reality." *Gerontologist* 39, no. 1 (1999): 118–20.

Minkler, Meredith. "Scapegoating the Elderly: New Voices, Old Theme." *Journal of Health Care Policy* 18 (1997): 6–12.

Minkler, Meredith and Carroll L. Estes, eds. *Critical Gerontology: Perspectives from Political and Moral Economy*. Amityville, N.Y.: Baywood, 1999.

Minkler, Meredith and Thomas R. Cole. "Political and Moral Economy: Getting to Know One Another." In *Critical Gerontology. Perspectives from Political and Moral Economy*. Edited by Meredith Minkler and Carroll L. Estes. Amityville, N.Y.: Baywood, 1999.

Mitchell, Margaretta."Imogene Through her Camera." Introduction to *After 90*. Seattle: University of Washington, 1977.

Mollenkott, Virginia Ramey. "Ageism." In *Dictionary of Feminist Theologies*. Edited by Letty Russell and J. Shannon Clarkson. Louisville, Ky.: Westminister John Knox Press, 1996.

Montgomery, Sy. "A Return to Native Foods." *Boston Globe* (March 7, 2000): A1.

Moody, Harry R. *Abundance of Life*. New York: Columbia, 1988.

———." Age, Productivity and Transcendence." In *Achieving a Productive Aging Society*. Edited by Scott Bass et al. Westport, Conn.: Auburn House, 1993.

———. "Bioethics and Aging." In *Handbook of Aging and the Humanities*. Edited by Thomas R. Cole et al. New York: Springer, 2000.

———. "The Humanities and Aging: A Millenial Perspective." *Gerontologist* 41, no. 3 (2001): 411–15.

———. "Overview: What is Critical Gerontology and Why is it Important." In *Voices and Visions of Aging*. Edited by Thomas R. Cole et al. New York: Springer, 1993.

Moore, Thomas J. "FDA Math Needs Warning Label." *Boston Globe* (Dec. 3, 2000): D1.

———. *Prescription for Disaster: The Hidden Dangers in Your Medicine Cabinet.* New York: Simon and Schuster, 1998.

———. "Why Estrogen's Promise Fell Short." *Boston Globe* (April 9, 2000): A1.

Moulson, Geir. "Japan Tops World Life Expectancy Rates." *Boston Globe* (June 5, 2000): A2.

Mulnard, Ruth et al. "Estrogen Replacement Therapy for Treatment of Mild to Moderate Alzheimer's Disease: A Randomized Controlled Trial." *JAMA* 238, no. 8 (February 23, 2000): 1007–15.

Munro, Alice. "Spelling." *The Beggar Maid.* New York: Knopf, 1978.

Myerhoff, Barbara. "Aging and the Aged in Other Cultures: An Anthropological Perspective." In *Remembered Lives: The Work of Ritual, Storytelling, and Growing Older.* Edited by Marc Kaminsky. Ann Arbor, Mich.: University of Michigan, 1992.

———. *Number Our Days.* New York: Simon and Schuster, 1980.

———. "Rites and Signs of Ripening: The Intertwining of Ritual, Time, and Growing Older." In *Age and Anthropological Theory.* Edited by David Kertzer and Jennie Keith. Ithaca, N.Y.: Cornell, 1984.

Myerhoff, Barbara and Virginia Tufte. "Life History as Integration: Personal Myth and Aging." In *Remembered Lives: The Work of Ritual, Storytelling, and Growing Older.* Edited by Marc Kaminsky. Ann Arbor, Mich.: University of Michigan, 1992.

Nelson, Hilde Lindemann. "Stories of My Old Age." In *Mother Time.* Edited by Margaret Urban Walker. Lanham, Md.: Rowman & Littlefield, 1999.

Neuhaus, Ruby and Robert Neuhaus. *Successful Aging.* Lanham, Md.: University Press of America, 1992.

Neysmith, Sheila. "Feminist Methodologies: A Consideration of Principles and Practice for Research in Gerontology." *Canadian Journal on Aging/La Revue Canadienne Du Viellissment* 14 sup. 1 (1995): 100–118.

Nikola, R. J. *Creatures of Water.* Salt Lake City, Utah: Europa Therapeutic, 1997.

Nydegger, Corinne N. "Family Ties of the Aged in Cross-Cultural Perspective." In *Growing Old in America,* 3rd ed. Edited by Beth B. Hess and Elizabeth Markson. New Brunswick, N.J.: Transaction Books, 1986.

O'Brien, Sharon J. and Patricia Vertinsky. "Elderly Women, Exercise, and Healthy Aging." *Journal of Women and Aging* 3 (1990): 41–65.

Ojea, Patricia and Barbara Quigley, ed. *Women's Studies 99/00.* Guilford, Conn.: Dushkin-McGraw-Hill, 1999.

Older Women's League. "The Path to Poverty: An Analysis of Women's Retirement Income." In *Critical Gerontology.* Edited by Meredith Minkler and Carroll L. Estes. Amityville, N.Y.: Baywood, 1999.

Ollenburger, Jane C. and Helen A. Moore. *A Sociology of Women,* 2nd ed. Upper Saddle River, N.J.: Prentice Hall, 1998.

Olson, Laura Katz, ed. *Age Through Ethnic Lenses: Caring for the Elderly in a Multicultural Society.* Lanham, Md.: Rowman & Littlefield, 2001.

———. "Women and Old Age Income Security in the United States." In *Aging in a Gendered World*. Santo Domingo: INSTRAW, 1999.

Onyx, Jenny and Pam Benton. "What Does Retirement Mean for Women?" In *Revisioning Aging. Empowerment of Older Women*. Edited by Jenny Onyx, Rosemary Leonard, and Rosslyn Reed. New York: Peter Lang, 1999.

Onyx, Jenny, Rosemary Leonard, and Rosslyn Reed, eds. *Revisioning Aging: Empowerment of Older Women*. New York: Peter Lang, 1999.

O'Rand, Angela M. and John C. Henretta. *Age and Inequality*. Boulder: Westview, 1999.

Ory, Marcia G. and Huber R. Warner, eds. *Gender, Health and Longevity: Multidisciplinary Perspectives*. New York: Springer, 1990.

"Our Mothers, Ourselves: Older Women's Health Care." In *Annual Editions Women's Health 98/99*. Guilford, Conn.: Dushkin-McGraw-Hill, 1998.

Ovrebo, Beverly and Meredith Minkler. "The Lives of Older Women: Perspectives from Political Economy and the Humanities." In *Voices and Visions of Aging*. Edited by Thomas R. Cole et al. New York: Springer, 1993.

Palmore, Erdman B. *Ageism*, 2nd ed. New York: Springer, 1999.

Pear, Robert. "Medicare Spending for Care at Home Plunges by 45%." *New York Times* (April 21, 2000): A1.

Peck, Richard A. and Iva Lim Peck. "Tai Chi Chuan for Pain Management." *The Pain Practitioner* 9, no. 4 (1999): 1–2.

Perry, Merry G. "Animated Gerontophobia: Ageism, Sexism, and the Disney Villainess." In *Aging and Identity: A Humanities Perspective*. Edited by Sara Munson Deats and Lagretta Tallent Lenker. Westport, Conn.: Praeger, 1999.

Phillipson, Chris. *Reconstructing Old Age: New Agendas in Social Theory and Practice*. London: Sage, 1998.

Porcino, Jane. "Psychological Aspects of Aging in Women." In *Health Needs of Women as They Age*. Edited by Sharon Golub and Rita Jackaway Freedman. New York: Haworth, 1985.

A Portrait of Older Minorities. Washington, D.C.: AARP Minority Affairs, 1995.

Posner, Richard. *Aging and Old Age*. Chicago: University of Chicago Press, 1995.

Pousada, Lidia. "Hip Fractures." *The Encyclopedia of Aging*, 2nd ed. Edited by George L. Maddox. New York: Springer, 1995.

Price, Christine Ann. *Women and Retirement: The Unexplored Tradition*. New York: Garland, 1998.

Price, Janet and Margrit Shildrick, eds. *Feminist Theory and the Body*. New York: Routledge, 1999.

Quadagno, Jill. *Aging and the Life Course*. Boston: McGraw-Hill, 1999.

———. "Social Security and the Myth of the Entitlement 'Crisis.'" *Gerontologist* 36, no. 3 (1996): 391–99.

Quinn-Musgrove, Sandra L. "Extended Caregiving: The Experience of Surviving Spouses." In *Women, Aging, and Ageism*. Edited by Evelyn R. Rosenthal. New York: Harrington Park, 1990.

Ram Dass. *Still Here: Embracing Aging, Changing, and Dying*. New York: Riverhead, 2000.

Ray, Ruth E. *Beyond Nostalgia: Aging and Life-Story Writing*. Charlottesville, Va.: University Press of Virginia, 2001.

———. "A Postmodern Perspective on Feminist Gerontology." *Gerontologist* 36, no. 5 (1996): 674–80.

———. "Researching to Transgress: The Need for Critical Feminism in Gerontology." *Journal of Women and Aging* 11, nos. 2–3 (1999): 171–184.

———. "Social Influences on the Older Woman's Life Story." *Generations* (Winter 1999–2000): 56–62.

RedHorse, John G. "American Indian Elders: Unifiers of Families." *Social Casework* 61 (1980): 490–93.

Reed, Alyson. "Health Care Special: Women, Disparities and Discrimination." *Civil Rights Journal* 4, no. 1 (1999): 42–48.

Reich, Robert B. "Broken Faith: Why We Need to Renew the Social Contract." *Generations* 22, no. 4 (1998–1999): 19–24.

Reinhardt, Uwe E. "How to Lower the Cost of Drugs." *New York Times* (January 3, 2000): A19.

Reinharz, Shulamit. "Friends or Foes? Gerontological and Feminist Theory." In *The Other Within: Feminist Explorations of Aging*. Edited by Marilyn Pearsall. Boulder, Colo.: Westview Press, 1997.

Rendell, Jane, Barbara Penner and Iain Borden, eds. *Gender, Space, Architecture*. London: Routledge, 2000.

Rentsch, Thomas. "Aging as Becoming Oneself: A Philosophical Ethics of Late Life." *Journal of Aging Studies* 11, no. 4 (1997): 263–72.

"Report Calls Substance Abuse, Addiction by Older Women 'Epidemic.'" *Women's Health Weekly* (June 15, 1998) 2–4.

"Researchers Warn of Drug Price Crisis." *Portland Press Herald* (July 27, 1999): 8A.

Riley, Matilda White and John W. Riley, Jr. "Structural Lag: Past and Future." In *Age and Structural Lag*. Edited by Matilda White Riley, Robert L. Kahn, and Anne Foner. New York: John Wiley & Sons, 1994.

Rimer, Sara. "Caring for Elderly Kin is Costly, Study Finds." *New York Times* (November 27, 1999): A8.

Rizza, Carolyn C. "Caregiving: a Deeply Felt Human Need." In *Social Gerontology*. Edited by David. E. Redburn and Robert P. McNamara. Westport, Conn.: Auburn House, 1998.

Robert, Stephanie A. and James S. House. "Socioeconomic Status and Health over the Life Course." In *Aging and Quality of Life*. Edited by Ronald P. Abeles et al. New York: Springer, 1994.

Roberto, Karen. "The Study of Chronic Pain in Later Life: Where are the Women?" *Journal of Women and Aging* 6, no. 4 (1994): 1–7.

Robertson, Ann. "Beyond Apocalyptic Demography: Toward a Moral Economy of Interdependence." In *Critical Gerontology*. Edited by Meredith Minkler and Carroll L. Estes. Amityville, N.Y.: Baywood, 1999.

Rodeheaver, Dean. "When Old Age Became a Social Problem, Women were Left Behind." *Gerontologist* 27, no. 6 (1987): 741–46.

Rodeheaver, Dean and Nancy Datan. "The Challenge of Double Jeopardy: Toward a Mental Health Agenda for Aging Women." *American Psychologist* 43, no. 8 (1988): 648–54.

Rosenthal, Evelyn R., ed. *Women, Aging, and Ageism.* New York: Harrington Park, 1990.

Rossi, Alice. "Sex and Gender in the Aging Society." In *Our Aging Society.* Edited by Alan Pifer and Lydia Bronte. New York: Norton, 1986.

Roszak, Theodore. *America the Wise.* Boston: Houghton Mifflin, 1998.

Roush, Wade. "Live Longer and Prosper." *Science* 273 (July 5, 1996): 42.

Rowe, John W. and Robert L. Kahn. *Successful Aging.* New York: Pantheon, 1998.

Ruddick, Sara. "Virtues and Age." In *Mother Time.* Edited by Margaret Urban Walker. Lanham, Md.: Rowman & Littlefield, 1999.

Russo, Mary. "Aging and the Scandal of Anachronism." In *Figuring Age.* Edited by Kathleen Woodward. Bloomington: Indiana University Press, 1999.

Sager, Alan and Deborah Socolar. "Let's Seek a Drug Price Peace Treaty." *AARP Bulletin* 42, no. 6 (2001): 29.

Sapiro, Virginia. *Women in American Society: an Introduction to Women's Studies*, 4th ed. Mountain View, Calif.: Mayfield, 1999.

Sarton, May. *As We Are Now.* New York: Norton, 1973.

Sankar, Andrea. "'It's Just Old Age': Old Age as a Diagnosis in American Medicine." In *Age and Anthropological Theory.* Edited by David Kertzer and Jenny Keith. Ithaca, N.Y.: Cornell, 1984.

Sceriha, Madge. "Women and Ageing: the Dreaded Older Woman Fights Back." In *Women's Health*, 3rd ed. Edited by Nancy Worcester and Marianne H. Whatley. Dubuque, Iowa: Kendall Hunt, 2000.

Schaie, K. Warner. "Intellectual Development in Adulthood." In *Handbook of the Psychology of Aging*, 4th ed. Edited by James E. Birren. San Diego, Calif.: Academic Press, 1996.

Scharlach, Andrew E. "Caregiving and Employment: Competing or Complementary Roles?" *Gerontologist* 34, no. 3 (1994): 378–85.

Scharlach, Andrew E., Esme Fuller-Thompson and B. Josea Kramer. "Curriculum Module on Aging and Ethnicity." Module 1: garnet.berkeley.edu/aging/ModuleMinority1.html (accessed 3-22-2002).

Scharlach, Andrew E., Esme Fuller-Thompson and B. Josea Kramer. "Curriculum Module on Aging and Ethnicity." Module 2: socrates.berkeley.edu/aging/ModuleMinority2.html (accessed 3-24-2002).

Schmidt, Robert M. "Preventative Healthcare for Older Adults: Societal and Individual Services." *Generations* (Spring 1994): 33–38.

Schor, Juliet. "The New Politics of Consumption." *Boston Review* (Summer 1999): 4–9.

Scott-Maxwell, Florida. *The Measure of My Days.* New York: Alfred Knopf, 1968.

Seltzer, Mildred. Review of *Women Growing Older: Psychological Perspectives* by Barbara Turner and Lillian E. Troll. *Contemporary Gerontology* 1, no. 3 (1994): 101–03.

Sharpe, Patricia A. "Older Women and Health Services: Moving from Ageism Toward Empowerment." *Women and Health* 22, no. 3 (1995): 9–23.

Sherman, David. "Geriatric Psychopharmacotherapy: Issues and Concerns." *Generations* 18, no. 2 (1994): 34–39.

Sinnott, Jan. "Developmental Models of Midlife and Aging in Women: Metaphors for Transcendence and for Individuality in Community." In *Handbook on Women and Aging.* Edited by Jean M. Coyle. Westport, Conn.: Greenwood, 1997.

Sison, Alan. "Mental Functioning May Predict Mortality in Elderly." *Medical Tribune,* Jan. 29, 2000: www.metrib.com (accessed 3-2002).

Skinner, John H. "Aging in Place: The Experience of African American and Other Minority Elders." *Generations* 16, no. 2 (1992): 49–51.

Smith, James. "New Directions in Socioeconomic Research in Aging." In *Aging and Quality of Life.* Edited by Ronald P. Abeles et al. New York: Springer, 1994.

Sorgman, Margo I. and Marilou Sorensen. "Ageism: A Course of Study." *Theory into Practice* 23, no. 2 (1984): 119–123.

Sotomayor, Marta. "Minority Elders and Managed Care Dilemmas." *Critical Issues in Aging,* no. 2 (1998): 18–22.

Stanford, E. Percil. "Diverse Black Aged." In *Aging and Inequality.* Edited by Robynne Neugebauer-Visano. Toronto: Canadian Scholars Press, 1995.

———. "Mental Health, Aging, and Americans of African Descent." In *Serving Minority Elders in the 21ˢᵗ Century.* Edited by May L. Wykle and Amasa B. Ford. New York: Springer, 1999.

Stanford, E. Percil and Donna L. Yee. "Gerontology and the Relevance of Diversity." In *Diversity: New Approaches to Ethnic Minority Aging.* Edited by E. Percil Stanford and Fernando M. Torres-Gil. Amityville, N.Y.: Baywood, 1992.

Stanley, Liz. "The Impact of Feminism on Sociology in the Last 20 Years." In *The Knowledge Explosion. Generations of Feminist Scholarship.* Edited by Cheris Kramarae and Dale Spender. New York: Teachers College Press, 1992.

Stannard, David. "Dilemmas of Aging in a Bureaucratic Society." In *Aging and the Elderly: Perspectives from the Humanities.* Edited by Stuart Spicker, Kathleen Woodward, and David Van Tassel. Atlantic Highlands: Humanities Press, 1978.

Stavig, G. R. et al. "Hypertension Among Asians and Pacific Islanders in California." *American Journal of Epidemiology* 119, no. 5 (1984): 677–91.

Steckenrider, Janie. "Aging as a Female Phenomenon." In *New Directions in Old Age Policies.* Edited by Janie Steckenrider and Tonya M. Parrott. Albany, N.Y.: SUNY Press, 1998.

Stolberg, Sheryl Gay. "Alternative Medical Care Gains a Foothold." *New York Times* (January 31, 2000): A1, A6.

———. "The Boom in Medications Brings Rise in Fatal Risks." *New York Times* (June 3, 1999): A1.

———. "Drug Switching Saves Money, But There is a Cost." *New York Times* (June 13, 1999): sec. 4, 3.

———. "FDA Pushes for Prescription Drug Guides." *New York Times* (June 4, 1999): A23.

————. "Gasping for Breath." 2-part series. *New York Times* (Oct. 18–19, 1999).

Stolberg, Sheryl Gay and Jeff Gerth. "How Companies Stall Generics and Keep Themselves Healthy." *New York Times* (July 23, 2000): 1.

Stoller, Nancy. "Innovative Models of Chronic Care: Lessons for Aging from Grassroots Movements." *Critical Issues in Aging*, no. 2 (1998): 15–17.

"Sugar: the Sweetening of the American Diet." *Nutrition Action Health Letter* (November 1998): 3–6.

"Surprises in a Study of Life Expectancies." *New York Times* (December 4, 1997): A9.

Svetkey, L. P. et al. "Black White Differences in Hypertension in the Elderly." *American Journal of Epidemiology* 137, no. 1 (1993): 64–73.

Swift, Jonathan. *Gulliver's Travels*. Edited by Robert A. Greenberg. New York: Norton, 1961.

Talbot, Margaret. "The Placebo Prescription." *New York Times Magazine* (January 9, 2000): 34–39.

Tappan, Frances M. and Patricia J. Benjamin. *Tappan's Handbook of Healing Massage Techniques*. Stamford, Conn.: Appleton and Lange, 1998.

Taylor, Anne L. "Coronary Heart Disease in Women." In *Serving Minority Elders in the 21st Century*. Edited by May L. Wykle and Amasa B. Ford. New York: Springer, 1999.

Temin, Christine. "The Faces of Alice Neel." *Boston Globe* (October 13, 2000): C1.

Tesh, Sylvia Noble. *Hidden Arguments. Political Ideology and Disease Prevention Policy*. New Brunswick, N.J.: Rutgers, 1988.

Thomas, Vicki. "Overdosing on Drug Ads." *Aging Today* 20, no. 5 (1999): 7–8.

Thompson, April. "Inside the Brain: New Research Prescribes Mental Exercise." *Aging Today* 20, no. 4 (1999): 8.

Thompson, Neil. Review of *Ageism, the Aged and Aging* by Ursala Adler Falk and Gerhard Falk. *Ageing and Society* 18 (1998): 379–80.

Toner, Robin. "Mother: Free, Equal, and Not at Home." Review of *Care and Equality* by Mona Harrington. *New York Times Book Review*. (Aug. 29, 1999): 29.

Tornstam, Lars. "Transcendence in Later Life." *Generations* 23, no. 4 (2000): 10–14.

Torres, Sara. "Barriers to Mental Health-Care Access Faced by Hispanic Elderly." In *Serving Minority Elders in the 21st Century*. Edited by May L. Wykle and Amasa B. Ford. New York: Springer, 1999.

Tournier, Paul. *Learn to Grow Old*. Tr. Edwin Hudson. New York: Harper and Row, 1972.

Townsend, Peter. "Ageism and Social Policy." In *Ageing and Social Policy: A Critical Assessment*. Edited by Chris Phillipson and Alan Walker. London: Gower, 1986.

Trager, Ellen Lutch. "Cheaper RXs for Seniors." *Boston Globe* (January 4, 1999): A13.

Tripp-Reimer, Toni. "Culturally Competent Care." In *Serving Minority Elders in the 21st Century*. Edited by May L. Wykle and Amasa B. Ford. New York: Springer, 1999.

Tronto, Joan."Age-Segregated Housing as a Moral Problem: An Exercise in Re-thinking Ethics." In *Mother Time*. Edited by Margaret Urban Walker. Lanham, Md.: Rowman & Littlefield, 1999.

Tyson, Ann Scott. "Old Women and Retirement: a Luxury They Can't Afford." *Christian Science Monitor* (July 17, 1998): 8.

Verbrugge, Lois M. "Disability in Late Life." In *Aging and Quality of Life*. Edited by Ronald P. Abeles et al. New York: Springer, 1994.

———. "The Twain Meet: Empirical Evidence of Sex Differences in Health and Mortality." In *Gender, Health, and Longevity*. Edited by Marcia G. Ory and Huber R. Warner. New York: Springer, 1990.

Verbrugge, Lois M. and Deborah L. Wingard. "Sex Differentials in Health and Mortality." *Women and Health* 12, no. 2 (1987): 103–43.

Villa, Valentine M. "Aging Policy and the Experiences of Older Minorities." In *New Directions in Old Age*. Edited by Janie S. Steckenrider and Tonya M. Parrott. Albany: SUNY Press, 1998.

Vincent, John A. *Inequality and Old Age*. New York: St. Martin's, 1995.

Wade-Gayles, Gloria. "Who Says an Older Woman Can't/Shouldn't Dance?" In *Body Politics and the Fictional Double*. Edited by Debra Walker King. Bloomington: Indiana, 2000.

Walford, Roy. *Maximum Life Span*. New York: Norton, 1983.

Walker, Alice. "In Search of Our Mothers' Gardens." In *In Search of Our Mothers' Gardens: Womanist Prose*. New York: Harcourt Brace, 1983.

Walker, Barbara. *The Crone: Women of Age, Wisdom, and Power*. San Francisco: Harper and Row, 1985.

Walker, Margaret Urban. "Getting Out of Line: Alternatives to Life as a Career." In *Mother Time: Women, Aging, and Ethics*. Edited by Margaret Urban Walker. Lanham, Md.: Rowman & Littlefield, 1999.

———, ed. *Mother Time: Women, Aging, and Ethics*. Lanham, Md.: Rowman & Littlefield, 1999.

Wallace, Steven P. "The Political Economy of Health Care for Elderly Blacks." In *Critical Perspectives on Aging*. Edited by Meredith Minkler and Carroll L. Estes. Amityville, N.Y.: Baywood, 1991.

Wallace, Steven P. and Elisa Linda Facio. "Moving Beyond Familism: Potential Contributions of Gerontological Theory to Studies of Chicano/Latino Aging." *Journal of Aging Studies* 1, no. 4 (1987): 337–54.

Wallace, Steven P. and V.M. Villa. "Caught in Hostile Crossfire: Public Policy and Minority Elderly in the United States." In *Minorities, Aging, and Health*. Edited by K. S. Markides and M. R. Miranda. Thousand Oaks, Calif.: Sage, 1997.

Wallack, Lawrence. "Japan's Heath Sacrifice." Letter to the Editor, *New York Times* (January 7, 2000): A22.

Wallis, Velma. *Two Old Women. An Alaskan Legend of Betrayal, Courage and Survival*. Fairbanks, Alaska: Epicenter Press, 1993.

Ward-Griffin, Catherine and Jenny Ploeg. "A Feminist Approach to Health Promotion for Older Women." *Canadian Journal of Aging* 16, no. 2 (1997): 279–96.

Weisstein, Naomi. Letter to the Editor. *Women's Review of Books* 17, no. 5 (February 2000): 4.

Weg, Ruth. "Beyond Babies and Orgasm." In *Growing Old in America*, 3rd ed. Edited by Beth B. Hess and Elizabeth Markson. New Brunswick, N.J.: Transaction Books, 1986.

Wendell, Susan. "Old Women Out of Control: Some Thoughts on Aging, Ethics, and Psychosomatic Medicine." In *Mother Time*. Edited by Margaret Urban Walker. Lanham, Md.: Rowman & Littlefield, 1999.

Wenger, G. Clare. "Dependence, Interdependence, and Reciprocity After Eighty." *Journal of Aging Studies* 1, no. 4 (1987): 355–77.

West, Maureen. "Vanishing HMOs Leave Rural Residents at Risk." *Arizona Republic* (February 8, 2000): A1.

Wheeler, Helen Rippier. *Women and Aging: A Guide to the Literature*. Boulder, Colo.: Lynne Rienner, 1997.

Whitbourne, Susan Krauss. *The Aging Individual: Physical and Psychological Perspectives*. New York: Springer, 1996.

Whitfield, Keith E and Tamara Baker-Thomas. "Individual Differences in Aging Minorities." *International Journal of Aging and Human Development* 48, no. 1 (1999): 73–79.

Whittaker, Terri. "Gender and Elder Abuse." In *Connecting Gender and Ageing*. Edited by Sara Arber and Jay Ginn. Buckingham: Open University Press, 1995.

Willett, Walter C., Graham Colditz, and Meir Stampfer. "Postmenopausal Estrogens—Opposed, Unopposed, or None of the Above." *JAMA* 238, no. 4 (January 26, 2000): 534–35.

Williams, Angie and Howard Giles. "Communication of Ageism." In *Communicating Prejudice*. Edited by Michael L. Hecht. Thousand Oaks, Calif: Sage, 1998.

Williamson, John B. and Sara E. Rix. "Social Security Reform: Implications for Women." *Journal of Aging and Social Policy* 11, no. 4 (2000): 41–68.

Winker, Margaret A. "Managing Medicine." In *The Practical Guide to Aging*. Edited by Christine Cassel. New York: New York University Press, 1999.

Wood, January. "'Productive Aging' Highlights Strengths." *National Association of Social Workers News* (Feb. 2001): 12.

Woodward, Kathleen, ed. *Figuring Age*. Bloomington: Indiana, 1999.

———. "Telling Stories: Aging, Reminiscence, and the Life Review." *Journal of Aging and Identity* 2, no. 3 (1997): 149–63.

———. "Tribute to the Older Woman: Psychoanalysis, feminism, and ageism." In *Images of Aging. Cultural Representations of Later Life*. Edited by Mike Featherstone and Andrew Wernick. London: Routledge, 1995.

Wray, L.A. "Health Policy and Ethnic Diversity in Older Americans: Dissonance or Harmony?" *Western Journal of Medicine* 157, no. 3 (1992): 357–61.

Wyatt-Brown, Anne and Janice Rossen, eds. *Aging and Gender in Literature: Studies in Creativity*. Charlottesville, Va.: University of Virginia Press, 1993.

Yee, Barbara W.K. "Gender and Family Issues in Minority Groups." In *Gender and Aging*. Edited by Lou Glasse and John Hendricks. Amityville, N.Y.: Baywood, 1992.

Yee, Barbara W.K. and Gayle D. Weaver. "Ethnic Minorities and Health Promotion: Developing a 'Culturally Competent' Agenda." *Generations* 18, no. 1 (1994): 39–44.

Yee, Donna L.. "Preventing Chronic Illness and Disability: Asian Americans." In *Serving Minority Elders in the 21ˢᵗ Century*. Edited by May L. Wykle and Amasa B. Ford. New York: Springer, 1999.

Yeo, Gwen. "Ethnogeriatrics: Cross-Cultural Care of Older Adults." *Generations* 20, no. 4 (1996–1997): 72–77.

Yeo, Gwen and Nancy Hikoyeda. "Asian and Pacific Islander American Elders." *The Encyclopedia of Aging,* 3rd ed. Edited by George L. Maddox. New York: Springer, 2001.

Zita, Jacqueline. "Heresy in the Female Body: The Rhetoric of Menopause." In *The Other Within*. Edited by Marilyn Pearsall. Boulder, Colo.: Westview, 1997.

Zuess, Jonathan. *The Wisdom of Depression*. New York: Harmony Books, 1998.

Index

AARP, 9, 29, 143
abuela, 42
acupuncture, 82
adverse drug reactions. *See* drugs, prescription
age: denial of, 7, 10–11, 23, 146–50, 153–56, 159, 203; integration, 46; passing, 11, 153; studies, 185; wave, 26, 30
age discrimination, 144, 157n1, 162–63
Age Discrimination in Employment Act, 144
ageism, 4, 5, 6, 78, 109, 130, 135–57, 157n1, 191, 130; internalized, 4, 120, 151, 153–56, 176
ageist humor, 155
ageist language, 140–42
aging: adjustment to, 119–20, 178; and appearance, 4, 20, 23, 24n2, 137–38, 140–41, 143, 146–50, 155, 184, 193–94; as decline, 5, 11, 13, 14, 22, 24n8, 35, 39, 46, 64, 69–70, 167, 168, 178, 203; demographics (*see* population aging); as development, 7, 18, 20, 23, 40, 152, 156, 167, 198, 199, 205; as disease, myth of, 40, 171, 190, 203; as extension of mid-life, 41; fatalism about, 39; fear of, 13, 30, 159–60, 199; ideologies of, 1–7, 25–33, 111, 152,
159–64; metaphors of, 26–27, 39, 184, 193; obituary images of, 149; physical changes with, 53, 72, 146–50, 90n3, 174, 194; politics, 25–33, 51–53, 93–112, 144–45; as recovery, 6, 104–5, 164, 204
AIDS, 59, 192
Africa, 115, 192; Sierra Leone, 118; South Africa, 4, 59; Chagga tribe, 9
Albright, Madeline, 149
Allen, Paula Gunn, 120, 175, 193
Allen, Tom, 58
alternative medicine, 61, 64–65, 66, 80, 81–86, 107, 110
Alzheimers Disease, 38–39, 104, 183; false diagnosis of, 54, 79; fear of, 38–39; ideology of, 39
American Indian women, 35, 101, 193; Onondaga, 192
American Indians, 14, 17, 32, 33n9, 38, 41, 43–44, 56, 97, 100–101, 107, 110, 118–19, 120, 166, 179, 198; diabetes among, 38, 101; health of, 100–101, 110; Native Elder Research Center, 101; Navajo, 9, 96, 166; oppression of, 166; Pima, 101; poverty of, 101; respect for elders among, 166, 175; sweatlodge, 101; transmission of culture, 43–44

American Society on Aging, 165
Americans for Generational Equity, 27, 33n3
Andrews, Molly, 152
androgyny, 45, 49n3
Angier, Natalie, 192
Annan, Kofi, 7
anthropology and aging, 9, 23n1, 101, 191–92
anti-aging, futility of, 141, 148, 156
Anzaldúa, Gloria, 120, 188
arpilleras, 21
Asian American men, 118
Asian Americans (Asian Pacific Islanders), 32, 41, 63, 96, 99–100, 118, 179, 198; Chinese, 14, 99, 100, 127; elders honored among, 100, 118; Filipinos, 99, 127; Japanese, 99, 119; Koreans, 14, 99, 100, 119; Vietnamese, 100, 119, 127
Asian American women, 118, 146; as caregivers, 123, 124
Atchley, Robert, 161
Avery, Byllye, 71
Ayurveda, 83

baby boomers, 79, 131, 148, 156
Bach, Peter, 98
Ball, Lucille, 142
Baltes, Margret, 14
Baltes, Paul, 76
Baltimore Longitudinal Study of Aging, 69, 186
Barer, Barbara, 16
Barker, Pat, 15
Barusch, Amanda, 116
Basting, Ann, 185
Bateson, Mary Catherine, 21
Bayly, John, 38
Bellow, Saul, 184
Benny, Jack, 142
Benoit, Meda, 87
Birren, James E., 186

bisexuals, 122
black men, 33n9, 118; and criminal justice system, 117
blacks, 5, 6, 7n1, 32, 41, 107, 110, 119, 120, 147, 165, 179, 188, 198; as caregivers, 125; health of, 88, 97–98; retirement of, 130
black women, 19, 35, 106, 116, 117, 120, 123, 131, 161, 186, 193, 197; as artists, 22; breast cancer in, 38, 71, 98; greater bone density of, 97; health of, 38, 71, 97–98; poverty of, 6, 116, 117; retirement of, 131
Blythe, Ronald, ix, 184
bodywork, 84–85, 90n13
borderlands, 121
Bortz, Walter, 71
Boston Globe, 8, 59
Boston Women's Health Collective, 109
brain, 53, 75–77, 85. *See also* mental function
Brandeis Center for Women's Aging, 109, 123
Brant, Beth, 166
breast cancer, 71, 88, 102, 104, 109
Brendel, Alfred, 22
breathing, 3, 21, 78, 81, 88, 168, 194
bridge jobs, 130
Brody, Jane, 112n4
Buddhists, 45, 73, 166, 167
Bush, Barbara, 146
Bush, George W., administration of, 51, 129
busyness, 15, 154, 159–65, 167, 171, 183, 204
Butler, Robert, 29, 42, 47, 54, 66, 135, 136, 171
Bytheway, Bill, 152

Callahan, Daniel, 26
Calmont, Jeanne, 87
caloric restriction, 73

capitalism, 36, 182

caregiving, 16, 122–28, 132, 134n7, 162, 163; and stress, 125–26; as women's role, 122–28, 132, 163. 167, 171n2, 176

Carpenter, Mary, 176

Carson, Rachael, 67

Cassel, Christine, 112

Cather, Willa, 19, 24n5

centenarians, 44, 171

Center for Aging, Religion, and Spirituality, 165

Center for Lesbian Health Research, 106

Chicanas, 42, 119, 124

Chicanos, 119, 179

Chinen, Allan, 185

chiropractic, 82

Chodron, Pema, 45

Christian, Barbara, 120, 193

civil rights movement, 135, 156, 205

Clark, Margaret, 35, 37

class, 20–21, 93–95, 115–18, 193

class privilege, 3, 21, 40, 45, 76, 112, 116–18, 128, 134n4, 177, 191

Clifton, Lucille, 147, 149

clinical ecology, 83

Clinton, Bill, 30, 51, 58, 129

Coalition of Labor Women, 123

Cofer, Judith, 147

coffee, addiction to, 74–75

Cohen, Lawrence, 180

Cole, Thomas, 13, 182, 185

Colette, 80

colleges and universities, impediments to learning created by, 46, 163. See also senior college

Colman, Hila, 163

colonization, 121, 153, 180–81; internal colonization, 4, 7. See also old, as a colonized people

Comfort, Alex, 136, 156

comfortable aging, 3, 111, 155, 167, 204

complementary medicine, 64, 66. See also alternative medicine

Concord Coalition, 27, 28

conscious aging, ix, 5, 80, 87, 108, 153, 156, 159, 163, 165, 204

Coontz, Stephanie, 16

Copper, Baba, 5, 20, 136, 145, 151, 152, 153, 163, 176

Cornell Center for Women's Healthcare, 109

cosmetic surgery, 148, 157n7

Coyle, Jean, 188

creativity and aging, 21–22, 24n7, 47–48, 158n11, 164, 185

critical gerontology, 180–86, 190, 195, 200n5, 200n6

crones, 137, 197–98, 201n14

culturally competent gerontology, 63, 101, 180–81, 188

culture and aging, 1–7, 9–23, 25–27, 35–49, 56, 63–67, 87–88, 110–11, 115–32, 135–57, 192, 203–5

Cunningham, Imogen, 20, 140

curanderas, 198

dance therapy, 72

Datan, Nancy, 199

deaf elders, 154

death and dying, 201n13

death, fear of, 135, 179

deBeauvoir, Simone, 20, 144, 163

Delaney, Sadie and Bessie, 71

dementia, 13–14, 39, 56, 125, 184; false diagnosis of, 110

Dennison, Ruth, 45

dentists, shortage of, 88–89

Department of Health and Human Services, 64

dependency, 7, 10, 11, 12, 14, 15, 17, 40, 126–27, 160, 181, 189, 204, 205

depression, 54, 71, 75, 79–80, 84, 99, 110, 125

DesMaisons, Kathleen, 75

diabetes, 70, 71, 72, 101

Diamond, Marian, 75–76
disability, 70, 107, 111
disabled elderly, 106
Disney movies, ageist and sexist stereotypes in, 138
divorce, poverty risk of for older women, 131
doctors, 61–62, 66, 108; and bribery of by drug companies, 58, 59, 68n3; deference to, 108; interaction with patients, 37, 38, 40, 61–62, 63, 78, 80, 89, 96, 102, 108, 142
Dole, Bob, 141
Dole, Elizabeth, 138
Donovan, Josephine, 17
double standard of aging, 143–44, 147, 157n6
Draxten, Nina, 20
Driving, 11, 12, 195; accidents of elders, 31
drug industry, 4, 57–61; ethical problems of, 58–61, 66; and generic drugs, suppression of, 59; lobbyists, 59, 62; marketing, 52, 58–59, 60, 63, 66, 67, 81, l03, 110, 160, 189; political influence of, 59, 60–61, 62, 205
drugs, prescription, 51–68; 188, 189; adverse reactions to, 53–57, 61, 62, 64, 79; alcohol and, 54; cell division and, 55; deaths from, 53, 55, 61, 62–63, 65, 66; dementia and, 56; dependency on, 61–62, 63, 64, 189, 190; high consumption of, 51–67, 68n2, 110, 189; high cost of, 51–52, 57, 66, 88; Medicare benefit, 51; "me too" drugs, 58, 63; psychotropics, 54, 56, 60–61, 62, 79, 102, 190; safety, 60, 62, 63, 67, 104; and side effects, 58, 66, 105; switching, 62
dualistic thinking, 126, 137, 147, 148, 153, 183–84, 186, 205
Durenberger, David, 27

Eastern philosophy, 110, 165, 167
economics of aging, 25, 27–33, 36, 65,
106–8, 111, 115–18, 123–24, 128–32, 144, 145, 162–63, 170, 181–82, 190
Eden Alternative, 12
Ekerdt, David, 161
elder abuse, 189–90
elders over eighty-five, 14, 16, 20, 21, 25, 44, 66, 170, 195
elderspeak, 141–42
Elders Share the Arts, 48
Emerson, Ralph Waldo, 10, 23, 169
emotions and aging, 77–81; anger, 19–20, 40, 77, 78, 97, 145, 166–67; in caregiving, 122–26; healing emotions, 80–81
Erikson, Eric, 161, 187
Erikson, Joan, 161
Estes, Carroll, 36, 180, 181
estrogen, 60, 104, 112n3
ethnicity, and aging, 95–102, 118–21, 132n2, 151, 152, 178; ethnic solidarity, 119
ethnogerontology, 95–97, 101, 119–21
exercise, 70–72, 88, 161

falls, 71, 84, 103–4, 108, 189
families of elders, 4, 5, 17, 28, 42, 118, 145–46, 187, 194
family caregivers, 122–28, 150
Fanon, Franz, 4
fear of an aging population, 25–32, 41, 126, 183, 190
federal support of elders, decline in, 126, 180
Feldenkrais Method, 85–86, 90n14
Felsteiner, Mary, 194
feminism, 148, 173–78. *See also* women's movement
feminist(s), 44, 108, 110, 123, 173–200; critique of gerontology, 186–91, 201n10; spirituality, 166; theory, 182, 190, 191–200
fertility, declining, and population aging, 1, 25

Finklehor, David, 77
Fisher, M.F.K., 147, 155, 168
folklore, ageist bias in, 138, 157n4
Food and Drug Administration
(FDA), 55, 59, 60, 62, 189
Forum on Religion, Spirituality, and
Aging, 165
foster grandparents, 43
Foucault, Michel, 181
Fox, Matthew, 166, 172n7
frailty, 13, 14–15, 37, 84, 86, 87, 111, 141,
160, 162, 177, 205
France, 116, 163
Franco-Americans, 185
Freedman, Marc, 46, 163
Freeman, Mary Wilkins, 19, 21
free radicals, 73, 90n6
Friedan, Betty, 77, 79, 149, 176
Friedman, Leonore, 167
Fuller, Margaret, 167
Furman, Frieda Kerner, 195

Gadow, Sally, 13, 15, 109, 189
Gage, Matilda Joslyn, 147
gay and lesbian liberation, 135
"geezer," 137, 156, 157n3
gender, 1–7, 13–16, 133n3, 173–200; and
ageist images, 142–44; and caregiving,
122–28; and health, 77–79, 87, 102–10;
and medication, 51–56, 60, 61, 67,
67n1; and power, 123, 126, 154–55;
and pressures to disguise aging, 147–50;
and retirement, 128–31, 134n9; and
service, 41–43; and sick role, 35–41
gender bending, 45
generational equity, 27–28, 33n3
gerastology, 174, 191–200
geriatricians, 56, 57, 60, 61
geriatrics, 61, 96, 109, 178
Germany, 27, 65, 74, 116, 138, 166
Gerontologist, The, 61, 191
gerontologists, 6, 20, 25, 41, 45, 52, 56, 60,
64, 74, 81, 86, 88, 93, 108, 118, 119–
21, 140, 160, 161, 165, 174, 175, 188,
194, 201n7
gerontology, x, 51, 52, 95, 102, 135, 142,
163, 178–86, 195, 196, 197, 199, 203,
204; feminist critique of, 186–91; male
bias in, 186–91
ginseng, 64, 68n6
Glaspell, Susan, 191
Goldman, Connie, 158n11, 160, 171n1
grandmothers, 119, 138, 140, 145–46, 178,
198
grandparents, 44, 140. See also social roles
Gray Panthers, 152, 158n9
gray pride, 151
"gray lobby," 106
"gray peril," 135
Great Britain, 46, 61, 65, 144, 184
Great Old Broads for Wilderness, 43
Grumbach, Doris, 21, 168
Gubrium, Jaber, 179
Gullette, Margaret, 185, 200n6
Gulliver's Travels, 138
Gutmann, David, 45

Haddock, Doris, 70
Hahn, Nhat, 167
Hahnemann, Samuel, 82
Hawaiians, 86
Hayden, Jacqueline, 13, 24n2, 149
Hazen, Haim, 181, 183
Healey, Shevy, 153, 197
health care: corporate control of, 36, 48,
109–10, 118; costs of, 30–31, 106–7;
lack of prevention, 103, 107–8, 111
health promotion, 30, 36, 39, 109, 203
Health Watch, 86
healthy aging, 68–89, 93–112, 190
healthy aging, programs for, 86–87
healthy aging research, 70, 73, 74–77, 79,
91n17, 96–104, 112n1
Healthy People 2010, 94

heart disease in older women, 102, 104, 109

Heilbrun, Carolyn, 19

Hendricks, Jon, 20

herbal medicines, 57, 74, 81, 90n7

Hildegard of Bingen, 166, 172n7

Hillyer, Barbara, 168, 194

hip fractures, 61, 71, 74, 89, 103, 188, 189

HMOs, dropping elders, 88

Holstein, Martha, 161–62, 166, 171n2, 195

homeopathy, 65, 81, 82

homeostasis, 69–70, 73

hooks, bell, 132, 188

Hoover Institute, 26

Hooyman, Nancy, 191

hospice, 135

housing, 194–95

humanities and aging, 165, 171n4, 182–86, 200n6, 201n9, 205

Hurtado, Aida, 120

"iatrogenic loneliness," 65

Illich, Ivan, 63

immigrants, 12, 17, 44, 124, 178; fear of, 27, 135

incest, 77, 78

individualism, 10–17, 23, 70, 107, 111, 127–28, 190, 191, 194, 204

Institute of Spirituality and Aging, 165

interdependence, 17, 23, 97, 111, 119, 132, 194, 201n12

intergenerational conflict, 25–29, 32, 33n3, 33n8; harmony, 10, 17, 32

internalized ageism, 153–56, 176

Inuit, 157n4

Jacobs, Ruth, 163, 165

Jacobson, Sharon, 196

Japan, 9, 25, 65, 107, 118, 153, 157n4

Jewett, Sarah Orne, 184

Johnson, Colleen, 16

Johnson, Don Hanlon, 167

Johnson, Lyndon, 29

Journal of Women and Aging, 191

Kaiser Permanente, 59

Kahn, Robert L., 2, 40, 46, 70

Katz, Stephen, 181, 200n6

Kaufman, Sharon, 185

Kennett, Jiyu, 45

Kivnick, Helen, 161

Kollwitz, Käthe, 21

Kuhn, Maggie, 158n9

LaBouvie-Vief, Gisela, 7

Labowitz, Shoni, 197

Langellier, Kristin, 185

Langer, Ellen, 12, 154, 167

Lansbury, Angela, 142

Latinas, 57, 116, 117, 121, 124, 136, 198; as caregivers, 123

Latinos, 14, 32, 41, 94, 98–99, 107, 119, 120, 125

learned helplessness, 17, 39

learning impediments, created by colleges and universities, 46, 163

legal issues, 144–45

lesbians, aging issues of, 21, 106, 121–22, 133n6, 195; invisibility of, 188

Lesbian and Gay Aging Issues Network, 122

lesbians and gay men, 18, 27

lesbian, gay, bisexual, and transgender elders, 106, 122, 187

Levinson, Daniel, 187

life expectancy, 31, 33n9, 95, 118; American Indians, 33n9, 118; blacks, 33n9, 118; gap between women and men, 33n9, 110; healthy life expectancy, 115, 132

life review, 6–7, 47–48, 49n4, 49n5, 163

life satisfaction studies, 179

literary images of aging, 15, 19–20, 21, 22,

147, 163–64, 166–67, 183–85, 191, 193, 205

longevity, x, 31, 44, 48, 93, 105, 176, 192–93, 195

Lorde, Audre, 148, 193

Luce, Gay, 166, 172n6

Lugones, Maria, 121

Lynott, Robert, 179

MacArthur Study of Aging in America, 2, 31, 70, 76, 186

Macdonald, Barbara, 41, 136, 145, 151, 152, 157n2, 176, 177–78

McKay, Clive, 73

Manahan, William, 74

Manitoba Cree, 35

Markson, Elizabeth, 39

massage, 83–84, 194

masturbation, 105

materialism and aging, 81, 168–70, 183

Maynard, Isabelle, 181

Mead, Margaret, 45

media coverage of aging, inadequacy of, 3, 20, 30, 36, 38, 46, 105, 121, 137, 140–41, 186; stereotypes in, 138, 142–44, 146

medicalization of aging, 14, 35–41, 51–67, 104–12, 148, 178, 180–81, 186, 188–89, 204

medical research, compromises in, 60

Medicare, 5, 9, 28, 29, 30, 31, 32, 33n8, 46, 83, 107, 112n4, 115, 204; cuts in home health care, 29, 106–7, 118, 192; fraud, 30; prescription drug benefit in, 51, 63

Meigs, Mary, 193

menopause, 72, 112n2, 193, 194, 198

mental function, 70, 154. See also brain

mental health, 77–81, 100

middle-class, 29, 82; bias in aging, 2, 3, 93, 94–95; elders, 48, 66, 87, 89, 107, 143; white women, 110, 116, 125, 130, 176, 179, 194

mindful aging, 12, 110, 160, 163, 164, 165–69. See also conscious aging

Minkler, Meredith, 28, 180, 182

minorities, aging of, 29, 32, 35, 47, 48, 94, 96, 106–7, 111, 112n1, 117–21, 132n1, 132n2, 180, 195; increasing numbers of, 96, 176; respect for elders among, 35, 118, 124; strengths of, 97, 119. See also American Indians; Asian Americans; blacks; Latinas; Latinos; people of color

Montefiore Senior Center of San Francisco, 45, 145

Moody, Harry R., 200n6

Moore, Thomas J., 53, 55, 60

moral economy and aging, 182

moral values and aging, 32, 42, 182, 196

Morgan, Anna, 73

mothers and daughters, 13, 125–27, 175, 197, 200n1

multiculturalism, 119–21, 133n5, 179–80, 196

Munro, Alice, 184

Murdoch, Iris, 38

Murray, Christopher, 118

Myerhoff, Barbara, 47, 150, 185

National Alliance for Caregiving, 123, 124

National Association for Home Care, 106

National Center on Addiction and Abuse, 55

National Center for Complementary and Alternative Medicine, 81

National Center on Women's Aging, Brandeis, 109, 123

National Council on Aging (NCOA), 109, 113n5

National Women's Studies Association, 177–78

Neel, Alice, 137

Nepal, 204

Nevelson, Louise, 21, 205

New Age spirituality, 166

New England Journal of Medicine, 60
New York Times, 27, 59, 140–41, 149, 163–64
Nhat, Hahn, 167
Noggle, Anne, 148, 157n7
nonconformity, 10, 40, 77, 161, 164, 194, 204
nurses, 106, 144
nursing homes, 4, 12, 13–14, 65–66, 83, 96, 102, 106, 122, 194; residents of, 15, 17, 43, 56, 61, 65–66, 83, 103, 144
nutrition, 53, 72–75, 89, 108

O'Connor, Sandra Day, 144
Office of Alternative Medicine. See National Center for Complementary and Alternative Medicine
O'Keeffe, Georgia, 21, 45
old, as a category, 5–6, 11, 120, 121, 136, 150–53, 154, 155, 173–74, 196, 197–98, 204
old, the: as a colonized people, 3–5, 12, 153, 154, 181; as a minority group, 145; as a percentage of the population, 25, 51, 145; status of, 9, 37, 135–157
Old Lesbians Organizing for Change, 122, 141, 152, 196
old women: clown role of, 4, 146; essentialist views of, 151, 197, 198, 199–200; fear of, 138–40, 147; hatred of, 139–40, 155, 198; health concerns of, 69–89, 93–112; invisible bodies of, 13, 109, 149; low status of, 9, 12, 103–4, 140, 190; as "Other," 5, 150–51, 174; powerlessness of, 123, 126, 154–55; productivity of, 122; robustness of, 110, 192, 193; silence expected of, 17, 37, 140, 168, 194; strengths of, 191–92, 197–98, 203, 205
Olsen, Tillie, 41
Olson, Laura Katz, 124
Omega Institute for Holistic Studies, 165

oppressor and oppressed, 147, 180
orgasm, 105
osteoporosis, 73, 75, 99, 104
overmedication, 4, 51–67, 68n2, 188, 203, 205
OWL (Older Women's League), 107, 128 130, 152

pain, 94, 103
paradigms of aging, 1–7, 52, 159–64, 170–71, 182–84, 187–88, 190, 204
paradoxes of aging, 45, 199, 203–5
pay gap, widening with age, 117
Pearsall, Marilyn, 177
peer care, 192
pensions, 96, 122, 128, 130, 131
people of color, 3, 27, 29, 32, 38, 48, 66, 87, 93, 94, 95, 96, 118–21, 130, 136, 152. See also minorities, aging of
performing age, 173, 174
Peterson, Peter G., 27
pharmacists, 62
Phillipson, Chris, 200n5, 200n6
Picard, Jeannette, 20
Pingree, Chellie, 58
placebo effect, 65
political economy, 181–82, 200n7
poor elders, 6, 32, 48, 87, 99, 117
poor whites, 38, 48, 87
poor women, 115–18, 124, 199
population aging, 25, 26, 33n8, 33n9, 51, 96, 132, 170, 176
Porcino, Jane, 105
positivism, 180
Posner, Richard, 31, 187–88
postmodernism, 173, 175, 181, 199
poverty, 6, 94–101; old women's risk of, 28–29, 32, 115–18, 124, 130, 132, 195; statistics, inadequacy of, 116
powerlessness, 37, 40, 190; "productive" aging, 2–3, 15, 161–63, 169–70, 171n2, 183, 199, 204

psychology of aging, 7, 9–23, 70, 77–81,
141–42, 145–57, 159–71; women's,
103, 110, 125–27, 129–30, 189, 193–
94, 195, 203–5
psychoneuroimmunology, 89
Public Citizen, 59

qi gong, 71, 72, 168
Quakers, 165

racism, 94, 95, 96v 97, 98, 119, 120, 136,
145, 147, 188, 193
Ram Dass, 162, 165
Ray, Ruth, 185, 195, 200n6
reciprosity, 32, 127, 182, 192, 201n12
re-entry women, 19
reflexivity, 188
regeneration, 39, 104
Reich, Robert, 29
Reinharz, Shulamit, 175
religious belief and aging, 97, 125, 165,
171n3, 191
reminiscence, 47, 48, 188, 189
Rentsch, Thomas, 162
research on aging, 11, 55–56, 65, 91n7,
96–97, 119–20, 25, 153, 154, 178–82,
191; feminist perspective on, 109, 186–
91, 195–96, 201n10; middle-class bias
in, 179–80, 204
retirement, 45, 128–32, 159, 161, 167,
170. *See also* social roles
Retirement Confidence Survey, 30, 33n5
Rich, Cynthia, 136, 176, 157n2
Riley, John W., 46
Riley, Mathilda W., 46. "roleless role,"
aging as a, 41, 47, 48
roles. *See* social roles
Rolf, Ida, 84
Roosevelt, Eleanor, 45
Rosenthal, Evelyn, 156
Rossen, Janice, 185
Rossi, Alice, 192

Rowe, John L., 2, 40, 46, 70
Roszak, Theodore, 162, 182
Rudman, Warren, 27

Sacramento Area Longitudinal Study in
Aging, 99
Sarton, May, 15, 166–67, 178
scapegoating elderly, 26–27, 182, 204
Schacter-Shalomi, Zalman, 165, 172n5
Schaie, K. Warner, 76
Schmidt, Robert, 69
Scott-Maxwell, Florida, 15, 164, 168
self-esteem, 11, 22, 71, 78, 142, 146–47,
153–57, 162, 167
self help, 108, 192
self-reinvention, 17–23, 24n4
self-reliance, 3, 10–17, 118, 124, 127
self-repair, capacity for, 70, 73
Seltzer, Mildred, 179
senior centers, 10, 37, 153
senior citizen, 58, 204
senior college, 46
Senior Community Service, 43
Senior Companions, 43
Senior Wellness Program of King County,
86
Sept 11, 2001, 27, 30
sexism, 137, 143–44, 170, 177, 187–88,
190–91
sexual abuse of girls, as aging issue, 77–79,
195
sexual harassment, 196
sexuality, 65–66, 105, 149, 183
sexual orientation, 121–22, 151
Sherif, Katherine, 55, 67n1
sick role, 35–41, 48–49, 63, 159, 183, 203
Simpson, Alan, 29
slowing down, 23, 64, 66, 81, 89, 154, 164,
165, 168, 169, 183
social construction of aging, ix, 1–7, 16,
25–27, 35–49, 51–67, 71, 87–88,
106–8, 119–20, 126, 145–57, 157n6,

159–64, 168, 173–74, 178–80, 185, 186–91, 197–98

social control, of elders, 4, 5, 63, 152, 161, 181, 197, 199

social inequality, 93–112, 115–32, 133n5

social roles, 35–49, 49n3, 129–30, 145–46, 203; environmental protectors, 43; grandparenting, 42; service, 41–43, 177, 178, 199 (*see also* caregiving); wisdom, 43–45, 48, 187, 199, 200; wise elder, 44, 198, 200, 203. *See also* retirement; sick role

Social Security, 5, 6, 26, 28, 29–32, 33n8, 98, 127, 128–31; anti-gay bias in, 122; gender bias in, 128–29; privatization of, 3, 30, 129, 134n8

Solti, Sir Georg, 15

Sontag, Susan, 147, 157n6

Spiritual Eldering Institute, 165

spirituality and aging, 80–81, 93, 160, 165–70, 179

Spretnak, Charlene, 166

standpoint theory, 196–97

Starhawk, 166

Steinberg, David, 42

stereotypes of aging, 26, 28, 62, 136–46, 152, 153, 154, 194, 200n8; of women's aging, 4, 44, 136–51, 177, 197, 198

storytelling, 6–7, 47–48

structural lag, 46–47, 162–63, 203

"successful" aging, 2–3, 15, 93, 161, 163, 194, 199, 204

sugar, addiction to, 75, 90n8

Sun City, Arizona, 86, 159, 160

Supreme Court, 135, 144–45, 157n1

survivorship, 20, 171

tai chi, 71, 72, 168

Talbot, Margaret, 65

TallMountain, Mary, 147

telomeres, 89

Tennyson, Alfred Lord, 160

Thomas, William, 12

Thoreau, Henry David, 169

thyroid disease, in older women, 83

time, sense of and aging, 167, 179

Tornstam, Lars, 179, 200n4

touch deprivation, 83, 105

Tournier, Paul, 6

Transcendentalists, 10, 169

transgendered people, 122

transportation, 11, 190

Unitarians, 165

University of the Third Age, 46–47

vaginal walls, thinning of, 105

vitamins, 73, 74, 90n7

volunteers, 163

Wade-Gayles, Gloria, 193

Walford, Roy, 73

Walker, Alice, 22, 191

Walker, Barbara, 139

Walker, Margaret Urban, 163, 177

Walking to Wellness, 71

Wallingford Wellness Project, 86

Wallis, Velma, 205

Wall Street, welfare for, 129

Walters, Barbara, 142

Washington Post, 59

Webster, Nancy, 87

Wenzel, Elizabeth, 22

Western attitudes, 32, 120, 121, 135, 139–40, 180, 183

Whisper the Waves, the Wind, 198

whiteness, 121

white privilege, 6, 125, 128, 166

Whitman, Walt, 169

widows, 105, 116, 130–31, 154, 187; declining incomes of, 131

Williams, Patricia, 188

wisdom of elders. *See* social roles

Wise, David A., 26

~

About the Author

Margaret Cruikshank, a native of northern Minnesota, taught English and gay/lesbian studies for many years at City College of San Francisco. She now teaches women's studies at the University of Maine, where she is also a faculty associate at the Center on Aging. She lives in a small coastal village in eastern Maine. Dr. Cruikshank's books include *Macaulay, Lesbian Studies,* and *The Gay and Lesbian Liberation Movement.* Her anthology of literature about aging, *Fierce with Reality,* grew out of graduate studies in gerontology at San Francisco State University. Her numerous articles cover many subjects. *Learning to Be Old* is not a blueprint for late life, but its author plans to follow its less taxing recommendations.

2277

wise elder. *See* social roles
witches, old women as, 138, 139–40
Wollestonecraft, Mary, 175
women of color, 3, 10, 104, 115, 119, 120, 121, 123, 125, 128 129, 146, 147, 148, 134n10, 188, 195, 199. *See also* Latinas, black women, Asian American women and American Indian women
Women of Color Health Data Handbook, 95
Women's Health Initiative, 104
women's movement, 41, 135, 156, 174, 175, 176, 205
women's studies, x, 135, 174–78, 185, 188, 196, 198, 199

Woodward, Kathleen, 47, 149, 185
Woolhander, Steffi, 54
Wordsworth, William, 81, 170
working-class elders, 3, 29, 43, 48, 94, 116–18, 129, 162; women, 19, 21, ? 124, 125, 128, 130, 132, 134n10
workplace discrimination, 144, 162–6?
World Health Organization (WHO), ? 115, 132
Wyatt-Brown, Anne, 185

"yellow peril," 135
Yeo, Gwen, 63
yoga, 71–72, 168

Zita, Jacqueline, 198

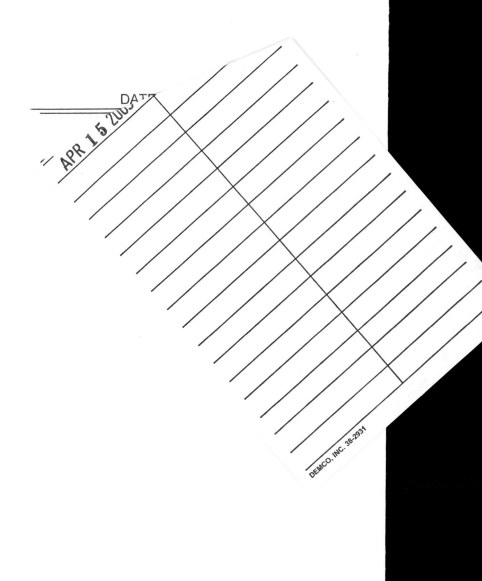

DATE

APR 15 2003

DEMCO, INC. 38-2931